*Reading in an Age of Theory*

# Reading in an
# Age of Theory

EDITED BY BRIDGET GELLERT LYONS

Rutgers University Press
*New Brunswick, New Jersey*

PN
81
R353
1997

Library of Congress Cataloging-in-Publication Date

Reading in an age of theory / edited by Bridget Gellert Lyons.
    p.   cm.
  Includes bibliographical references (p.).
  ISBN 0-8135-2430-X (alk. paper)
  1. Criticism.  2. Reading.  3. Rhetoric.  4. Poirier, Richard.
I. Lyons, Bridget Gellert.
PN81.R353  1997
801'.95—dc21                        96-45633
                                          CIP

British Cataloging-in-Publication information available

*For Richard Poirier*

# CONTENTS

# PREFACE

Since *In Defense of Reading*, a collection of essays he co-edited with Reuben Brower, appeared more than thirty years ago, Richard Poirier has been one of the most brilliant advocates of "close reading." This earlier volume is a reminder of what a contested activity close reading was, even in 1962. As the book's preface indicates, the "mere" reading of texts was under attack as anti-historical, even anti-intellectual: an exercise for which specialized training in literary study was hardly necessary. And as the editors' defense makes equally clear, attentive reading should never have been confused with the sterile hunt for ambiguities, symbols, and ironies which gave New Criticism a bad name in its later phases, or with the separation of literature from history: "Surely those who now call for a 'return to literary history' cannot be thinking that history is a 'thing' that we can study without first helping to construct it." Every text is embedded in its cultural moment (a fact too obvious to belabor in 1962 as it is now) and is as much a participant in its intellectual and social environment—an environment which must necessarily be our own reconstruction—as a receptor of a historical "context."

The concerns animating the essays in the current volume are similar, although the intervening years have made scholars addressing the question of reading more conscious of "theory"—of developed and articulated rationales and methods for understanding literary texts. Literary theory has now gained an ascendancy in elite graduate schools and among the publishers of academic journals and monographs that was scarcely imaginable in 1962, and some of the results have been energizing. For adherents and practitioners, the methodologies often borrowed from related disciplines (linguistics, psychology, anthropology, etc.) have reanimated literary study, saving it from the repetitive and self-enclosed readings of an exhausted field, and from a professoriate that could never be as objective in its scrutiny of great works as it claimed to be. For opponents, theory has become a threat because it has displaced the study of literature altogether, so that some students (and their teachers) consider the reading of literary works a secondary or even dispensable activity.

In effect, an alert attention, of the kind Poirier has always practiced and advocated, to the energies and movements of language refers to the concerns of more systematic theories while resisting subservience to their methodologies. Against those who have condemned close reading as regressive he has always claimed that rightly done, it yields insights analogous to the abstractions of theory. Close reading of complex texts can discover the contradictions and insufficiencies of the language on which an author depends, just as programmatically "deconstructive" readings do. But while he finds it reductive in the most literal sense to treat any text as an illustration of a theoretical or ideological system, Poirier has always argued against those who would use this common-sense proposition as an excuse for ignorance of contemporary theories, and of the intellectual situation which gave rise to them. One reason for the respect accorded him by his graduate students is that he is so conversant with modern formulations about literature without ever being dominated by them.

For Poirier, the quest for unified critical argument can be the enemy of attentive listening, and therefore of good reading. Such a quest was as misguided under the aegis of an older generation of scholars who flattened out any difficulties to be found in the works of Milton and Shakespeare by making these authors conform to a Christian-humanist ideology, as it is today when pursued by those who impose on complex literary works the predictable machinery of particular theoretical positions. Some of the most revealing and expressive aspects of language, Poirier has insisted throughout his career, are tonal, "vague," and barely articulate: for a great writer, such almost hidden tones carry with them resonances and conversations with other writers, other uses of related phrases or rhythms in their own past. To listen to a writer as he or she deserves is to attend, as one does in conversation with good friends, to patterns of repetitions, to the particular verbal contexts that elicit pleasure or fear, self-protective gestures or unexpected revelations, conformities or surprising knowledge. For this reason, Poirier has always focused on the performative aspects of literature, not alone in his 1971 book *The Performing Self*, and on its disruptions and discontinuities rather than on its articulations of order. The writers he has studied most intensely and read with most pleasure—including James, Frost, Gertrude Stein, and Shakespeare—have been masters of voice, of inflection and tonal subtleties, not creators of symbolic or allegorical schemes.

Poirier's commitment to close reading in all of its aspects has made him the most demanding and rewarding of teachers. His avoidance of theoretical or formulaic systems has been an inspiring challenge to his students, even if it has sometimes frustrated them. Students dazzled by the rich responses he gives —and elicits from them—to the works they are studying are nonetheless daunted by the refusal of method, of rules that can be transferred and applied to other works. Yet this is precisely what he will never supply. Even though a knowledge of the codifications that are the staples of many literature courses is necessary—whether these are conventions of genre, systems of prosody, labels for rhetorical figures, or networks of literary affiliation and influence—they are always insufficient to account for the complex sounds and movements of any work interesting enough to be studied. Each work is unique, however related to preceding or surrounding ones. For students, this constitutes a formidable challenge. What if they are not capable of reading "without a net," to adapt Frost's phrase? As a graduate student recently complained: "What if one doesn't have perfect pitch the way he [i.e., Poirier] does?"

But though students are invariably awed by Poirier's brilliance and by the difficulty of emulating him, his detailed editorial advice to them on papers and dissertations—as to contributors to *Raritan*, the cultural journal he edits and which has been recognized as one of the most interesting and influential in the country—always surprises them by its practicality. To creators of overambitious dissertation projects he says "I want a plan of *work*—what will you be doing in the library tomorrow? Next week?" His penetrating comments in the margins of papers ask for clarity and accuracy. Inimical to totalizing critical method-ologies, he nonetheless requires rigorous argumentation. A good reading is not simply an exercise in ventriloquism, in paraphrasing a text: it must make an argument of some cogency to readers knowledgeable about the subject.

This has always required intelligent practice: as Brower said in his intro-ductory essay in *The Defense of Reading*, remarkably few students understand what a "point" in a paper is. Fellow-teachers in Humanities 6 at Harvard and in Introductory Literature at Rutgers were often partly fellow-students as these communal courses tried to create exercises to inculcate the interwoven skills of textual responsiveness and relevant generalization. For an impressive number of students, both graduate and undergraduate, the education they received has been seminal—never to be forgotten—and successful in terms of professional careers. David Bartholomae (University of Pittsburgh) and Donald McQuade (Berkeley) are two of Poirier's students who have become nationally known in the field of teaching of writing: at least partly, as they would be the first to acknowledge, because of the training in reading that they received from him.

Even for those who have not become professionals there has never been any doubt of the seriousness and importance of accurate and responsive reading. The language of literature, they learn, is simply a concentrated version of lan-guage they encounter every day, crucial to social interactions and the emotions associated with them: love, friendship, resentment, hostility, indifference. Since most people navigate such feelings and experiences with at least some success and understanding, the challenge has been to make them apply their skills as readers of the conversations in which they regularly engage to the complex forms of language to be found in literature: "You would be run over by a truck if you read the experiences of your life as sloppily as you're reading this text," he would tell his undergraduates.

Since literary language for Poirier is thus a heightened form of the language we all use, pleasure-giving as well as communicative, it requires from listeners the attentiveness due to any conversation that is to be taken seriously, and as speakers or writers an awareness of our expressive possibilities, a refusal to succumb to clichés and formulas, and a heightened consciousness of how we actually sound to others. It is no accident that many of his closest professional colleagues have also been good friends through the years, as the current volume richly attests. The expressive and responsive qualities he values in good critics are also those he values in his friendships.

The essays in this volume pay tribute to Poirier as one of the leading scholars and critics in the country, the author of seminal books on American literature and culture, a founding editor of the influential Library of America, as well as the principal editor of *Raritan*. They honor him not only by choosing as their subject some of the authors about whom he has written so tellingly himself—James, Frost, Emerson, and Shakespeare—but by focusing on the "life of language" as it exceeds codification.

The first two essays, Ross Posnock's and Edward Said's, address the most general critical issues. After analyzing Poirier's critical affinities with Emerson and American pragmatist philosophers, Posnock extends Poirier's emphasis on process to a writer he did not deal with in *Poetry and Pragmatism*: W.E.B. Du Bois. Said describes his dissatisfactions with New Criticism as a Ph.D. student in the sixties, but also with some current theoretical approaches which have become detached from the cultural issues that originally gave them urgency. Leo Bersani demonstrates to a class why Sartre's initially exciting, extractable philosophy in *No Exit* is less rich and alive as literature than La Fontaine's fable of the two pigeons, even though the latter's "moral" seems simplistic and even banal.

Others analyze their focal authors (or the characters they create) as readers: David Bromwich shows that Edmund Burke "read" his own political stance and that of the French revolutionaries through the lens of *King Lear*, and Barry Qualls reads *Wuthering Heights*, as Emily Brontë may have done, against two models of narrative exemplified in the Bible. Two analyses demonstrate the inadequacy of critical paradigms to the life of James's characters: Margery Sabin discusses two novellas to demonstrate that neither sociological nor aestheticizing models can do justice to the interpersonal yet private consciousness of the protagonists, and Millicent Bell shows how the principal characters of "Madame de Mauves" are themselves aware of the over-simplifications of the American versus European scheme so often taken to explain much of James's fiction. Modifying the argument that Poirier made about Jane Austen and Mark Twain in *A Defense of Reading*, Thomas Edwards shows that in her last novel, *Persuasion*, Austen came closer to questioning the authority of social language than some of her critics gave her credit for.

The two essays on Frost are exemplars of close reading alert to the poet's cultural context: the Americanization of commonplace European literary tropes in John Hollander's discussion of Frost's birds and, in Anne Ferry's analysis, the connections between Frost's titles and his poems, compared to the practices in this regard of more obviously modernist poets such as Williams, Eliot, and Stevens. Two other essays, by Frank Kermode and Robert Garis, focus on the function of rhetoric in drama: Shakespeare's dramatic integration in late plays, such as *Coriolanus*, of a repertoire of rhetorical devices from his early plays, and Ibsen's expressive use of deliberately unmetaphorical language.

Fittingly, the last selection in the volume is a poem. David Ferry's brilliant and evocative translation of a Horatian Ode conveys its themes of friendship and affection obliquely but unmistakably even to those whose ears are normally endowed, let alone to someone with perfect pitch: through rhythm and allusion, through the sounds of the speaking voice.

*Bridget Gellert Lyons*

# CHAPTER 1

# *Reading Poirier Pragmatically*

ROSS POSNOCK

$\mathcal{T}$o appreciate the importance of Richard Poirier's most recent book, *Poetry and Pragmatism* (1992), one must recall a time when such a title risked baffling most readers. This reaction reflects pragmatism's unstable place in twentieth-century intellectual history. Until and even after Dewey published *Art as Experience* (1934) the notion of a pragmatist aesthetics was generally regarded as little more than an oxymoron. America's one indigenous philosophy was widely viewed as the loyal servant of the era in which it was born—the crass, utilitarian Gilded Age, whose acquisitive ethos it sought to justify and celebrate. In a particularly influential assessment, Lewis Mumford in 1925 found William James and Dewey to be emblematic of "pragmatic acquiescence." Mumford heaped scorn on what he saw as Dewey's impoverished, instrumentalist view of life that reduced human experience to little more than practical activity. Remarkably, only in the last dozen years has this caricature been decisively overturned. Intellectual historians now agree that Mumford grievously misread Dewey, who was already moving towards an aesthetics as Mumford was castigating him.

Indeed, Dewey's intellectual mobility, his belief that in "the moment of passage . . . is that of intensest life," has come to be seen as in itself part of his greatness and of pragmatism's promise.[1] In the last thirty years of his life, Dewey revealed his capacity to challenge some of his deepest beliefs—in Enlightenment rationality—and to radicalize others—in liberalism and in democracy. Pragmatism's devotion to revision, experiment, and risk, to what Dewey called the "intellectual disrobing" of ceaseless inquiry without transcendental grounding, helps account for the contemporary renewal of pragmatism's prestige. Since intellectual prestige in America almost always means importing European standards, rich affinities have been traced between pragmatism's rejection of the Cartesian subject, foundationalism, and epistemology and the animating themes of various continental, post-structuralist thinking. And acknowledged affinities are now beginning to be appreciated: Adorno's admiration for Dewey, Derrida's for Peirce, Habermas's for Mead. Thanks to philosophical pragmatism's foremost champion, Richard Rorty, one may now, without embarrassment, mention James and Dewey in the same sentence with Nietzsche, Wittgenstein, Foucault. "We should see Dewey," Rorty remarks, "as having already gone the route Foucault is traveling."[2]

In this light, Richard Poirier's latest book can be read as intervening to turn Rorty's insight homeward and recover a "scandalously neglected figure" who preceded both Dewey and Foucault but who still awaits recognition as a powerful resource for cultural work.[3] That figure is Emerson, the contemporary of Nietzsche, who found him intoxicating to read, and the thinker whom James and Dewey revered as an intellectual forefather. Linking all of these thinkers is a shared belief that (to repeat Dewey's phrase) power resides in "the moment of passage." Dewey's words tally with James's remark that reality is "still in the making," but they seem also to allude to Emerson, who says, in "Self-Reliance," "power ceases in the instant of repose; it resides in the moment of transition." Poirier is the first to show that Emerson's principle generates "a form of linguistic skepticism" that William James disseminated while teaching philosophy at Harvard when Frost, Stein, Stevens, and Eliot attended. As transmitted through James, Emerson's skepticism significantly shapes the pragmatism that is expressed in the work of these great figures (5).

Emerson inspires the kind of criticism Poirier practices and initiates his book's principal concern—the experiments in language conducted by the "extended tribe of Waldo" (principally those mentioned above, but also Thoreau, Dickinson, Dewey, Whitman, Eliot, and Williams). Poirier redescribes its members as "Emersonian pragmatists" who share a "liberating and creative suspicion as to the dependability of words and syntax" (5), a skepticism premised on the fact that language is a cultural, historical inheritance that at once entraps us and incites our evasive action. This action manifests itself in the act of troping, whereby the human will turns language from predetermined meanings and fashions and refashions new figures to live by. To retain energy, troping can only be a "momentary stay against confusion" (to borrow Frost's famous phrase), a stay that functions as "less a solution," in James's words, than as "a program for more work."[4] Poirier shows the incessant, antagonistic, and exhilarating effort of Emerson and the "line of force" he engenders to keep words in motion and thereby escape (or at least loosen) the gravitational pull of the conventions and conformity that make language possible in the first place.

What gives compelling power to Poirier's Emersonianism is not a worship but a troping of the philosopher who is conventionally regarded as the faintly embarrassing monument to our most cherished *isms*: exceptionalism, individualism, optimism, and ahistoricism. In continuing the "Emersonian reflections" of *The Renewal of Literature*, *Poetry and Pragmatism* reveals that such reflection entails toppling Emerson from his pedestal of cultural authority by inflecting him with the Nietzschean and pragmatist commitment to the way-wardness of genius, its performative energy that challenges "those clarifications of purpose and design which are essential to public and institutional life."[5]

*Poetry and Pragmatism* is certainly the most important work on the subject since Dewey's. Though a relatively short book, admittedly "partial," Poirier's is criticism of "density," a word he values over "difficulty," which he asso-ciates with a modernist mode of self-impressed pomposity. In contrast, density describes writing that at first seems clear or casual but which becomes, upon reflection, reverberant and imponderable. Density is usually accompanied, says Poirier, "not by the extruding allusiveness of modernism but by the covert allusiveness of troping."[6] The last four words convey precisely both Poirier's own technique and his subject. And because his troping at times alludes to some of his previous books, *Poetry and Pragmatism* crystallizes into a kind of summa, if we can cleanse that word of its grandiosity and finality and turn it towards action and expectation.

Poirier has always been wary of the definitive, and though an eminent cultural authority, he has remained on uneasy terms with many of American culture's basic assumptions, especially about literature as redemptive authority. Instead, he has made his intellectual career one of continuous troping, for this activity requires a discipline of work that nurtures the human capacity for creative conduct. The work of writing literature and of reading it, says Poirier, can do no more than "provide exemplary metaphors for action in the world" (95). In today's cultural climate such modesty will satisfy neither the contemporary cultural right's nostalgia for moral order nor the left's demand for radical curricular change. Both sides disguise what they implicitly share: a complacent assumption that literature's splendid linguistic recalcitrance can be comfortably harnessed to the tenets of an ideology—be it liberal humanism or cultural critique.

For over thirty years Poirier has contested any effort to arrest literature's "extravagance," its propensity for "vagrancy" and the "superfluous," key words for Thoreau, James, and Emerson, words whose connotations Poirier brilliantly probes. Poirier's master trope of performance regards literature as a "form of energy" that is not "a source of comfort and order but rather of often dislocating, disturbing impulses," as he remarked in the preface to his most self-consciously strategic book *The Performing Self*. The ways in which Poirier has adroitly managed his master metaphor, steering it past the siren calls of orthodoxy, with its temptations of repose and inevitable irrelevance, have been various, subtle and richly instructive both in terms of what it tells us about navigating a literary career in post-war America and, more important, as a profound enactment of what it means to be an Emersonian intellectual. Yet to construe this last phrase in conventional terms is to risk misreading Poirier completely.

By stripping Emerson of the encrusted identities of his cultural monu-mentality, Poirier seeks to permit Emerson "to *be* Emerson." This deliberately paradoxical claim in *The Renewal of Literature*—that "Emerson has been a pervasive presence, but he has not been allowed to *be* Emerson"[7]—receives, perhaps, its richest, if subtlest, gloss in *Poetry and Pragmatism*. Near the end of the introduction, after showing Emerson's efforts to find a way to evade the paradox that language at once enables and betrays the effort to represent the immediate flow of one's experience, Poirier asks, "how is one to cope with this situation without collapsing into silence?" (28).

"The answer," says Poirier, lies in the phrase "the soul Becomes," an allusion to a passage in "Self-Reliance": "This one fact the world hates, that the soul *becomes*." For Poirier, "the soul" here "is first named, as if, with its definite article, it were an entity; note, too, that its realization as an entity is immediately and forever delayed, its presence transferred to an ever elusive future, by the word '*becomes*.' The soul never 'becomes' a thing or a text; it exists in the action of becoming" (28).

Poirier's "answer" in this passage, his identification of what he calls Emerson's "saving principle," is a pivotal moment in Poirier's latest book and is a way to explain how Emerson can be "allowed to *be* Emerson." Poirier's italics echo Emerson, as both "to *be*" and "*becomes*" are inflected with the creative energy of process without telos. "To *be* Emerson" is to dissolve as entity, as monument, as mythology, and to exist in the action of becoming as it is enacted in the movements of his prose, in writing that creates "ever ponderable, ever enlivening, ceaselessly vibrant energies of language" (31). To *be* an Emersonian reader is to dwell within this linguistic turbulence, charting its flowings and resisting the refuge of fixed meaning for immersion in the confusions and agitations, the contradictions that always mark our "barely negotiable" relation to language. To *be* the greatest Emersonian critic, that is, to *be* Richard Poirier, involves generating one's master trope of performance as disruptive action out of the fact that the mind "goes antagonizing on," as Emerson says in "Experience." It feeds off the energy released in the struggle to swerve from what we require—the repose offered by all that precedes us, be it embodied in genetic, linguistic, or cultural inheritance. More concretely, Poirier's commitment to Emersonian reflection impels him to devise ways to resist absorbing the act of work into the monumentality of textuality.

To repeat Poirier's query: "How is one to cope with this situation?" Poirier's response has been to create an oeuvre that is best read (to borrow his words about Emerson) not as a "series of more or less discrete texts each holding in trust a source of wisdom," but as overlapping voices in a prolonged conversation, voices that affirm, repeat, clash and revise each other (29). And his answer has also been to fashion communal cultural forms that exist in the action of becoming; that is, he has initiated generative, ongoing cultural projects—*Raritan*, *The Library of America*—that perform and re-form the endless work of culture. In sum, the Emerson who has been the beacon guiding Poirier's course teaches the invaluable "art of *not* arriving," which is what Poirier calls the dexterous and subtle mode of reading that first Reuben Brower and then Poirier, Paul de Man, and others taught at Harvard in the fifties as a more skeptical version of the New Criticism (182).

But to call Emerson a beacon too blandly describes a relation far more intimately entangled, a relation that might be glimpsed in Poirier's explanation as to why "Emerson remains the greatest of his tribe." Not content to describe our vexed relation to language, Emerson's "writing *enacts* the struggles." He dramatizes "his agitations when confronted with the evidence that the words he is putting down on paper, including words of resistance and dissent, are themselves products of 'previous human thinking'" (27). Emerson's willingness to "suffer" for language's betrayals makes him "a truly sacrificial figure," who, in his writing, "moves as victim and victor" (31). Poirier's figuring here suggests that Emerson offers himself as a corpus to be ingested as sustenance for his inheritors, a logic that recalls Henry James's remark made soon after the death of his brother William. Henry wrote that "he is a possession, of real magnitude, and I shall find myself still living upon him to the end. My life, thank God, is impregnated with him."[8]

Infused with Emerson, Poirier has been living upon him from the start of his career. And to recognize their intimacy is crucial if we are to grasp both the intra-textual structure of Poirier's oeuvre and the remarkable and intricate self-reflexivity of *Poetry and Pragmatism*. This work is so impregnated with Emerson and the pragmatist tradition that Poirier's commentary can be read, at nearly every turn, as descriptive also of how he himself, rhetorically, has made a career of troping. What this double reference provides is the rare opportunity to witness a critic going beyond exposition and analysis, which is criticism's usual domain, and entering the realm of enactment, that pragmatist poetic space where action, not entity, is all.

Rather than asserting his work's self-reflexive resonance, Poirier insinuates it through inflection and, above all, repetition. When we consider that these modes of indirection are discussed in detail in *Poetry and Pragmatism*, where Poirier says that the performing self of Emersonian pragmatism "responds less by assertion than by inflection" (142), we can begin to discern this double register. We can hear it more fully by noting that performance has particular pertinence here since this book originated as a series of vocal performances, as lectures expanded in print but still "meant for the ear" (3). And meant also for an "audience hospitable to exploratory and digressive movements in an argument" and "grateful, now and then, for a few clarifying repetitions" (4).

Announcing repetition as one of his techniques, Poirier soon makes it a theme central to his important argument that far from believing in absolute originality, Emerson conceives it as "repetition with a difference" (18). Man, declares Emerson, is born "but to be a Re-former, a Re-maker of what man has made," or, more famously, "every man is a quotation from all his ancestors." Revising that quotation becomes our life's work. The static state of textuality threatens to proclaim an illusory (because unconditional) and deadening originality. Emerson mitigates this by understanding every text as reconstructing "some previous texts of work, work that itself is always, again, work-in-progress. . . . each being a revision of past texts to meet present needs" (17). This also aptly describes Poirier's own oeuvre of interweaving Emersonian reflections. Repetition, like language, is a socializing force tethering to earth the flight into the infinite towards which original genius aims. Poirier is really the first to make vivid the value of the earthbound Emerson, the immanent rather than transcendental thinker, the Emerson of complicity and limits who asks us "to submit to the *poverty* of subjectivity" (73).

Among those writers who comprise the Emersonian "line of force," Poirier finds that their relation to past literature tends to be poised rather than anxious, as if "these writers simply feel *entitled* to such repetitions" because ordinary idiom and the things of this world are funded with poetic, cultural associations available to everyone (104). At times, insouciance prevails in their attitude toward the past, as in Emerson and Frost's figuration of thinking as skating stylishly and gracefully on the surfaces of previous ideas and texts (65). This skating is a way, says Poirier, of "saying you are in a slippery but by no means anxious relation to earlier creations, texts, or truths. It can also put you into an actively skeptical, antagonistic/flirtatious relation to your own writing, especially as you discover that it, too, might, as the word hits the pages, be gravitating dangerously toward 'pretended absolutes'" (66). Poirier offers the example of Emerson, whose self-interrogation occurs most dramatically when he turns on the very phrase—self-reliance—that he has honored by making it the title of an essay. Emerson abruptly demands, "Why, then, do we prate of self-reliance?"

This whole passage from Poirier enjoys its own "antagonistic/flirtatious" relation to two of his previous texts. Not only does the Emerson just quoted appear in *The Renewal of Literature* in a discussion about the propensity of literary works to develop an energy subversive of their own "internally generated rhetorical structures." But twenty years earlier, in *The Performing Self*, Poirier had enacted his own moment of self-troping when, in disagreeing with Herbert Marcuse's idealist belief in art as a higher form of life, he noted: "literature in Marcuse is a kind of 'world elsewhere.' And (as I've tried to suggest in a work of that title) it can never be. Given the nature of language . . . no book can, for very long, separate itself from this world."[9] As if correcting the many readers who misread (and continue to misread) his title as indicating an endorsement of aestheticist withdrawal, and perhaps wishing to clarify this issue left unresolved in that book, Poirier sought to deflate his titular phrase (itself borrowed from *Coriolanus*) that had taken on an unfortunate life of its own and threatened to become a "pretended absolute."

The most obvious way that Poirier has troped textuality and made his works open to change, open to conversing with and, at times, challenging, one another is his habit of reissuing his books (so far three of the previous five) with new prefaces, new inflections to meet present needs. But he has managed less obvious, more internal intra-textual inflections. Before discussing a particularly striking one, it might be best appreciated after looking at how Poirier treats the political implications of Emersonian pragmatism's effort to have us regard reading and writing as endless work with language. This work "just might possibly *begin* to help change existing realities, and only then if the work is carried on endlessly" (95). Beyond this deliberately tentative statement describing the relation of literature to "social or communal efficacy," Poirier will not go.

He resists, even though William James, Dewey, and other pragmatists went further, often acting as if literature had, potentially, far greater social consequences. And he resists at a time when many on the contemporary cultural left clamor to make literature and criticism an instrument for social justice. Bothered by what he calls "the loud mouth of contemporary criticism," with its demand that literature offer far more than a "momentary stay against confusion," Poirier asks that deconstructive skepticism be more often directed at "the language of criticism itself and *its* claims to large significance" (167). Such claims, whether found in James and Dewey or on the cultural left, betray "a compulsion to evade the fact" that to work intensely with language is so "special a discipline that it can legitimately hope . . . to have only a minimal effect on existing realities" (94). The pragmatists, according to Poirier's persuasive argument, recognized "their own extraordinary degree of literariness" yet disguised it (in virile metaphors of writing as hard labor and in "aphoristic availability") to avoid its "socially alienating effects."

For Poirier, reading is "most rigorously historical" when one accepts the challenge to do for oneself "some version of the work being done word by word *in* the writing," its "twists and turns of words." This labor requires us as readers to come as close as possible to "duplicating the actions which went into the writing—actions inevitably of cultural resistance as well as of conformity" (97–98). To chart the movements of words rather than to fix their meaning is the task of pragmatist reading, a practice whose procedures were first made explicit by William James in "The Stream of Thought" chapter in *The Principles of Psychology*. Poirier brilliantly shows that James's linguistic skepticism is not only Emersonian but inseparable from James's acute awareness of the relations between things. Our rigid focus on things themselves, says James, has the effect of minimizing or ignoring relations.

Our reading habits reflect this bias; they remain stunted by scanting transitives (verbs, adverbs, prepositions, conjunctions) and attending only to the substantives (nouns) in sentences. The privilege granted substantives, declares James, "works against our perception of the truth" (quoted 143). To unsettle this priority requires what James calls a "reinstatement of the vague" as a way, says Poirier, "to take the edge off words themselves, to blur and refract them," and thereby unstiffen our normal way of reading which, given our preference for fixity and certainty, habitually inclines us towards a sentence's conclusions and key words (139). Poirier notes that James's effort to loosen the hold of substantives in favor of transitives and relations is already anti-patriarchal and "implicitly feminist": his ideal grammar leads to his anti-imperialist politics "and not the other way around" (152).

To witness what pragmatist reading can do we need only observe Poirier's response to Emerson's claim that "power ceases in the instant of repose; it resides in the moment of transition from a past to a new state . . . in the darting to an aim." Focusing on the transitive "in" quickly disturbs the conventional image we have of the Emersonian self. For by saying that power is not a result of transition but rather "*in* it, and nowhere else," Emerson is also implying that the source of power, the self, is not the solid rock of self-reliance that his rhetoric of radical individualism advertises. Rather, says Poirier, the self is neither an entity nor a function, but startlingly precarious, transitional, inferential, appearing "only *in* its doings, *in* its workings, *in* its actions with words—*in* movements which turn back against any self, or on any assemblage of words as it may have been constituted even a moment ago" (67). Poirier's attention here to the work of Emerson's transitives succeeds in troping the received wisdom that extols (or vilifies) Emerson as our archetypal imperial self. Indeed, says Poirier, "Emerson is actually opposed to individualism in the customary or social sense in which the term is most often used" (29).

One lesson of William James's seminal pragmatist reorientation of reading is that, says Poirier, "familiar, homey words cannot be dispensed with. . . . We must learn once again to hear sounds already deeply embedded in the caves of the human mouth and of the human ear," sounds relegated by most philosophers "to the fringes of discourse" (136). Poirier urges that "we listen caringly" for these "scarcely audible phrases and words," for they can be reshaped by poets attuned to what Frost called "the sound of sense." Frost is so receptive to transitives that he reworks them to "catch those tones or sounds of speech that can substantially inflect or even reverse the meanings normally assigned to words" (136). What results are poems where meaning is insinuated or inflected rather than asserted.

In this Jamesian context, Frost's "Mending Wall" becomes, for Poirier, a conflict between a believer in substantives—the stolid neighbor who laconically affirms that "good fences make good neighbors"—and the poem's speaker, who has faith in transitives, "in whatever moves things from static positions" (151). Given the prominence of "wall" in the title and the fact that the stubborn neighbor's aphoristic string of substantives is the poem's most famous line, the poem seems clearly biased against the transitive. But by reading pragmatically one can see otherwise:

> Something there is that doesn't love a wall,
> That sends the frozen-ground-swell under it
> And spills the upper boulders in the sun,
> And makes gaps even two can pass abreast.

The strategic vagueness of the initial "something" (a favorite word of

Frost's) starts a "movement that manages to scramble surrounding efforts at clarification" until it hits a blank "wall" (145). The sound of this opening line, observes Poirier, "creates a mystery, or what the poem itself calls a 'gap.' This gap is not filled by summary bits of wisdom, like 'good fences make good neighbors.' . . . No, good neighbors are made by phrases whose incompleteness is the very sign of neighborliness: 'something there is.' Anyone can go along with that," for it creates "chances for companionability; this 'something' doesn't love walls; its love is given instead to the 'gaps' in walls wherein people may join" (150–151). In stressing the "gaps" that "something" makes to be the occasion for a transition to tentative human bonding, Poirier's reading itself responds to a gap—an interpretive one, in his 1977 analysis of "Mending Wall"—that was deliberately left open. In this earlier discussion, Poirier had resisted closure.

To see how this gap was formed we need to recall that in his previous reading, in his great book on Frost, Poirier's inflection fell on the act of making in the opening of the poem's fourth line: "and makes gaps," part of his point being that "if fences do not 'make good neighbors' the *making* of fences can." But in passing, Poirier noted that most readers ignore that the playful speaker (and not the rigid neighbor) is the one "committed to the making and remaking" of "human structurings": "the point is usually missed, along with most other things importantly at work in this poem."[10] In light of his most recent reading, this casual acceptance in 1977 that his own discussion might be incomplete becomes a fertile vagueness or gap, a pointing toward "other things" (echoing Frost's "something") that await to be partially realized in the future, that is, by his current inflection on "and makes *gaps*." In short, by juxtaposing these two readings of Frost's poem, Poirier's intra-textual repetition with a difference becomes visible as a means of enacting, not merely describing, the pragmatist commitment to transitives, to generative deferrals of clarity. These incompletions ask us to respond to gaps not as evidence of linguistic crisis or of the abyss (the overheated diction of some deconstructionists), but rather as invitations to make a transition, to keep moving, to keep reading (149). "Something" remains to be understood: "the poem ["Mending Wall"] never does or can directly yield all the significances I want to find in it" (150).

The "art of not arriving," which requires near acrobatic poise, is inscribed not only in Poirier's critical practice but is writ large in the cultural politics of his career. More than twenty years ago he suggested that English studies need only remain "in motion" to avoid conformity, be it to the old left's fear of trendiness, the new left's demand that literature be socially engaged, or the academic conservative's plea for business as usual. To all of these factions, Poirier's performing self, with its cry of "more disruption" of academic hierarchy (a plea redolent of its historical hour—1968), became threatening, for it eluded any precise political labels. This reinstatement of the vague seems to have been precisely his point, a way of troping the available intellectual models of the day. He had performed his most notorious troping a year earlier, in

1967. As a member of the editorial board of *Partisan Review*, that old left bastion of modernism and Marxism, Poirier challenged the journal's ossified high cultural agenda by describing in its pages what he had been "learning from the Beatles."

The essay of that name enacts his anti-hierarchial effort to make performances other than literature—"dance and sports . . . film or popular music . . . newspapers, political speeches, advertising . . . the conduct of the classroom itself"—available for academic study. Before we blame or praise Poirier as a godfather of contemporary cultural studies, it is important to add that he proposed opening up English studies but not at literature's expense. Rather, he believed that widening the bounds of criticism would give literature a chance to prove "not its cultural superiority . . . but its superiority as a training ground for all other efforts in the struggle for expression."[11] This kind of saving distinction is fatally missing from the programs of today's curricular reformers.

Neither old left, new left, nor neoconservative, Poirier's stance might be described as "radically conservative" (what he calls Emerson) or, more aptly, as pragmatist. Because of their pragmatist love of transition, revision, and restless analysis, cultural critics like Henry James, Kenneth Burke, and John Dewey tend to be written off as politically naive or worse. Poirier has been no exception. More than one critic flustered by Poirier's Emersonian elusiveness has sought to fix him in the caricature of an ahistoricist aesthete, a label whose political content has varied over the years. In the seventies, his work was associated with the anti-political formalism of the avant-garde; in the nineties some on the left have regarded it as symptomatic of an exhausted, betrayed Cold War rhetoric of American exceptionalism that persists in dividing reality into simple oppositions.

The easiest way to prove the emptiness of this last characterization is to point to Poirier's discussion in *Poetry and Pragmatism* of what he regards as Emersonian pragmatism's most glaring "fault line"—its political naïveté (121). This theme surfaced in his earlier study of Frost, where Poirier noted the poet's blindness to social systems, his lack of "historical vision." Now Poirier bluntly, and correctly, identifies William James's weakness for "vapid political rhetoric" that celebrates America as God and nature's nation blissfully innocent of corruption. In a canny remark, Poirier finds James's belief "that the enemy is never within America's economic-social system, it is only whatever is opposed to America," as sounding "like a preparation for the mentality of the Cold War" (119). And in a footnote Poirier takes issue with Rorty's recent neo-Jamesian claim that the Cold War was a "good war." According to Poirier, the war has done "unacceptable damage to the victor country's sense of itself" and its relations to otherness in general. Poirier calls his dissent from Rorty "crucially pragmatic," by which he means that the war cannot be called good because, as he sees it, the war's conduct depended on the United States becoming frozen in "an immaculate conception" of itself that justified indifference or hostility to any and all who failed to subscribe to this myth (204–205). I think that on this point Poirier would be closer to Rorty's hero, Dewey. After all, Dewey was acutely sensitive to the dangers of self-righteous Americanism. In *Freedom and Culture* (1939), Dewey warned Americans that a "complacent and self-congratulatory" belief in the inherent health of their own political system betrayed a profound ignorance of the fragility of democracy. Dewey's unsparing estimate of American democracy as founded not on fixed doctrine but on "an unflagging, unceasing" faith that has to be enacted daily testifies to the rigor of his pragmatism, its refusal to leave cherished certitudes undisturbed.[12]

Sharing this skepticism is another illustrious member of Dewey's generation, W.E.B. Du Bois, a student at Harvard in the 1880s who imbibed pragmatism directly from William James. In conclusion, I want briefly to show why Du Bois should be regarded as part of the "extended tribe of Waldo." And in expanding Waldo's tribe I am following Poirier's lead, for he himself has recently been adding new voices such as Frank O'Hara. Scholarly work on Du Bois's relation to James has largely been confined to the latter's influence on "double consciousness," the famous phrase from Du Bois's masterpiece *The Souls of Black Folk*. But the impact of Du Bois's beloved professor was not merely local and contained. Nor was it restricted to Jamesian psychology. Du Bois called himself "a devoted follower of William James at the time he was developing his pragmatic philosophy."[13] And in another memoir he noted: "The turning was due to William James."[14] This short sentence recalls that James encouraged him to move from studying philosophy to history and social problems, but it also neatly distills the philosopher's catalytic impact upon Du Bois's predilection for the mobility of troping. Sociologist, historian, novelist, essayist, and poet, Du Bois's is a career of turnings, of finding freedom in moments of transition, of moving between. Skeptical of the preordained, preferring to improvise under pressure of changing historical circumstance, Du Bois declared that "no idea is perfect and forever valid. Always to be living and apposite and timely, it must be modified and adapted to changing facts."[15]

Du Bois seems to have internalized pragmatism as a method and style of thinking, for it tapped and channelled what he called his restless "anarchy of the spirit which is inevitably the goal of all human consciousness."[16] He shared this spirit with James, that self-described "anarchistic sort of creature" who cherished "a world of anarchy . . . with an 'ever not quite' to all our formulas, and novelty and possibility forever leaking in."[17] Du Bois construed Jamesian pragmatism, with its pluralistic immersion in indeterminacy and chance, as in effect a philosophical anarchy whose lesson to Du Bois, the social scientist, was that "he could not stand apart and study *in vacuo*." Abandoning the insulation of a spectator theory of knowledge (to borrow Dewey's phrase), Du Bois opened himself to a "certain tingling challenge of risk."

Du Bois's decidedly Jamesian phrase is apt, for it describes the visceral stance of his writing during twenty-four years (1910–1934) as editor of the

NAACP journal *The Crisis*. He calls his work in that quarter-century "sociology" inspired by "Jamesian pragmatism." I have been quoting from a remarkable yet seldom cited 1944 career retrospective, "My Evolving Program For Negro Freedom."[18] It charts the various "re-adaptations" he has been improvising over the course of his career. His pragmatist sociology counts as the most dramatic revision, for it set Du Bois "in the midst of action" and "continuous, kaleidoscopic change of conditions." The hectic pace of the "hot reality of real life" rendered his "previous purely scientific program" (his Atlanta University studies) old before it was even analyzed. Driven by journalistic immediacy, Du Bois's pragmatist sociology attempts not to discover physical laws of action but instead to "measure the element of Chance in human conduct." At the helm of *The Crisis*, Du Bois "faced situations that called—shrieked—for action" if "social death" was to be averted, and that left no time for the patient testing of scientific observation. Yet neither could he simply work "fast and furiously" by "intuition and emotion"; thus Du Bois seeks to be responsive to the raw unfolding of events while simultaneously pursuing "ordered knowledge" of the race problem which "research and tireless observation" would supply.[19] Du Bois is working in the grain of pragmatist science as James construed it: his effort is to practice science as immersion in and reflection upon gross experience, rather than science as preoccupied with technical verification and a specious objectivity.

Summing up his pragmatist stance, Du Bois writes: "I was continually the surgeon probing blindly, yet with what knowledge and skill I could muster, for unknown ill." This is a metaphor of crisis, of authority stripped of authority and flirting with chaos as it confronts the hazards of unmastered experience in a "tramp and vagrant world, adrift in space." These are James's words describing the pragmatist universe where Du Bois reconstructed authority with the permanent risk of chaos built in. Above all, pragmatism inspires in Du Bois a mode of conduct that precisely accords with the mobility of his "double consciousness" of "unreconciled strivings," a tension Du Bois internalizes as the structure of his vision and of his prose.

Du Bois would not merit inclusion in the tribe of Waldo if his respect for the incalculable was not also embodied in the calculating elusiveness of his style. One way to describe the stylistic triumph of *The Souls of Black Folk* is its enactment of an understanding—rare even to this day—that Jamesian pluralism is not merely tolerance of multiplicity but, more precisely, the recovery of what James calls the "unclassified residuum," that which slips the concept's grasp and encourages the "reinstatement of the vague," to borrow a phrase from *The Principles of Psychology*.[20] In *Souls* Du Bois carries on this reinstatement of the vague as a political and aesthetic project. In a seldom-examined assessment of *Souls* he published in 1904, Du Bois speaks of the "penumbra of vagueness and half-veiled allusion" that he has spun around "a clear central message."[21] While he notes that this vagueness has made some readers "impatient," it is "the nature of the message" that is at least partly responsible. That message is summarized in "The Forethought" to *Souls*: "Herein lie buried many things which if read with patience may show the strange meaning of being black. . . . I have sought here to sketch, in vague, uncertain outline, the spiritual world in which ten thousand thousand Americans live and strive."[22] To excavate meanings long repressed under the weight of racist stereotype, Du Bois must step "within the Veil" of segregation and raise it so that the reader "may view faintly its deeper recesses." Hence his immanent stance requires that vagueness be a condition of perception. Du Bois also assimilates the Veil of vagueness into a serpentine prose style that dissolves the stark rigidities bred by Jim Crow. In its elaborate delicacy and deliberate fusions and confusions of pronoun references, his style blurs divisions and grants respect for the intricacy of black experience. It demands the reader's openness to complexity. Vagueness becomes a tactic (admittedly risky) to frustrate stock responses by arousing the reader's sympathetic patience. The patience Du Bois urges was another practice he acquired in his aesthetic initiation in Europe: "I had been before, above all, in a hurry. I wanted a world, hard, smooth, and swift."[23]

By embroidering his first non-academic book with the aesthetic textures he had imbibed first-hand, Du Bois signals his intention to make *Souls* a modernist artifact and not a collection of magazine articles. Difficulty and indirection become his chosen modes, the only ones flexible enough to do justice to the "strange experience" of "being a problem." Du Bois is thoroughly aware that his experiment is modernist. In his 1904 statement he speaks of renouncing "the usual impersonal and judicial attitude of the traditional author" as a loss "in authority but a gain in vividness." He mentions the "intimate tone of self-revelation," the "distinctively subjective note that runs in each essay." The epistemological decentering Du Bois describes aligns him with modernism as it exchanges what might be termed an imperial mode of authenticity for a liberated modernist one. Du Bois topples the Olympian assumption of authorial omniscience for the new authenticity of vulnerability. The impersonal clarity of the imperial mode is replaced by freely confessed ambivalences and uncertainties, what Du Bois calls in 1904 "abrupt transitions of style, tone and viewpoint," all leading to a "distinct sense of incompleteness and sketchiness."

Du Bois's pleasure in troping and his strategic vagueness argue for his inclusion in Poirier's pragmatist literary history, but also vividly confirm and extend that "line of force." That is, Du Bois's splendid appropriation of his Jamesian inheritance testifies implicitly to the power of Poirier's narrative. The most apt, most pragmatist, response to the absence of Du Bois from Poirier's book is to regard it as a gap in a text whose author has taught us to regard his gaps not as defects but as invitations for future tropings. In distilling the meditations of a lifetime of remarkable work with language, *Poetry and Pragmatism* dwells in the pragmatist poetic space of enactment. In banishing "that stolid word *about*" (in James's phrase), it becomes entirely its own reward.

## Notes

1. John Dewey, *Art as Experience* (New York: Minton, Balch and Co., 1934). The present essay is an expanded version of one that first appeared in the *Yale Review* 80, no. 3 (1992): 156–169.
2. Richard Rorty, *The Consequences of Pragmatism* (Minneapolis: University of Minnesota Press, 1982), 63.
3. Richard Poirier, *Poetry and Pragmatism* (Cambridge: Harvard University Press, 1992), 6. Hereafter page references are cited in parenthesis in the text.
4. William James, *Pragmatism* (Cambridge: Harvard University Press, 1975), 31.
5. Richard Poirier, *The Renewal of Literature* (New York: Random House, 1987), 76.
6. Poirier, *Renewal*, 131.
7. Poirier, *Renewal*, 19.
8. Henry James, *Letters*, ed. Leon Edel (Cambridge: Harvard University Press, 1984), 4:562.
9. Richard Poirier, *The Performing Self* (New York: Oxford University Press, 1971), 68.
10. Richard Poirier, *Robert Frost: The Work of Knowing* (New York: Oxford University Press, 1977), 104–105.
11. Poirier, *Performing Self*, 85.
12. Poirier's critique of James only makes more puzzling his tendency in *Poetry and Pragmatism* to scant Dewey's achievement of a remarkably supple pragmatism that, like Poirier's, might be said to take Frost's line (from "A Servant to Servants") "the best way out is always through" as its watchword. Thus Poirier does not recognize that Dewey, who had little patience for James's naïveté, might serve as a corrective to Emersonian pragmatism's lapses into exceptionalism and other forms of historical myopia. Only to Emerson and not to Dewey does Poirier ascribe "the rare courage of an uncertainty that will at all costs speak its mind" (112). And only inferentially can we discern that Dewey alone of the pragmatists was without "distaste for social or economic theory" (119). These evasions of Dewey are consistent with a lack of any sustained engagement with the pioneering *Art as Experience*, with its Emersonian emphasis on art as the "interaction of energies" colliding with "reciprocal resistances" (Dewey).
13. W.E.B. Du Bois, *The Autobiography of W.E.B. Du Bois: A Soliloquy on Viewing My Life from the Last Decade of Its First Century* (New York: International Publishers, 1968), 133.
14. W.E.B. Du Bois, *Writings* (New York, The Library of America, 1986), 582.
15. Du Bois, *Writings*, 776.
16. Du Bois, *Writings*, 652.
17. Quoted in Ralph Barton Perry, *The Thought and Character of William James* (Boston: Little, Brown, 1935), 2:700.
18. W.E.B. Du Bois, "My Evolving Program for Negro Freedom," in *What the Negro Wants*, ed. R. Logan (Chapel Hill: University of North Carolina Press, 1944), 57, 58.
19. Du Bois, "My Evolving Program," 56–57.
20. William James, *The Will to Believe* (Cambridge: Harvard University Press, 1979), 222; *The Principles of Psychology* (Cambridge: Harvard University Press, 1983), 246.
21. W.E.B. Du Bois, *Book Reviews*, ed. Herbert Aptheker (Millwood, NY: KTO Press, 1977), 9.
22. Du Bois, *Writings*, 359.
23. Du Bois, *Writings*, 587.

# CHAPTER 2

# The Franco-American Dialogue: A Late Twentieth-Century Reassessment

## EDWARD W. SAID

*I*n the opening pages of his massive history of the twentieth century the distinguished British historian Eric Hobsbawm talks about the unevenness of his method in the book and the "shaky foundations" on which it finally rests. As the author of three magisterial volumes on the nineteenth century, Hobsbawm says that he found himself confronting the history of his own time with a far less sure grasp of its literature, sources, and ultimate interpretive meaning than he had commanded for his earlier studies of the modern past. In the end this did not deter him, since the major themes he wished to treat in the twentieth century corresponded to and overlapped with his own life's experiences; far from disqualifying him as historian, this congruence enabled him instead to write as a "participant observer." Moreover, he says a little later, the tendency of present generations to live in a sort of "permanent present" in which the past has been all but obliterated, impels a historian of that present to restore the past with an urgency that consequently makes the historian "more essential at the end of the millennium than ever before."[1]

On a much more modest scale, it seems to me that any assessment of the extraordinarily fruitful and interesting contemporary cultural encounter that I shall discuss here must be based on a similarly flawed historical and interpretative mode. For to assess the recent Franco-American dialogue in literary theory is to try to deal with something both extremely close and essentially unfinished. There is therefore no alternative but to be personal and somewhat impressionistic in the manner of a participant observer, although we are fortunate that a great number of actual texts that are part of the encounter are still available, read, and used. I shall consequently operate on the assumption that what I shall talk about will in effect be a public history tied to verifiable changes and continuities in the contemporary history of critical practice, despite the quite personal tone of my remarks.

As someone who came to the United States in the early 1950s as a schoolboy, and remained there for my entire university education, I can testify to the fact that until the mid-1960s literary studies were almost completely unaffected by any French critic or theorist of the kind that was later to play so central a role in English, as well as foreign language departments. I spent four years as a Princeton undergraduate between 1953 and 1957, during which time I took almost an equal number of courses in English as in French: none of them ventured anywhere near what today we would call either theory or criticism. I do not mean to suggest, however, that I am sorry about this. On the contrary, the single-minded, relatively positivistic and highly empirical approach to the study of literature at Princeton made it possible for undergraduates of that generation to become acquainted with an impressive roster of writers and periods, all of them examined and appreciated as providing us with both an aesthetic and historical experience. In my own case at Princeton, I also had the benefit of the presence there of R. P. Blackmur, a remarkably eccentric genius whose work as a critic constitutes what I still consider to be the major achievement in American criticism. Blackmur was an autodidact and a poet; he had neither finished high school nor attended university, but because of his astonishingly refined readings of modern poetry had attracted the attention of Allen Tate, who had brought him to Princeton, where he soon became—how or by what procedures I have never been able to understand—professor of English. Although I did not study with him directly, I did hear Blackmur lecture, and perhaps more important, I read him, and because of his surprising powers as an academic entrepreneur, I read and heard the many interesting people he managed to bring to Princeton.

It is not widely known that Blackmur was the first major American critic to take Erich Auerbach seriously and to present him, along with Jacques Maritain, Hermann Broch, and Erich Kahler, to an American audience. To read Blackmur on criticism was to encounter literary theory for the first time in a severe and yet strangely beautiful form. He was of course loosely affiliated with the New Critics, but unlike them was not at all bound to Episcopalian and agrarian values, and above all by no means confined only to a carefully circumscribed Eliotesque swathe of English literature. Blackmur's interests ranged over the whole of European and American literature, and alone of all his peers he was as much a master in the explication of difficult poetry as he was of difficult fiction. I was especially impressed by his later essays, written in an extremely gnarled and eccentric style, which explored for the first time in my experience arcane questions of literary form, and metaphysical approaches to the study of theory. An eclectic and completely self-taught *bricoleur*, Blackmur would typically rely on Croce, Augustine, Jung, and Maritain, and he was one of the first Western critics to take seriously and write extended meditations on the work of other critics. More than anyone else he opened the study of literature to theoretical reflection, freeing students and scholars from the provincialism of the New Criticism.

After Blackmur there were two critics who pioneered the study of theory in the United States, Northrop Frye and Kenneth Burke. Both were much more systematic than Blackmur—both in fact were inveterate systemizers—although neither in my opinion had anything like his personal genius. Frye's *Anatomy of Criticism* and Burke's various grammars, as he called them, did attract a fair amount of attention in the late fifties and early sixties, but neither man for a long time acquired the status of an establishment figure, to be read and incorporated into the canon of literary studies. It is one of the themes of my remarks here not only that such once marginal figures as Burke and Frye themselves did in fact become influential and canonical, but that the literary and intellectual culture of the last three decades absorbed and domesticated nearly everyone who had once been an outsider, a rebel or an iconoclast. This is as true of the North Americans as it has been of people like Barthes, Foucault, Benjamin, and Bakhtin. I shall also be suggesting throughout that what to me has made all such figures interesting and valuable is what in and about their work did not get absorbed, that particular *quidditas* rooted in the irreducibly individual and unregimentable practice of a particularly ingenious and active mind. Criticism is primarily performance, not prescription.

There was, of course, one American critic who pioneered the notion of criticism and the arts not as monumental and, in the case of criticism, moralistic and judgmental, but as performative and energetic: Richard Poirier. His *The Performing Self* appeared in 1971 but contained essays he had written during the 1960s on an extraordinary range of subjects, from dance, to literature, to popular culture, politics, and, underpinning the collection, the theory of criticism. This book was the first that directly connected criticism not just to the past but to the present and the future; like Barthes, Poirier showed how a brilliantly resourceful "close reader" could read society as a whole host of signifying activities, and also demonstrated that critical writing could be as pleasing, as inventive, and as surprising as Arnoldian critics believed it should *not* be. As a reflection on the institutions of literature both in and outside the academy *The Performing Self* was an iconoclastic book, displacing the rigidified attitudes that prevailed in critical study in order to make itself available to the demands of great athletes like Lawrence and Mailer: and, of course, Poirier reflected on these changes with a new consciousness.

But let me return to my narrative. If I were to ask myself what the prevailing ambiance of critical consciousness was like before the French influence was to manifest itself in the mid-1960s I would have to describe a landscape of on the whole quite amazing intellectual and theoretical poverty. I recall that when I first entered Harvard (then considered the leading American graduate school) as a doctoral student in the autumn of 1958 the one intellectually distinguished figure there was the English critic I. A. Richards, with whom I took my first seminar. He was the only professor who seemed to transcend the professional, but nevertheless solid, grounding in a loosely historical approach to literature that Harvard provided through its faculty of well-known scholars. And yet I found Richards strangely disappointing, even though it was in his classes on Platonism in English Poetry that I first heard the names of Ludwig Wittgenstein, C. S. Peirce, and F. H. Bradley applied to a literary, rather than a professional philosophical context. Richards had the strange capacity of raising the most abstruse philosophical and metaphysical issues—for example, the notion of the mind as a poetic object—and then reducing them to what seemed to me to be rather humdrum utilitarian models, complete with diagrams and cartoons. He was then vestigially in his Basic English phase, so whatever he opened up in the way of concepts and problems he tended soon after to shut down into comic sketches. It was a most frustrating encounter, made even more unsatisfying when about a month before the seminar was supposed to end, his secretary walked in and said that Richards would be unable (for reasons of indisposition) to meet us again that semester. I have thought of the whole episode as a symbol not only of Richards's own foreshortened career, but for the way Anglo-American criticism in the twentieth century has refused opportunities and trails to follow offered it by its own, often quite ingenious insights.

What I have been describing characterizes the state of English studies on the eve of what was to be a tremendous transformation, largely as a result of the sudden infusion of French theory in the mid-1960s. For most of this century English, and not American, studies held center stage in American higher education, and indeed within the humanities as a whole. Of course there is more in the way of volume, and perhaps even of quality, to study in English literature than in American, but it is still a strange fact that alone of all the major Western democracies academic experts in the United States did not feel it somehow necessary to put the study of American texts at the core of the literary curriculum. And it is perhaps even more curious that this odd anti-nationalism—snobbish Anglophilia some would call it—was resisted only by a relative handful of outsiders like Perry Miller and F. O. Matthiessen at Harvard, or the basically freelancing Edmund Wilson, who struggled to give American literature pride of place inside university English departments.

To add one more bit of autobiographical lore to this recital: I remember that it struck me as peculiar that having grown up studying English literature and culture as an Arab schoolboy living in the British colonial countries of Palestine and Egypt, I came to the United States to find a similarly colonial situation prevailing. You studied English literature in America as part of an ideological package that stressed continuities, traditions, and trends constituted by what was supposed to be the dominant culture, but which was essentially Tory, Church of England, and Oxbridge, an ensemble inflected by the land-owning classes and having little to do with the social and historical realities of much of the immigrant culture of the United States. Moreover, little attention was paid to the dissenters within English literature like Blake and Shelley, for instance, and when eccentrics such as Gerard Manley Hopkins were read and studied, they were assimilated to an ahistorical element entirely saturating the works in analyses of irony, metaphor, and strictly formal considerations.

Nor were the French, German, Spanish, and Italian departments much better. All of them were similarly constricted by an approach that might be described as a combination of connoisseurship and cultural appreciation. While at Harvard I discovered some relief in Comparative Literature, which for its syncretism and historicism as practiced by Auerbach, Curtius, and Spitzer, and by their American counterparts like Harry Levin, seemed to be an opening out from the narrowness of Anglo-American New Criticism. It is hard for me to say whether my experience was typical or not, but I distinctly recall how when on my own I discovered such unfamiliar figures from the past as the young Georg Lukács (whose *Histoire et conscience de classe* I first read in the French translation by Kostas Axelos, in 1958 I think) and Vico, I was emboldened to abandon the unpromising horizons inside which I had been educated and I began to look quite purposefully and deliberately for help in other quarters. At that point in the late fifties, Heidegger and Sartre were of course available, but it was Husserl and Merleau-Ponty, plus a chance encounter with the works of Georges Poulet and Gaston Bachelard that set me off in a new direction. My first book, a study of Joseph Conrad's letters and short fiction, was stamped with the vocabulary and the concerns of phenomenological criticism, all of it European and aggressively non-English.

I do not think it is an exaggeration to say that the sudden influx of theory into the American university occurred in large part as a result of a quite amazingly powerful and influential conference that occurred at Johns Hopkins University in October 1966. It was organized by several people at Hopkins, but principally by Richard Macksey and my much-regretted dear friend, the late Eugenio Donato.[2] By a quite amazing combination of entrepreneurial genius and intellectual daring the two men arranged for a truly heroic list of participants from France to come to Baltimore en masse, and indeed to America for the first time. The list included Barthes, Todorov, Vernant, Hippolyte, Lacan, Derrida, Lucien Goldmann, Charles Morazé, and Poulet, all of whom made a lasting impression on the American academic and cultural environment. René Girard and Paul de Man, both of them then resident and working in the United States, were also at the Johns Hopkins conference as discussants and lecturers: their work became much more widely known as a result of those October days.

Many of the French visitors returned to the United States quite regularly after the conference, and they in turn triggered off the disproportionately high number of European theoretical visitors to French and general literature departments in the United States: after 1966 Julia Kristeva, Jean Genette, Serge Doubrowksy, Sara Kofman, Michel Foucault, Hélène Cixous, Michel de Certau, and others like them became frequent participants in American academic life. In addition, the Hopkins conference stimulated American literary interest not only in philosophical antecedents like Nietzsche, Hegel, Rousseau, Freud, and Heidegger, but also gave rise to a flood of translations of German and Russian theoreticians, among them Benjamin, Bakhtin, the Russian formalists, Szondi, Adorno, and Kracauer. Similarly, the rediscovery of Gramsci, Lukács, Althusser, and even Marx through new translations brought those earlier writers into the purview not only of philosophical and historical study, but of literary analysis.

But what of traffic going in the other direction, from the United States to France? My impression has been that it was far from equal with the importation of French theory into the United States. An early clue was provided me by a couple of chance encounters with Roland Barthes, the first of them at the 1966 Johns Hopkins conference. Guests to the meetings were housed in a hotel at some distance from the university. A bus was provided us for the trek out in the morning and the evening trip back. As a young and unknown participant in the conference I was particularly engaged by Barthes's paper on *écrire* as an intransitive verb, one of his most brilliant performances, but I was too timid to enter the public debate that swirled around it. I noted that much of what he and Derrida said at the time quite explicitly depended on Lévi-Strauss and Emile Benveniste, whose structuralist explorations in language seemed to me to resemble some of Kenneth Burke's speculations in what he called *logology*, a word he coined for his book *The Rhetoric of Religion*. So on one of the bus trips out to our meetings I approached Barthes, my fellow-passenger, and after complimenting him on his paper rather nervously, suggested an affinity between what he seemed to be doing and what Burke, of whom he had never heard, was also doing. I recall also that Joseph Frank, later the distinguished biographer of Dostoevski and the author of a quite famous essay entitled "Spatial Form in Modern Fiction," was also on the bus, and we had both noticed the similarity between what he had discovered about writing and many of the structuralist analyses being presented at Johns Hopkins, none of which made any reference to the work of Frank or Poirier, to mention another innovative critic. In any event, Barthes expressed genuine interest in Burke, even to asking me to jot down a list of titles for him; no, he had never heard of Burke but was certainly going to look up his books.

About two years later I ran into Barthes in Chicago, at the big Modern Language Association Convention where he was giving another of his wonderfully elegant and slyly allusive talks. He had time for a cup of coffee—I was flattered that he seemed to remember having met me at Hopkins (but perhaps he was just being polite)—and we chatted amiably about this and that. Quite innocently, and with no purpose other than to find out whether he had enjoyed making the discovery for himself, I asked him how he had liked Kenneth Burke. "Kenneth Burke? Mais qui est-il?" was his slightly puzzled but genuinely interested rejoinder. I was of course both crushed and mystified. Why wouldn't someone whose mind was as volatile and as searching as Barthes's *not* want to seek out a like-minded colleague across the Atlantic, and why wouldn't a list such as mine prove to be of compelling interest to so inquisitive and restless a spirit as Barthes's?

I opined that Burke was not interesting to him because like everyone else Barthes was almost completely surrounded by his world, with its own structures of feeling, audiences, professional colleagues, history, and social formations. I found this to be unusually true of the French theorists whose works and presence so often found nearly unqualified acceptance in the United States and Britain. By the early seventies Foucault, Barthes, Derrida, Lacan, and the others were appearing in English translation at roughly the same time that their works started to be sold in Paris bookshops. In addition, articles and books about them began to pour forth in English, far exceeding the secondary literature they seemed to generate in France itself. My own university, Columbia, instituted a kind of permanent visitorship in the French Department, to be filled by three theorists from Paris, rotating one in each year in what came to be called a troika arrangement. The same was true at other prestigious universities. Plenary sessions at the MLA, and indeed whole conferences about the French New Criticism dotted the academic calendar, and more important than all this a massive change occurred in the vocabulary and the deployment of terms of American criticism.

Very little of this was reciprocated in France, or in the French writing that was becoming a staple of intellectual discourse in the United States, Canada, and Britain. Particularly memorable on intellectual grounds was the lively debate on "theory" between Edward Thompson and Perry Anderson, which seemed to have no echo in France. There is, I must admit, something admirably confident about the self-quarantined style of French intellectual life, with its entirely unchallenged assumptions about the universality of French concerns. Thus it seemed to be assumed that the world had to take note of how Foucault and Derrida were at odds, because such a local disagreement was in effect something of transcendental importance for everyone else. But this insular confidence also reflected a perverse heedlessness that allowed itself to ignore many of the important works done outside France that either refined and elaborated what Foucault, as an instance, had presented, or that directly refuted his studies and his methods, often with quite devastating results. I always felt that it was a pity that Foucault seemed to pay very little attention to what his many students in the United States (and elsewhere) said about his work, and how from even his staunchest admirers he might have considerably increased the range and power of his almost entirely French-based work. This was particularly true of works like his *Histoire de la Folie*, *Les Mots et les choses*, and *Surveiller et punir*, the potential of whose arguments for modification was quite considerable, but which obdurately made the case for a politics of confinement and epistemological authority that seemed universal when, barring a number of exceptions, in fact it was remorselessly French in its import and argument. There is something poetically just therefore in the fact that one of the most important books on Foucault to appear after his death—James Miller's *The*

*Passion of Michel Foucault*—was an attempt to read even his earliest, and most apparently impersonal works as a covert autobiographical grappling with his personal sado-masochistic problems. So that far from being public histories, works like *Surveiller et punir*, according to Miller, expressed the man's innermost private neuroses: their formidable scholarship was marshalled and deployed in a sense to objectify personal obsessions.[3]

There was an especially regrettable missed opportunity for real Franco-American dialogue when Foucault and Noam Chomsky met in Amsterdam in 1972 for a television debate organized and moderated by Fons Elder. I did not myself see the encounter, but I certainly read with great interest a transcript of what transpired that was published in a difficult to find book called *Reflexive Water*. Neither Fons Elder nor his two guests appeared to be talking about the same thing most of the time, and even though the spectacle of three such intelligent interlocutors talking past each other is still quite funny to behold on paper, the underlying seriousness of what went on is hard to miss. Chomsky has said that he assumed Foucault was a Maoist; he had only read one or two of Foucault's works before the program, and therefore had no very clear idea why the two of them were matched up in the debate. Certainly Foucault gave no evidence that he knew much about Chomsky's peculiar combination of anarcho-syndicalism and Cartesian idealism. Yet here were two of the most influential dissenting analysts of authority and power showing that they belonged to two completely different moral universes, with Foucault both contemptuously and dismissively rejecting Chomsky's attempts to talk about justice and humanity and Chomsky pressing on regardless, even though he seemed scarcely to comprehend what it was that Foucault was trying to say.

I do not want to be misunderstood. In speaking of the inequality of the Franco-American dialogue I am suggesting only that there seemed to be a greater readiness, indeed eagerness, on the part of American critics to take up French concerns than the other way round. This is by no means to say that critics like Barthes, Foucault, and Derrida (who, by the way, was and continues to be involved in numerous American debates) had no interest in the American cultural scene: they did, as witness the number of times they appeared on university campuses and accepted invitations to speak. Some visitors from France like Tzvetan Todorov showed a distinctly American and generally non-French influence in his work, but such cases were exceptional. Again to speak impressionistically, there was a far greater American need for new infusions of method and vocabulary than was felt by French critics, who had already fought their battles and achieved their various intellectual victories by the time their work made it across the Atlantic.

This brings us to the question of how and what theories travel, a subject I have been interested in for some time. No culture is watertight, and no nation can completely seal its borders against foreign influences. There are as many (if not more) constant borrowings, translations, and crossings between cultures as there are between individual nations. What was it in 1966 that made

American criticism so receptive to thinkers like Barthes, Foucault, Althusser, Lacan, Derrida, and the others?

Let me speak in a summary and retrospective way about four characteristics generally perceived by us in America in such very different works as Foucault's *Les Mots et les choses*, Barthes's *Critique et verité*, *S/Z*, and *Mythologies*, Lacan's *Ecrits*, Goldmann's *Le Dieu caché*, Derrida's *L'Ecriture et la différence*, Althusser's *Pour Marx*. The first thing to be noted is how novel these works are, and how original in idea and performance each one of them is. There was a kind of restlessness about the sixties in the United States that hardly needs recital here. Some of it had to do with the anti-war movement and the rise of the counter-culture, but in the academic study of the humanities, in literature specially, most scholars of my generation were already chafing at the Anglophilia, the narrowness, the sheer exhaustion of the New Critical method. How liberating to encounter the daring epistemological sweep of Foucault's linguistic, economic, and biological descriptions as they illuminated *Don Quixote* or the works of de Sade, Mallarmé, and Nietzsche, or of Althusser's analyses of the major epistemological breaks at the center of Marx's oeuvre. I recall in particular my enthusiastic reading of Goldmann's *Le Dieu caché*, which I wrote about in 1965, in which I discovered a dazzling coherence and a rigor lacking in Anglo-American scholarship. Goldmann combined Lukács's aesthetic insights into the nature of form in *Die Seele und die Formen* with a subtle analysis of the power relationships in seventeenth-century France that created and sustained the Port-Royal community; he then turned his critical gaze on the fragments of Pascal's *Pensées*, revealing how their aphoristic style and tragically paradoxical, antinomian vision was not just in correspondence with the socio-historical realities, but an aesthetic development of them.

The sense one got from Barthes's liberating polemics against Raymond Picard in the little book on Racine, or his coruscating sentences on behalf of critical independence and creativity, or his amazing demonstrations of "semio-criticism" in *S/Z*, his wonderful book on the Eiffel Tower, and in *Mythologies*, is that the act of criticism itself had a witty dignity and a social range unsuspected by some of the mournful practitioners of Anglo-American critical writing. It was not only that he could produce a remarkable essay on Loyola's *Spiritual Exercises*, but how he said what he did with a conscious effort to be new, to be audacious, and unpredictable. With Barthes in particular, even when he was going over territory ploughed by others, there was a lightness of touch allied to a modest theatricality that made the presentation of the argument and evidence—normally left to the greyest of proses—a delight to encounter. For a change, thanks to Barthes, one felt that critics should be more like Wilde than Matthew Arnold, since Wilde, like Barthes, was moved by desire, not duty.

Much the same tonic thrust was delivered by other "new" critics contemporary with Barthes, with all sorts of unexpected rewards gathered along the way by writers of my own slightly younger generation. Underlying all that, however, was a quality of irreverence that translated itself across the board into a hostility to established authority, whether that authority was political, intellectual, or social. This is the second characteristic of new French criticism that was welcomed into American academic writing, in particular the writing of young scholars and critics, most of whom were under forty (in fact I cannot recall a single older scholar who in his or her work displayed, much less flaunted the impress of French theory as so many junior scholars did). Two of the most quoted and influential works by Barthes and Foucault respectively were "The Death of the Author" and "Qu'est-ce qu'un auteur," essays that boldly displace what Foucault called the "author-function" from the realm of pure agency onto discourse and the regulated interchange of signs. The American critic Clara Parke has suggested in a sympathetic piece on Barthes that the insurrectionary anti-authoritarianism in his attacks on the author perhaps goes back to the strict paternalism and rigorous regimentation of French schooling. And this, she goes on in a mode reminiscent of Arnold's essay on the role of academies, reflects itself in the entire structure of French cultural life, with its centralized academies, dictionaries, schools and hierarchies, for which there is no exact equivalent in American life. She concludes that perhaps Barthes and Foucault have a reason to kill off the authoritative author, or surrogate father, but is it not ridiculous for Americans to feel the same urge?[4]

The answer has to be "no," since all societies, as both Foucault and Barthes demonstrate in their work, are stratified, organized, regulated, despite the appearances of greater freedom in some more than in others. The difference between the French and American situations so far as criticism was concerned, however, is that with few exceptions American critics intended their critique of authority as something entirely academic, whereas the French tried to deal with problems in the society at large. Until he was made a professor at the Collège de France, Barthes was a complete outsider in the academic system; hence, to a great degree, Professor Raymond Picard's Sorbonnian animus against him, the established insider contemptuously dismissing the unprofessional procedures of the brilliant gate-crasher. Barthes's deliberate pollution of his literary concerns with sociological and semiotic language opened the criticism of established literary figures like Racine to the scrutiny not only of other disciplines but to a wide general public. One can see this in *Le Degré zéro de l'écriture*, where writing is treated as social performance, not as private language-game. No one needs to be reminded of Foucault's work on behalf of French prison reform.

But along with the anti-authoritarianism of Barthes, Foucault, Lacan, and so many others was the consequent (if not always admirable) ambition to replace an old system with a new one. You could read *S/Z* as Barthes's attempt to produce a structuralist equivalent of academic orthodoxy, but that was not, I think, the work's main virtue. Unfortunately in the United States, structuralism, or rather structuralist-sounding readings (most of them forgotten) were produced to show affiliation with something outré and European. I myself never found Barthes's falling-back on Greimas or even Benveniste, whom I very much admired, completely convincing, although to some of his French and American disciples it did seem as if he was trying to ground his work in a scientific method that could be exported and reproduced beyond his own seminar room. And whether they wanted it or not Foucault and Derrida were seen as initiators of a new system of thought, which gained them battalions of acolytes and epigones.

One immediate result was that words like "episteme" and "discourse," which Foucault had labored with excruciating difficulty to try to define, now clotted the prose of everyone who wrote criticism; similarly the habits of deconstruction—puns, emphases on instabilities of meaning, the monotonously recurring words *difference*, *logocentrism*, and *undecidable*—became as common as *metaphor* and *irony* had been a few years earlier. What disappeared in transit across the Atlantic was not only the particular situation out of which archaeology and deconstruction developed, but the laborious processes, the visible difficulties with these concepts that Foucault, Derrida, and the others had actually worked through, and which made for a great deal of their interest. Trans-Atlantic readers by and large seized on the words as if they were magic wands by which to transform humdrum scholastic readings into eye-catching theoretical "texts." In fact the word "text" supplanted competing words like "essay" or "article," and took on a new prestige in the United States. But not for nothing was Foucault one of the last to be imitated, since more than any of the others, his books were the results of great bibliographic saturations, something not easily reproduced by simple mimicry.

Except for Foucault, Vernant, and Goldmann, one of the features of new criticism, or structuralism, or theory—the exact word is unimportant—was its ahistoric and its often aggressively formalistic quality. Curiously, that quality was what made Barthes a writer so attractive to read. But the disregard of the gravity and density of history in American texts influenced by French writing of the seventies and eighties was emulated quite freely by even newer converts. Let me give an example. One of the most influential books of the period was Hayden White's *Metahistory*, which appeared in 1973. White's argument is now familiar, based as it is on categories of tropes that he sees as governing both the vision and the fundamental historical structure of writings by Michelet, Marx, Croce, and a few other great nineteenth-century historiographers and historians. I don't have any problem with White's main claim that there is no way of getting past historical texts without attending to the way their linguistic structure determines their epistemology. This of course is a Barthesian and Foucauldian insight. Yet to my mind White leaves out both the drives behind the writing (why it is, for example, that Marx writes history in the first place, or why Nietzsche felt himself to be so provoked by what he called the uses and abuses of history) and also any mention of the quite urgent veridic claims made by his authors. In other words, in focussing entirely upon textuality, he quite startlingly neutralizes or even eliminates the instigatory force of history, its cumulative and verifiable weight, which makes any particular subject possible only in *that* time and society, not in some other.

What seemed to be lacking in the United States was not just a new mode of doing historical research, but rather a solution to the impasse American criticism had reached. On the one hand the New Criticism associated with Eliot, Richards, and the Southern Agrarians had more or less exhausted itself, and on the other, the older style historical and social critics—exemplified at their best by such scholars as Lionel Trilling, M. H. Abrams, W. J. Bate—had recoiled in consternation from anything resembling theory, as the first signs of French criticism taking root began to be apparent. In part, the cult of theory was perceived by critics like Trilling as a sixties phenomenon; they turned away from what they saw as a wanton celebration of Dionysian passion, Marxist liberation, and straight-out generational rebellion of the sort that brought the Columbia and Berkeley campuses to a complete standstill in 1968. The intellectual preparation for those upheavals, according to Trilling, was to be found in the work of R. D. Laing, Norman O. Brown, and Herbert Marcuse, whose works were, I think, correctly perceived as undermining not only the academic and bourgeois order, but even the possibility of liberalism itself. In response to the hostility of the academic establishment and its quite seriously disapproving attitude to the new, French theory—though not its patient, slow work, nor its homegrown genius—became a rallying cry in fields quite distant from literary study: sociology, anthropology, political science, history, education. The result was a thinning of theory, so to speak, and its rapid instrumentalization. A small sign of the impatience with history and cultural density in the United States was that whereas book after book of Foucault's interviews began to appear with extraordinary speed, it took years before Foucault's historically minded contemporaries and teachers in France became known and translated. One thinks in particular of the work of Georges Canguihelm and François Jacob.

The final characteristic of French theory that made a strong impact in the American academy was its radical multi-disciplinary effect on the stability and traditional continuities of the academic disciplines. The category of *écriture*, as first adumbrated by Barthes but then expanded by Derrida and others, had the effect of dissolving the boundaries enclosing what was believed to be an objective object. "Literature," the poem itself, as the New Critical adage had it, could be taught and studied, venerated and appreciated, without fear that its underlying, albeit largely unexamined social coherence would be dissolved. Above all, the literary object was believed to be distinct from other forms of writing, principally criticism, which was supposed to exist in relationship to a poem as servant to master (the metaphor of servitude was often used). And underlying literature was its support in humanism, a notion that despite its fuzziness gathered unto it all the academic and liberal pieties supposedly derived from early authorities like Pico della Mirandola, Shakespeare, and Montaigne.

Very little of this survived the essentially demystificatory energies of French writing, whether in Barthes's attacks on institutional erudition, Foucault's brilliant archaeologies (the complexities of which were almost immediately shrunk by his less imaginative disciples and then conscripted for use under the slogan of "the death of man"), or Derrida's grammatological explorations, the earliest of which were genuinely resourceful exercises in ambiguities of meaning rivalled only by William Empson in the Anglo-American tradition. Humanism as an ideology was subjected to heavy bombardment, even though many of the ideas for this attack came from earlier thinkers, well exploited by the French, like Freud, Marx, and Nietzsche. I remember with great clarity how invigorated I felt when I read the earliest French revisionary readings of Nietzsche in books and essays by Deleuze and Foucault. Not only did I see things that I had not dreamed were there—mostly Nietzsche's prophetic insights into the nature of language and interpretation, and the immense philosophical importance he had attached to the very idea of philology—but I also felt that major writers in the field of philosophy, for instance, did not necessarily exclude me because I happened not to be certified as a philosopher. And thus very slowly the idea that each field had its own special techniques protected by guilds and traditions and its own internal coherence anchored in humanistic procedures stemming from the dignity of man—all this in time fell under suspicion and was discredited enough to make its adherents defensive.

Nor was this all. The attack on humanism and disciplinary celibacy liberated new fields and activities into existence. Popular culture encroached on the academic study of literature, as did film and video. Ethnic studies and the beginning of what was later to be called post-colonial literature, which in the United States meant literature not written by male inhabitants of the major metropolitan centers in England and the United States, were released into academic respectability as the result of theory in general, most of it French but later to include the Frankfurt School as well as American, African, and Asian critical theory. A salutary effect of this for English studies was that whole historical periods, first Romanticism, then Renaissance studies, then American literature, then the rest of the major Atlantic literatures, were subjected to scrutiny as fields that were constructed in a particular way to reflect the class and gender interests of well-established authorities. Most important of all, the already burgeoning energies of feminism were given a significant boost by the work of Julia Kristeva principally, but then also by that of Cixous and Irigaray. All of this took very strong hold in the American academic curriculum, provoking, as everyone knows, an angry counter-reaction, the most famous symptom of which was Allan Bloom's *The Closing of the American Mind*. Although Bloom's intent was in its own way to release the American mind from its bondage to French theory and Nietzsche, and women, and ethnics, his curricular prescriptions amounted to an extremely narrow and even perverse reading list as a method for educating the tiny elites who deserved education. Greek literature and a few Enlightenment philosophers were the only lucky masters to survive Bloom's ungenerous squint; and as to how so meager and arid an attitude as his was to lead to real intellectual emancipation, no one, least of all Bloom himself, was able to explain.

Perhaps the most profound effect of the new multi-disciplinary shock with its anti-humanist emphasis (the result of French theory of the late sixties and early seventies) was the anti-foundationalism that emerged in American philosophy. The key figure here is Richard Rorty, whose book *Philosophy and the Mirror of Nature* (1979) argued the case for anti-foundationalism and anti-essentialism more effectively than anyone before or after. Rorty's path to this position obviously was excavated and charted through his own readings in American pragmatism, but he had absorbed the deconstructionist and archaeological principles articulated by Derrida and Foucault. This position found its way into the work of a diverse group of critics, including Stanley Fish among the better-known theorists. But there was also a considerable overlap between the early French anti-foundationalists and Jean-François Lyotard, whose little book on post-modernism contained a similar message and became exceptionally influential in the new intellectual growth industry of post-modernist studies. Rorty's later work derived from the idea that since philosophy is a language, it is not therefore "a third thing intervening between self and reality," but offers instead the possibility of community according to the contingency of language-users sharing similar circumstances. Philosophy is not a search for truth, but a conversation. These rather less strict positions were presented in his 1989 book *Contingency, Irony and Solidarity*, a book that is important for laying out his criticisms of philosophers (especially Foucault and Derrida) with whom he previously agreed and still admires, but who are now seen by him as making real politics and philosophy impossible.[5]

Rorty's importance as commentator and exceptionally clear propounder of views is that in his work we can see the liberal corrective for the excesses both of the French theoretical left and the American neoconservatives. I don't mean to say that he actually did clear a middle ground between these two extremes, but rather that his work records a shift that was bound to take place over time, as older revolutionaries settled into positions of benign authority and somewhat socially aloof respectability. In any event I should not forget to say here that most of what I have been describing was probably enabled not so much by a free transit of ideas from France to Britain and the United States, but by some basic changes in the structure of American society that made the trans-Atlantic welcome so warm. One is that the number of university students, and hence of professors, recorded an increase of several quantum leaps in size after the Second World War. This in turn created a much larger consumer group for new ideas and methods. Secondly, an increase in the student population meant also an increase in the mobility of ideas and communication which as Hobsbawm very convincingly shows, turned student groups—who received new ideas with exceptional eagerness—"not only into politically radical and explosive [groups] but [groups that were uniquely] effective in giving national, even international, expression to political and social discontent." Hobsbawm mentions another factor in the spread of ideas via the university, mainly the unprecedented number of women, especially married women that entered the working class during the boom years of the 1960s.[6] Along with huge numbers of new emigrants, these new populations were restless and enthusiastic standard-bearers of new interests, new appetites, new ideas of self-betterment.

And yet a mere fifteen years after the Hopkins conference, and after many translations of French theory and criticism had appeared, there was a rather sudden sense that the bubble was bursting. The Paul de Man case had a lot to do with this. While I do not want to exaggerate its importance, I do not want either to minimize the special symbolic power over American academics of the revelations made of Paul de Man's evident collaboration with the Nazis in his youth in German-occupied Belgium. His death in 1983 furnished the occasion for a passionate debate not so much about de Man himself, but about deconstruction and "advanced" criticism of a vaguely European provenance. *Signs of the Times*, a book by my former student David Lehman, was published in 1991, and seemed to blame de Man for the collapse of liberal education, for untrammelled radicalism, for the unrestricted wave of theory, for the destruction of traditional values, all of them in some way ascribable to what de Man's putative Nazism represented. What had once been uncritical receptivity to the latest in French theory, from the excesses of Bataille to the dizzying performances of deconstructive readings of nearly everything, all of this was replaced now by a sense of crisis (as in William Cain's *The Crisis in Criticism*), by various obituaries for a now etiolated and febrile decadence, which is what theory had turned into. That many of the great figures had themselves died—the list is an impressive one and includes Foucault, Althusser (whose murder of his wife added to the general disillusion with theory), Barthes, and Lacan—increased the overall desolation of a scene that had once been vibrant with energy and optimism.

Yet I think it is fair to say that all was not well from the outset, despite many and obvious positive results of the trans-Atlantic cross-fertilization, uneven though it was. What interested me in the whole wave of theory that erupted in Paris during the 1960s was its origins in French cultural and political life, without which, I argued in my book *Beginnings* (1974), it could not be properly assessed. There was an essential difference, therefore, between theory as a response to specific situations—theory, that is, as a way of handling the overwhelming complexities of immediacy itself, theory as giving form to powerful feelings of anti-authoritarianism, of reconceiving the idea of intellectual mission (as was the case with Foucault and Barthes in particular, but also Derrida and Lacan), of theory as furnishing a starting-point for intellectual reflection—and, on the other hand, theory perceived as a method for solving problems, theory as something as repeatable as a set of rules, theory as a language isolated for specialized use. In the United States that confusion between seeing theory as response to immediacy and seeing it as a method was made almost from the start. A considerable number of new university courses and programs began to be offered during the 1970s, most of them producing reading lists of prominent authors (Foucault, Barthes, Derrida, etc.) arranged like items on a menu. The most frequent practice was to take one literary work, say *Hamlet*, and then read it week after week "according to the structuralist, or Marxist, or Foucauldian method," as if one could move from one mode to the other the way a car shifts gears. Such a mentality underlies the work of Gerald Graff, who like an impresario arranges and rearranges interpretive conflicts into palatable reading lists and "conflicts" for his courses.

I can think of several universities where theory was detached from the study of literature, and given its own niche as a program, department, or even institute, thus further promoting the notion that you could "have" theory the way you picked a profession such as dentistry or law. In my own department it is now rare to find graduate students who spend more than about twenty percent of their time reading books of literature; most of the time is spent in reflecting on, elaborating, refining, commenting on a handful of theories, most of them themselves reflections of reflections. Worst of all has been the degeneration of language. The idea that theory might be of use to persuade readers or to get a constituency, which was certainly the aim of the French models that continue to be read, scarcely exists anymore. Now, theory is like a badge of affiliation: it has its own indecipherable jargon, its own like-minded coteries of experts, its own specialized and protectively enclosed guild of members. To be incomprehensible has become a sign of profundity.

I don't want to suggest that such refinements in and of themselves were always either wrong or in some way immoral. But what I do want to insist on is that there has been a remarkable change in the way theory arose in France, and the way it has evolved in the United States. What made the French originals interesting, as I have said, was how they constructed their theoretical explanations of continuities and discontinuities in culture; Foucault's archaeologies, for instance, posit an account and an explanation for the way statements are made under one epistemological regime and then under another. His reason for performing these impressive demonstrations has something directly to do with the discipline in France of the history of ideas, with the structure of authority and power, and finally with his sense of a need for change. There is a directly contemporary reference in his work which is both social and intellectual. By the 1980s in the United States the contemporary references had become unimportant, since even academic Marxists had no connection to an ongoing political struggle outside the university. Depoliticized and decontextualized, the theoretical methodology pursued became a discourse of high expertise. Writing theory about theory, I believe, therefore slenderized and professionalized a practice that in the past, and in the case of the French theorists I have been discussing here, arose out of an existential contingency that made their work intellectually exciting and interesting in the first place.

An exceptionally instructive example of what I mean is to be found in an essay by Wlad Godzich on de Man on Derrida. Godzich argues that with each use as a method, a theory is further domesticated. Thus his own essay "The Domestication of Derrida" is an illustration of the predicament. To work through the various aporias detected in Derrida by de Man is finally to arrive, as Godzich does at the end of his own essay, at a hall of mirrors alone with Hegel, where in the ensuing passage Godzich gives us a reflection upon reflection:

> But the identity of thought and being is not immediate, otherwise the problem would not have arisen immediately, nor would philosophy have had any historical roots. As Hegel thinks of mediation, it is based upon the recognition of the contingency of the contingent. The mode of my being in the world translates itself through actions which I undertake and by which I transform both the world and myself; but what matters in such a formulation is that, in each case, the instrument of the action is mediated: I am the instrument of the transformation of the world, and it is through this externality that I transform myself. Mediation is a structure of indirection. Thought proceeds in similar fashion since consciousness apprehends itself only as consciousness of something else. In ordinary thinking, natural consciousness does not keep track of this mediation. It takes itself as immediate consciousness of the external. It is only in a movement of return upon itself, that reflection, as mediated reflection upon itself, apprehends this movement. This leads to the re-examination of truth, for, if in the first instance, truth was the adequation of thought to being, but thought and being are mediations of each other, then the propositions of truth are valid only insofar as we produce their conditions of emergence. But, and here the paradox grows, this is nothing more than a primary utterance forgotten by simple reflection.[7]

Despite Godzich's brilliance, it is hard for me to imagine what problems of understanding or interpretation this analysis is meant to solve. Of one thing we can be sure: that it is writing at several removes from anything that resembles direct experience. Besides, and more to the point, it tends to confirm the charge made by Christopher Norris in *Uncritical Theory: Postmodernism, Intellectuals and the Gulf War* that there has been a tendency in post-structuralist thought (that would include Rorty and Fish) to eliminate the notion of truth altogether in favor of such ideas as consensus, local conditions, interpretive community. The most egregious case of all is that of Jean Baudrillard, whose work reduces material reality to the status of a fictive word-game. The occasion of Norris's quite justified ruminations on this peculiarly post-modern variation on the *trahison des clercs* theme was the failure of modern Western intellectuals to respond adequately to the assault on humanity and politics as symbolized by the Gulf War. Baudrillard is singled out by Norris as particularly fatuous and sublimely offensive in his claims before the war that it couldn't take place, and after it that it hadn't taken place. All this, says Norris, it due to the political and moral nihilism induced by a misreading of deconstruction:

> . . . one could cite many passages from Derrida's work where he asserts that deconstruction is not, as his opponents would have it, a

discourse with no further use for criteria of reference, validity, or truth; that it squarely repudiates the "anything goes" school of postmodern hermeneutic thought; and that to deconstruct naive or commonsense ideas of how language hooks up with reality is not to suggest that it should henceforth be seen as a realm of open-ended textual "free-play" or floating signifiers devoid of referential content. In ethical terms likewise, it is a gross misunderstanding to suppose that deconstruction ignores or suspends the question of interpretive responsibility, the requirement that texts should be read—or utterances construed—with a due respect for those other-regarding maxims (of good faith, fidelity, attentiveness to detail, etc.) which prevent it from becoming just a super-subtle game, a license for all kinds of readerly extravagance.[8]

I'm not sure I would completely agree with Norris that Derrida's work provides its own careful safeguards against the excesses Norris quite correctly ascribes to American and other critics influenced by French theory. But it is the case with the later Derrida, as it was also with the later Barthes and Foucault, that for good or bad their work became a good deal more personal, expressing autobiographical instincts and interests that were quite different from the more intellectual and scholarly, and certainly public, concerns of the work that made them famous. I think, for example, that the Barthes of *Incidents*, or *La Lumière du Sud-Ouest*, or "Au Palace ce soir," recently published as *Incidents* in the United States, has something pathetic and forlorn about it, quite at odds with the ironic and virtuosic style he had perfected in such books as *S/Z* or *La Tour Eiffel*. I am probably in a minority in my opinion of Foucault's *History of Sexuality* as a great letdown after the many important books that preceded it. The larger point, I believe, is that there is a connection between this winding down of the bravura period in French intellectual life and the dissipation of energies, the jargonism, and the inconsequential quality of American post-structuralism, with its paper-thin hermetic treatises, its peculiar idolization of Baudrillard and Lyotard, and its relative neglect of really interesting and intellectually challenging figures like Gilles Deleuze.

Perhaps the period between the mid-sixties and the mid-eighties can be characterized as having dramatized the stark difference between French theory and its trans-Atlantic reception. In the former, whatever else there was, there was always a sense of intellectual mission. With few exceptions (one of them being feminism) that sense of mission was not present in the work of most American and British academics who relied on French theory for their work. For once the novelty died down somewhat, theory became a passé or outdated thing, to be overtaken in one wave after another of fashion and orthodoxy by post-modernism, post-colonialism, post-Marxism, and the many varieties of post-structuralism. There has been a greater erosion than before in appreciations of the historical texture that literature, which expresses an historical experience, is made up of.

The saddest thing is that intellectual life in the university is dominated by a new kind of anti-intellectualism, in which ethnic, gender, and guild interests have become a substitute for veridic claims and rational examination. And in France, to the extent that I am able to understand what is happening there, the situation is different only in style, not so much in kind. Some weeks ago I was on the campus of Princeton University and saw a sign announcing a symposium to be held under the rubric of "New French Thought." The occasion was the Ecole Normale's two hundredth anniversary, for which half a dozen new (to me) names were to be presented; they were described as "the younger generation of philosophers, historians, and social commentators who represent the new liberal humanistic bent of French intellectual life." How different in ambition, tone, and claims this was from the Johns Hopkins symposium of thirty years ago. Maybe it is still too early to tell what trans-Atlantic borrowings might follow this latest formation, but that the results will be less far-reaching seems to me a virtual certainty.

### Notes

1. Eric Hobsbawm, *The Age of Extremes: The Short Twentieth Century, 1914–1991* (New York: Pantheon, 1995), 3.
2. The two edited the conference's proceedings for what was to become an extraordinarily influential book: Eugenio Donato and Robert Macksey, eds., *The Language of Criticism and the Sciences of Man: The Structuralist Controversy* (Baltimore: Johns Hopkins University Press, 1970).
3. James Miller, *The Passion of Michel Foucault* (New York: Simon and Schuster, 1993), 201–203.
4. Clara Claiborne Park, *Rejoining the Common Reader: Essays, 1962–1990* (Evanston: Northwestern University Press, 1991), 206–228.
5. Richard Rorty, *Contingency, Irony and Solidarity* (Cambridge: Cambridge University Press, 1989), 14.
6. Hobsbawm, *Age of Extremes*, 298, 311.
7. Jonathan Arac, Wlad Godzich, Wallace Martin, eds., *The Yale Critics: Deconstruction in America* (Minneapolis: University of Minnesota Press, 1983), 37.
8. Christopher Norris, *Uncritical Theory: Postmodernism, Intellectuals, and the Gulf War* (London: Lawrence and Wishart, 1992), 17.

CHAPTER 3

# Love is for the Birds:
# Sartre and La Fontaine

LEO BERSANI

*T*he heroism of teaching literature was
brought home to me last spring by my students' inability to admire and to enjoy
La Fontaine. However much I tried, I ran up against an impregnable wall of
indifference: the fables were, at best, charming, but how could anyone claim
they were intellectually challenging? I now realize that I contributed to this
failure of appreciation by placing La Fontaine immediately after Sartre. In the
Berkeley French Department, 103 is one of two semester-length courses offered
as a required transition between Lower Division language courses and Upper
Division offerings in French literature and culture. I organize my section of 103
along traditional generic lines: we start off with some short prose fiction, move
on to a few plays, and end with about five weeks of poetry. There was nothing
more than an organizational rationale for the peculiar, perhaps unprecedented,
juxtaposition of Sartre and La Fontaine: the former's *No Exit* was the last work
in the section on theater; selections from the *Fables* initiated the readings in
poetry. Sartre ended one group of works and La Fontaine started another, and
I was unprepared for any carry-over from one to the other. But the students
were much less sensitive than I to formal and generic discontinuities between
Prose Fiction, Drama, and Poetry, and much more responsive to degrees of
excitement generated by·everything we read. For them the course was divided
between the intellectually meaty works (a few poems by Baudelaire, *No Exit*,
and Voltaire's *Candide*) and the great bores (La Fontaine, Giraudoux's *Inter-mezzo*, and Flaubert's *A Simple Heart*).

Sartre, then, provided the grounds for a generally negative judgment of
La Fontaine. The grounds were philosophical: Sartre's ideas were more profound than those of La Fontaine. It was hard for me to dispute this, especially

since the definition of a profound idea had come from Sartre—which made it inevitable that he would emerge triumphant. *No Exit*, like other literary works by Sartre, leads up to the enunciation of its philosophical thesis. Just as Roquentin's understanding of his "nausea" conveniently provides us with a one-sentence encapsulation of the sense of Sartre's *La Nausée* ("L'essentiel c'est la contingence"), *No Exit* builds up to Garcin's (Sartre's) famous formula for human relations: "Hell is other people!" ("L'enfer c'est les autres.")[1] What students generally, and understandably, want is an explanation of that formula: *why* are other people hell? I could of course have passed out sections of *Being and Nothingness* that make this argument much more profusely, but since this might be taken as a demonstration that an incoherent literary work can somehow become coherent by more satisfactorily articulated versions of its sense drawn from other works, I tried to flesh out the argument with other passages from *No Exit* itself, extrapolating more or less philosophically from the play's action and dialogue.

The three characters who represent humanity in Sartre's version of hell will make each other suffer for all eternity, and yet they can't do without each other. The moment that really turns students on is when Garcin hurls himself against the door of the room in which he, Estelle, and Inès have been locked up, shouting to whatever Authorities might be listening that he'd rather suffer from all of hell's traditional tortures ("your red-hot tongs and molten lead, your racks and prongs and garrotes") than go on enduring "this agony of mind" (42) ("cette souffrance de tête, ce fantôme de souffrance")—the torture of simply being with his two hell-mates.[2] What makes this particular moment so compelling is that, against all expectations, the door opens—but none of them leaves. This adds to the climactic Sartrean thesis (which is announced soon after this) the complexity of something like a choice. If "hell is other people" meant simply that others are malevolent, there might still be an escape from hell. We could turn inward, safe in the knowledge that however infernal intersubjectivity may be, subjectivity *tout court* will always be a source of comfort and renewed strength. But it is, perversely, intersubjectivity that the characters choose by refusing to leave. To understand why, we have to look more closely at the detested suffering without which these three can't "live."

Take Garcin. The director of a pacifist newspaper in his native Argentina, he was shot for trying to leave the country after a war broke out. Instead of announcing to the military authorities his refusal to serve in the armed forces (which would have landed him in prison), he had, so he claims, decided it would be more effective to speak as a "witness" against the war ("Je voulais témoigner, moi, témoigner"!) from Mexico City, where he hoped to launch another pacifist publication.[3] But now he's not sure about the reasons for his attempted departure: was it in order to continue the pacifist struggle abroad, or was he simply afraid of being killed in the war? Garcin begins by welcoming the "time" he will have in death. Hell at first seems to him almost a marvelous opportunity, as he says, to put his life in order, to probe his conscience in order to be sure he was leaving Argentina for the right reason. Eternity may be a monstrously extended period of moral leisure, one in which Garcin would finally be able to answer the question that tortures him: Am I a coward?

The trouble is, according to *No Exit*'s argument, that he needs someone else to provide the answer. Introspection is inherently inconclusive. To look inside is to discover that in addition to all the good reasons he had for fleeing, "fear and hatred and all the dirty little instincts one keeps dark—they're motives too" (39). Excitement in the classroom mounts as students are brought to see in this overwrought little play an immensely successful popularization of a significant move in modern philosophy: the putting into question of the Cartesian *cogito* as a mode of knowledge. "I think" can no longer be followed by a confidently enunciated "therefore." The solitary consciousness, far from certifying being, produces the very doubt Descartes triumphantly experienced as erasing. It is only in the eyes of others that human subjects can see themselves as having being, which, in the context of *No Exit*, also means what we would call today having an essentialized identity. It is only outside of himself that Garcin might find the illusory hero-identity he can't find within himself.

But what if the other chooses to send back a quite different image—that of a coward-identity? In *No Exit*, Estelle is more than willing to assure Garcin that he's not a coward, but, as he says, she doesn't count. She'll say anything he wants to hear provided she gets from him (from a man), in return, the confirmation of *her* identity as a desirable woman. It is only Inès, the infernally intelligent lesbian, that Garcin can trust—trust not to say he is a hero unless she really believes it. So he will spend eternity trying to persuade her to allow him to be the man he can't ever know he is without her. And since she detests him for making Estelle turn away from her, she will naturally never bestow upon him a hero-essence. Inès may, as she says, be nothing more than "a mere breath on the air, a gaze observing you, a formless thought that thinks you" (45), and yet no one else can tell him what his acts add up to. Death has made impossible the one escape life does offer: time, that is, the possibility of other acts, of projecting oneself into other choices that can give the lie to whatever being others malevolently ask us to read and to recognize in their congealing, essentializing look.

This is fairly nourishing for the freshmen and sophomores who take 103. *No Exit* deliciously but toughly raises such heavy issues as: the relation between self-reflexive thought and self-knowledge, the ontic grounds of the social, and the relation between action and identity. By comparison, poor La Fontaine—and, for that matter, all of French classical literature—can easily seem intellectually impoverished. The fable that made my chance juxtaposition of Sartre and La Fontaine seem like a pedagogical godsend—an unplanned opportunity to examine the status and the identity of "ideas" in literature—was *The Two Pigeons*.[4] Certainly *that* work would never lead to the excited questions, agreements, and protests to which *No Exit* had given rise. Two pigeons love each other tenderly. One of them, however, gets bored at home and decides to take a trip—not a very long one, he tells his desolate, sobbing companion ("For I'll have had enough before three days have passed"), and upon his return the story of his adventures will be a source of "extreme pleasure" for the other pigeon. Sobbing himself as he takes leave of his cherished companion, the restless one quickly falls prey to all the misfortunes that can fall upon a hapless bird: a storm, a "pigeon" that turns out to be a lure for a trap, a narrow escape from a hawk's sharp claws, and a wound from the sling of a boy ("un fripon d'enfant"). The poor pigeon drags himself back home to be united once again with his beloved companion. "I leave it to be guessed," La Fontaine concludes, "with what extreme delight their sorrows they allay."

The story is over, but the fable continues for another nineteen verses. This is the fable's "moral," which actually becomes, after the first five verses that admonish happy lovers never to leave one another ("Be all things each to each, what though all else default"), a more personal reflection on the part of the fabulist. The general lesson is particularized by La Fontaine's insistence that when *he* has loved, he wouldn't have exchanged the places "[honored by the step] and whereon the bright glance fell" of his beloved "For all the Louvre and all it hid, / And all the starry firmament and Heaven's vault." The memory of those sweet times even leads the fabulist away from his subject. In the fable's last six lines, it is no longer a question of the folly of leaving a loved one for the illusory pleasures of far-off places; now La Fontaine wonders if he'll ever again know the happiness of loving. Is he too old? He even suggests that he may no longer have the courage to love again, a confession that takes the form of a discreet challenge to himself ("Ah! si mon coeur osait encore se renflammer!"). At least, La Fontaine seems to be saying, the foolish travelling pigeon had a lover both to leave and return to. His very folly is a luxury *I* may no longer have; more succinctly, in the fable's final verse: "Ai-je passé le temps d'aimer"?

Try interesting a group of twenty-year-olds in that! First of all, the ideas in *The Two Pigeons* are distressingly weak. Love is the greatest happiness we can know. Nothing can compensate for the loss of that happiness. Perhaps the major misfortune of life is to live beyond the time when we are still capable of love, or still courageous enough to take the risk of loving. This is a fable for old men. Only some one fearful of never having another lover could find such pathos in the pigeons' separation and reunion. Thus the fable's moral sentimentalizes intimacy, exaggerates its value. An implicit yearning for youth blinds the fabulist to all those ambiguities (all the insecurity, all the ill-will) of intersubjectivity that make Sartre's "Hell is other people" so tough-mindedly realistic. The intellectual substance of *The Two Pigeons* can be reduced to the narrator's personal plight. What is (mildly) interesting about the poem is what also makes it intellectually thin: the fact that the fabulist is drawn to this tale out of sentimental nostalgia, as both a reminder of, and a momentary relief from, his affective aridity. At least *No Exit* owes nothing to such personal pressures.

Sartre's ideas, in addition to having the glamor of being pessimistic about human relations, can stand on their own. "Hell is other people" can be defended as a philosophical proposition. The rest of the play fleshes out the argument instead of revealing the weakness of the flesh behind the argument.

The sensible thing to do would have been to drop the comparison and to teach La Fontaine on his own terms: what he added to the ancient fables that were his inspiration, how his language re-invented a particular literary tradition, how, in *The Two Pigeons*, the personal voice intersects with the universal, the thematic commonplace (individual experience at and as a "lieu commun") characteristic of French classicism. The inherent anthropomorphism of the animal fable is, for example, at once indulged in and corrected by La Fontaine. The pigeons may speak to each other like characters in a tragedy ("L'absence est le plus grand des maux: / Non pas pour vous, cruel"), but it is La Fontaine's exquisite sensitivity to their physical pigeon-ness that accounts for such touches as the description of the wet traveller's body as "*chargé* de pluie" and the precision with which the fabulist distinguishes between the bird "dragging" its wings behind him and "pulling" his feet forward ("traînant l'aile et tirant le pié") as "half-dead and more than halfway lame," he returns home. There is also, for me, the historical interest of that parenthetical remark about children ("that age is heartless") which suggests how confidently La Fontaine, and his contemporaries, took for granted a view of childhood (and of the civilizing effects of growing up in society) which Rousseau and his followers would strenuously put into question a century later. There are, finally, in this deceptively easy poem, such elliptical effects as the one produced by the transitional gap between the first two verses. In summarizing the fable, it seemed to me natural to say: "Two pigeons love each other tenderly. One of them, however, gets bored at home and decides to take a trip." But there is no "however" in the poem—that is, nothing to suggest an opposition between the pigeon's love and his restless boredom. Nothing has happened to make him bored, and his boredom isn't exactly opposed to his love. It is an episode (the *passé simple* of "*fut* assez fou") *within* the extended and uninterrupted time of his love ("deux pigeons s'*aimaient*"). Had La Fontaine used a transitional connective, it would have been "and" rather than "however."

Suddenly *The Two Pigeons* doesn't seem that far removed—thematically, at any rate—from *No Exit*. What if both of them were "about" intersubjectivity? And what if *The Two Pigeons*—for all the banality of its sentimental lesson—were more "profound" on that subject than Sartre's play? If that were the case, it could only be proven through an analysis, in each case, of the relation between the thematic center and the rest of the work. If we let these centers stand by themselves, there can be no real competition between "Hell is other people" and

O lovers, happy lovers, must you fly the nest?
    Fly then, but never far away.

Fly to a world of beauty fixed between you two,
   Forever different and new.
Be all things each to each, what though all else default.

But how are these statements addressed within the two works? The peculiar comparison of Sartre and La Fontaine provided an unexpected opportunity to study not only how the literary work addresses its readers, but also how it speaks to itself, or claims not to speak to itself—which is a notable feature of the Sartrean literature of ideas. In *No Exit*, Sartre works to make us not hear the responses to (which are also the origins of) his philosophical thesis. His characters, interestingly, most fully realize they are dead when they can no longer hear sounds from their lives. The voices of Garcin's journalistic colleagues fade away; Estelle can no longer hear her friends talk about her. They're dead because the line has gone dead; voices have stopped travelling. "I feel so empty, desiccated," Inès says when she can no longer see or hear the young couple who have come to rent the apartment she shared with Florence, "really dead at last. All of me's here in this room" (30) ("A présent, je suis tout à fait morte. Toute entière ici").[5]

"Toute entière ici": this lack of extension beyond the here and now could also be thought of as an authorial directive. This is the way Sartre wants to be read: the sense of my philosophical message is entirely within its enunciation. What "hell is other people" means is "entirely here," fully contained within the formula itself. The rest of the play fortifies this self-containment if we think of it, as Sartre wants us to do, as a mere illustration of the thesis, or, in dramatic terms, as the build-up that vindicates the thesis, makes its enunciation necessary. Everything preceding that celebrated formula can be locked up within it. It has nothing more than an amplifying effect, increasing its philosophical volume. Denis Hollier has said that for Sartre literature is a news bulletin: tonight's headline is "hell is other people," last week it was "what is essential is contingency."[6] The writer is the lucky or astute reporter; he "does" the intersubjective or the ontological scene better than his colleagues. His bulletins are philosophical scoops.

There is, then, a probably unintended relevance to Sartre's notion of the prose writer (as he spells it out in *What is Literature?*) in Garcin's profession as a journalist. Unfortunately, literature tests both that notion and the philosophical theory itself—existentially . . . , and it is perhaps because Sartre thought of literature as advertising and confirming ideas that he was, apparently, blind to his own work's subversion of ideas. In *Nausea*, not only does Roquentin's extravagant use of metaphor rhetorically contradict his idea of things as simply *there*, wholly unavailable to language; the specific metaphors he uses also invite a psychologically reductive interpretation of his nausea. Contingency is always attacking him "from behind," and the entire philosophical edifice is exposed through what is meant to be its novelistic support as a fearful fantasy of anal rape. *No Exit* continues that fantasy, so to speak, through

Garcin's emphasis on being a man among other men. Early in the play, when scenes from life are still visible to him, he sees some of his former friends sitting around a newspaper office: "The air [smells] of men and cigar smoke," he says with nostalgia. "I used to like living among men in their shirt-sleeves" (13). Later on, exasperated by Estelle's and Inès's talk, he complains: "If they'd put me in a room with men—men can keep their mouths shut" (23).

Philosophically, the play directs us to think of Garcin's inability to be certain that he's not a coward as a universal dilemma of consciousness: inwardness cannot confirm identity. And Inès, the tough lesbian who has been chosen to make Garcin suffer eternally, tortures him on his own terms. That is, she implicitly agrees with him that the issue is whether he left Buenos Aires as a hero or fled as a coward, whereas Garcin might have provided her with a more subtle instrument of torture—not was he a hero, but rather what did his wanting to be a hero mean? As Sartre's stand-in, it is perhaps not surprising that she fails to pick up on what might, after all, be taken as Garcin's most interesting piece of information about himself: "Listen! Each man has an aim in life, a leading motive; that's so, isn't it? Well, I didn't give a damn for wealth, or for love. I aimed at being a real man. A tough [*un dur*] as they say. I staked everything on the same horse" (44). *Un dur*: the hero-coward polarity weakly sublimates Garcin's more fundamental—more visceral—obsession with *staying hard*. The trouble with Estelle—with straight women in general—is that they make a man go soft. Garcin says as much in repelling Estelle's advances: "Go away. You're even fouler than she [Inès]. I won't let myself get bogged in your eyes. You're soft and slimy. Ugh! [*Bangs on the door again.*] Like an octopus. Like a quagmire" (42). No wonder Garcin prefers Inès, the only real man in the play. "So it's you whom I have to convince; you are of my kind" (44). Inès is in fact better, harder, than Garcin, which is why she can subjugate him. It is better to be enslaved by a hard man than to be liquefied, perhaps even dissolved, by swamp-like femininity.

In Sartre, philosophy is notoriously gendered. Far from making a case for the viability of a literature of ideas, *No Exit* discredits the very ideas it proposes. To take Sartre's thesis with the kind of seriousness he expects from us, we have to isolate it from the rest of the play. He asks us to think about an idea rather than read a text. This is close reading understood as the arresting of meaning's movement. "Stop here; this is my play's meaning." But when the rest of the work is thought of as serving this central and unambiguous (if complex) thesis, literature, as it were, takes its revenge by reducing the thesis itself to a derived or secondary position. The prominence of the idea turns out to be a defensive strategy—and while this obviously doesn't have to be the case whenever there is an equally bald enunciation of a philosophical argument in literature, *No Exit* usefully if unintentionally demonstrates how literary meaning is always in excess of any such enunciation. "Hell is other people" takes on a new intelligibility when it is placed in relation to Garcin's surly machismo.

And that of course is the danger, for Sartre, of putting his ideas in a play.

He had to imagine people for whom such ideas would be urgently meaningful. The idea becomes *their* idea—not a disembodied argument about inter-subjectivity, but their way of getting a hold on their troubled relations to other people. The fact that abstract ideas help people to manage their experience is in no way an argument "against" abstract ideas, but it should lead to a reflection Sartre does not make about the status of such ideas—about their always potential mobility and vitality, what he might, after all, have been qualified to discuss as their existential fragility *and* energy. In *No Exit*, this might have meant less fretting about manly heroism and some suggestions about the convenience, for these particular characters, of thinking about other people as "hell." The failure to allow *that* idea to be moved around, even assaulted, has the unfortunate result of legitimizing the most reductive interpretation of the idea—the one I have offered of its being a cover-up for a frantically gendered version of human relations, a male version of otherness itself as a castrating female.

La Fontaine, on the contrary, becomes more interesting when we attend to the play between the fable and its moral. The view of the poem as an aging man's sentimental idealizing of love depends on our assuming that the fable's significance is adequately contained in its moral, is "entirely there" (as Sartre wishes us to find *No Exit* satisfactorily accounted for by "hell is other people.") But the fable performs a certain irony about its own thematic conclusions. The difficult—and important—point to make to students is that, as far as emphasizing the moral's intellectual insignificance goes, La Fontaine got there before they did. He proposes, however, not a reductive interpretation of the moral but rather a reading of it as one element in a much richer performance. And this performance can even accommodate the reductively biographical reading of the fabulist's paean to love. For we're not allowed to settle on any of these meanings. The banality and the sentimentality of the moral in *The Two Pigeons* are the intellectual risk La Fontaine takes in order to keep us on the move, to make us circulate among various ways of forming meaning in literature. And perhaps only the greatest intellectual security allows the poet to be so casual about the value of his ideas, to question, ultimately, the usefulness in describing the moves of consciousness, of isolating a category to be labelled, as "ideas."

If, in *The Two Pigeons*, La Fontaine celebrates the inestimable value of love, what he means by love is far from certain. "Love" is highlighted through-out the poem: in the tautology of the very first verse ("Deux pigeons s'aimaient d'amour tendre"), in the invocation to "lovers, happy lovers" that initiates the second section, and as the final word of the entire fable. "Aimer"—which literally begins and ends the poem—is clearly what it's all about. And yet there are certain problems—problems, first of all, of gender. Whereas Sartre confidently knows what side of the great male-female divide he's on, or desperately wants to be on, La Fontaine peculiarly fails to specify the gender, or genders, of his avian protagonists. Do we have a male and a female pigeon—or two male pigeons? La Fontaine has them refer to each other three times as "brother."

Why would a male pigeon refer to a female pigeon as "brother"? It is of course possible—and the fable has frequently been read this way—that the type of love in question is one of intense friendship rather than a sexually passionate love— *philia* rather than *eros*. But not only does La Fontaine insist on the "tender love" between the two pigeons; their language also evokes sexual passion. If someone unfamiliar with the fable were asked to identify the author of the words "L'absence est le plus grand des maux; / Non pas pour vous, cruel," he would surely say Racine, whose sexually obsessed lovers often address similar reproaches to the "cruel," unloving objects of their desire. Furthermore, in the second section La Fontaine is clearly talking about romantic and/or sexual love. Would he have to wonder if he might dare to love again if he were thinking of a new friendship? Can *philia* eliminate all other interests ("Tenez-vous lieu de tout, comptez pour rien le reste")? And we at once recognize that adorable "shepherdess" under whose laws he has happily served in the past as the romantically idealized loved one of pastoral literature.

The fable may, then, have given rise to a moral inapplicable to it— without the fabulist even appearing to be aware of the discrepancy. But would someone this sophisticated move from a story about friendship to a moral about romantic passion without at least suggesting both the similarities and the differences between two types of love—or indicating why this story about a momentarily fickle friend moves him, the fabulist, to reflect upon passion? No: it seems certain that both sections of *The Two Pigeons* are about eros, and as if to forestall our thinking that he has passed somewhat inattentively from friendship to sexual love, La Fontaine makes the pigeons' story sound much more passionate than his own amorous adventures. The clichéd if elegant reference to vows made in the pact to serve an "aimable et jeune bergère" contrasts sharply with the more maturely Racinian echoes of the two pigeons' tale: the reproaches, the desperate effort to keep the beloved, the bad faith on both sides.[7] What are we to make of such passion between two "brothers"? Are these two pigeons gay?[8]

Such a question could easily seem like a new low point in gay studies. Does it make any sense to ask about the sexual orientation of pigeons? But the pigeons of fables are of course not only pigeons, and when birds speak like human beings as convincingly as they do in La Fontaine's poem, then questions you would only ask about people are probably inevitable. If this particular question is irrelevant (and I think it is), it is because La Fontaine makes it irrelevant after appearing to invite us to ask it.[9] It is as if a heterosexually form-ulated moral could be inferred from an apparently homosexual fable because the fabulist's *idea of love* makes him somewhat inattentive to such distinctions. And it *is* a certain "idea" that *The Two Pigeons* develops, one, however, which no single formula can adequately contain. It emerges from a dramatic relation between the moral and the rest of the fable, from a performative tension between the two.

The praise of love is a function of its accidental, or, perhaps more exactly, slightly insignificant character. In the second part, La Fontaine claims that when he was lucky enough to be in love he wouldn't have exchanged that happiness for the treasures of the Louvre "and all the starry firmament and Heaven's vault," but in the context of both the fable and its moral, very little supports that claim. The restless pigeon is happy in his love, so happy that he cries when he bids farewell to his "brother" (whose words had shattered him ["ébranla son coeur"]). But that happy attachment counts for little when it is pitted against—what exactly? Something very vague, indeed: this pigeon doesn't know what he wants to see; he is moved simply by curiosity ("le désir de voir") and, more significantly, by "boredom," and by what La Fontaine calls his "humeur inquiète."[10] "Inquiète" returns at the end of the poem, this time applied to the fabulist, who, abandoned by "so many objects so beguiling and so charming," is guided by nothing but his own restlessness ("Faut-il que tant d'objets si doux et si charmants / Me laissent vivre au gré de mon âme inquiète?"). La Fontaine would have us believe from the very start that he is superior to the pigeon who, as he pointedly says, was so mad—"fut assez fou"—as to wish to travel far from home. But the pigeon is at least temporarily cured of his restlessness; La Fontaine may be condemned to live his remaining years "au gré de [son] âme inquiète." It is true that the fabulist longs for the intimacy the pigeon frivolously renounces, but there are also suggestions that the former's restless solitude is a choice. He doesn't ask if he will ever be loved again or even if someone he will want to love will enter his life; rather, he wonders if *he* will dare to love again. Is there a charm powerful enough to "arrest" him, to center him once again? ("Ne sentirai-je plus de charme qui m'arrête"?)[11]

The fabulist, unlike the imprudent traveler whose tale he has told, may be permanently on the move—not necessarily travelling physically, but unanchored, spiritually scattered. Intersubjectivity in *The Two Pigeons* is what stops and centers the human. We are unhappily but irresistibly centrifugal. The pigeon sobs as he leaves for the voyage he can't renounce; we pass "the time of loving" when there is no longer any object of desire strong enough to immobilize our "âme inquiète." Types of intimacy (heterosexual or homosexual, for example) are irrelevant to this dramatic reflection on an unhappy (if also seductive) mobility of being. Love is what we call a certain point of rest, a relation that appears to be adequate to the energies of desire. *The Two Pigeons* is, however, generally unpersuasive about the power of love. Not only is there the pigeon's boredom *within* his happy love; in the moral, love is either a gravely uncertain future possibility or a depersonalized memory, one in which the beloved is hyperbolized, and derealized, as a literary convention. Restlessness in *The Two Pigeons* is a structural defect of consciousness—as if consciousness, as in Pascal, were programmed for pleasures no human experience can deliver. We can hear these Pascalian resonances in the very rhyming of "humeur inquiète" and "âme inquiète." In both cases "inquiète" rhymes with its opposite: "mon âme satisfaite" in the first instance, and "arrête" in the second. Love is nothing more than an episode in that polarity of centeredness and dispersal.

The hyperbolic praise of love is the fabulist's rhetorical strategy to counter the pull away from the center, the restless wandering. But it is also a compliment to love—and this adds something very non-Pascalian to the reflection on *ennui* and our *âme inquiète*. Both the hyperbole and the banality of the pastoral references in the moral are an extraordinary tribute to love's power to calm an ontological anguish. I say "extraordinary" because, as I have been suggesting, the poem doesn't really authorize that tribute, and so it is at once generous and deceptive. In the face of the *humeur inquiète* that continuously draws us away from those we have the luck to love, La Fontaine's urgent appeal to lovers assumes, or rather constitutes a community that might at least pretend to be stronger than our anti-communal drives. If there is not much "behind" the discourse to support it, the discursive play is itself socializing and civilizing.

To teach La Fontaine should, if we are lucky, replicate that civilizing experience. It counters a potentially terroristic faith in the self-centered idea—the idea that asks us not to see the experience it more or less successfully manages—with a training in critical mobility. If the Sartrean idea encouraged discussion, which it certainly did, it also locked us up in ideas that could be debated. A debate on La Fontaine's ideas would be inconceivable, for none of them is "entirely here" or "entirely there." They are rather in the trajectory *from* here *to* there (and back), and on the face of the sort of discussion *that* requires, debate seems a primitive form of sociability. La Fontaine invites us to move among his positions rather than to argue about the validity of his ideas, and the intellectual sociability we enjoy in accepting that invitation is itself an attractive, if modest, refutation of Sartre's somber thesis.

### Notes

1. Jean-Paul Sartre, *La Nausée* (Paris: Gallimard, 1938), 166; *No Exit*, trans. Stuart Gilbert, in *No Exit and Three Other Plays* (New York: Vintage Books, 1955), 47. Subsequent page references to this edition of *No Exit* will be given in the text. *No Exit* was first published in French as *Huis clos* in 1945.
2. Sartre, *Huis clos* suivi de *Les Mouches* (Paris: Gallimard, 1947), 86.
3. Sartre, *Huis clos*, 77.
4. See the Appendix for both the French and an English translation of *Les Deux Pigeons*. Francis Duke's translation, which is given here, is perfectly serviceable. It stays very close to the French, and since I wish to draw the reader's attention as much as possible to the original, that is sufficient merit. For a more impressively poetic experience of La Fontaine in English, I recommend Marianne Moore's extraordinary transposition of the *Fables* into seventeenth-century English poetic diction and the very different, but perhaps no less impressive, translation-conversation with La Fontaine published by Bruce Boone and Robert Glück, *La Fontaine* (San Francisco: Black Star Series, 1981).
5. Sartre, *Huis clos*, 64.

6. Denis Hollier, *The Politics of Prose / Essay on Sartre*, trans. Jeffrey Mehlman (Minneapolis: University of Minnesota Press, 1986), 94.

7. On the part of the restless one, the suggestion that he wants to travel mainly in order to have amusing and instructive stories to tell his brother; on the part of the abandoned one, the attempt to frighten the other with hastily improvised evil omens ("Un corbeau / Tout à l'heure annonçait malheur à quelque oiseau").

8. There is an amusing history of critical attempts to deal with the sex—or sexes—of La Fontaine's birds. In the nineteenth century, Henri Régnier announced that they represent two male friends (an opinion shared by today's eminent French seventeenth-century scholar, Marc Fumaroli), and Emile Faguet claimed that when, in the second part of the fable, La Fontaine addresses lovers, he has simply "forgotten" that he was speaking of brothers in the first part. (Régnier, *Oeuvres de La Fontaine* [Paris: Hachette, 1838–92], 2:361. Faguet is quoted in Leo Spitzer, "L'art de la transition chez La Fontaine," *Etudes de style* [Paris: Gallimard, 1970], 186.) Closer to us, Spitzer declared that "the reminiscences of Virgil's Dido which are found in the discourse of the pigeon who remains behind cannot be explained unless one admits that La Fontaine saw this speaker as a woman." But, as far as strictly internal evidence goes, it may be the impudent traveler who is "a woman." Toward the end of the first part of the fable, La Fontaine refers to this pigeon as "*la volatile malheureuse*"—choosing the feminine gender for a word which, in the seventeenth century, was at times given as masculine (in the *Dictionnaire de l'Académie*) and at other times as feminine (by the lexicographer Richelet). But then both pigeons may be female—which would bring us back to the possibility of a gay fable . . . Spitzer's comment, from a 1959 article in *Studi francesi*, is reproduced and translated in an essay by Michael Vincent, who, addressing the gender confusions in the fable, argues that intertextuality operates here to disallow such anthropomorphic questions as the pigeons' sex (or sexes). ("Fragmented Love's Discourse: Textuality and Sexuality in La Fontaine's *Les Deux Pigeons*," *Papers on French Seventeenth-Century Literature* 9, no. 17 [1982]).

9. It is not irrelevant because of a presumed failure to make the heterosexual-homosexual distinction in seventeenth-century France. There was of course no analysis of "the homosexual character," but homosexual tastes were clearly noted, with varying degrees of acceptance and reprobation. The Princess Palatine, the wife of Louis XIV's brother, was scandalized by the "horrible vice" she found "so much in vogue" at the French court, a vice to which, she gratefully announced, her "good and honest" German compatriots were immune. What "disgusted [her] even more than all the rest" were all the women at Versailles in love with other women. (Christiane Lalloué, ed., *Princesse Palatine: une princesse allemande à la cour de Louis XIV* [Paris: Union générale d'éditions, 1962], 92.) This passage was brought to my attention by my colleague Leonard Johnson.

10. It is also by no means clear that the pigeon's trip immunizes him against future attacks of restless boredom. It is not, after all, as if he compares the joys of love to the pleasures of travelling. His trip has been a disaster, and he comes back to his "brother" "half-dead." In the future, might he not tell himself that he will have better luck if he sets out on another voyage—better weather, no more mistaking decoys for real birds, no nasty kids with slings . . . ?

11. With "stuns," Boone and Glück nicely render the immobilizing impact of "arrête."

# Appendix

## *Les Deux Pigeons*

Deux pigeons s'aimaient d'amour tendre.
L'un d'eux, s'ennuyant au logis,
Fut assez fou pour entreprendre
Un voyage en lointain pays.
L'autre lui dit: "Qu'allez-vous faire?
Voulez-vous quitter votre frère?
L'absence est le plus grand des maux:
Non pas pour vous, cruel. Au moins, que les travaux,
Les dangers, les soins du voyage,
Changent un peu votre courage.
Encor si la saison s'avançait davantage!
Attendez les zéphyrs. Qui vous presse? Un corbeau
Tout à l'heure annonçait malheur à quelque oiseau.
Je ne songerai plus que rencontre funeste,
Que faucons, que réseaux. "Hélas! dirai-je, il pleut,
"Mon frère a-t-il tout ce qu'il veut,
"Bon soupé, bon gîte, et le reste?"
Ce discours ébranla le coeur
De notre imprudent voyageur,
Mais le désir de voir et l'humeur inquiète
L'emportèrent enfin. Il dit: "Ne pleurez point:
Trois jours au plus rendront mon âme satisfaite;
Je reviendrai dans peu conter de point en point
Mes aventures à mon frère.
Je le désennuirai: quiconque ne voit guère
N'a guère à dire aussi. Mon voyage dépeint
Vous sera d'un plaisir extrême.
Je dirai: "J'étais là; telle chose m'avint.
Vous y croirez être vous-même."
A ces mots, en pleurant ils se dirent adieu.
Le voyageur s'éloigne; et voilà qu'un nuage
L'oblige de chercher retraite en quelque lieu.
Un seul arbre s'offrit, tel encor que l'orage
Maltraita le pigeon en dépit du feuillage.
L'air devenu serein, il part tout morfondu,
Sèche du mieux qu'il peut son corps chargé de pluie,
Dans un champ à l'écart voit du blé répandu,
Voit un pigeon auprès: cela lui donne envie.
Il y vole, il est pris: ce blé couvrait d'un las
Les menteurs et traîtres appas.

Le las était usé; si bien que de son aile,
De ses pieds, de son bec, l'oiseau le rompt enfin.
Quelque plume y périt, et le pis du destin
Fut qu'un certain vautour à la serre cruelle
Vit notre malheureux qui, traînant la ficelle
Et les morceaux du las qui l'avait attrapé,
   Semblait un forçat échappé.
Le vautour s'en allait le lier, quand des nues
Fond à son tour un aigle aux ailes étendues.
Le pigeon profita du conflit des voleurs,
S'envola, s'abattit auprès d'une masure,
   Crut pour ce coup que ses malheurs
   Finiraient par cette aventure;
Mais un fripon d'enfant (cet âge est sans pitié)
Prit sa fronde, et du coup tua plus d'à moitié
   La volatile malheureuse,
Qui, maudissant sa curiosité
   Traînant l'aile et tirant le pié,
   Demi-morte et demi-boiteuse,
   Droit au logis s'en retourna.
   Que bien que mal elle arriva
   Sans autre aventure fâcheuse.
Voilà nos gens rejoints; et je laisse à juger
De combien de plaisirs ils payèrent leurs peines.


Amants, heureux amants, voulez-vous voyager?
   Que ce soit aux rives prochaines;
Soyez-vous l'un à l'autre un monde toujours beau,
   Toujours divers, toujours nouveau;
Tenez-vous lieu de tout, comptez pour rien le reste.
J'ai quelquefois aimé: je n'aurais pas alors
   Contre le Louvre et ses trésors,
Contre le firmament et sa voûte céleste,
   Changé les bois, changé les lieux
Honorés par les pas, éclairés par les yeux
   De l'aimable et jeune bergère
   Pour qui sous le fils de Cythère
Je servis engagé par mes premiers serments.
Hélas! quand reviendront de semblables moments?
Faut-il que tant d'objets si doux et si charmants
Me laissent vivre au gré de mon âme inquiète?
Ah! si mon coeur osait encor se renflammer!
Ne sentirai-je plus de charme qui m'arrête?
   Ai-je passé le temps d'aimer?

### The Two Pigeons

Two Pigeons shared a tender love;
But one, being bored with life at home,
Made up his foolish mind to rove
Away, and through the world to roam.
"What shall you do?" exclaimed the other.
"Why must you desert your brother?
Absence is the worst of blows;
But, cruel, not to you! Would that a wanderer's woes,
    And risks, and cares, might serve for you
    A little to amend your view;
And later in the year you might fare better too!
Wait till the zephyrs stir; who's goading you? A crow
Just now croaked warning that some bird would be brought low.
I'll dream of nothing but of travelers distrest
And hawks, and nets. I'll say: 'Dear, but the weather's wet;
    And are my bother's wants all met,
    Hot supper, warm bed, and the rest?'"
    This plea brought turmoil to the heart
    That on so mad a voyage would start;
But curiosity and restlessness at last
Prevailed, and he responded: "Wipe your tears away,
For I'll have had enough before three days have passed.
I'll soon be back, and in a circumstantial way
    I'll tell my brother my adventures
For his pleasure. Anyone who nothing ventures
Can't make conversation either. When you know
    My tale, you'll find it royal fare.
I'll say: 'That's where I was; this happened thus and so' —
    You'll think you actually are there."
Upon these words they wept, and said a fond good-bye.
The wanderer wings away. And now a cloud sails near,
And makes him seek some safer hiding-spot close by.
He finds a tree such that the tempest even here
Lashed at the Pigeon through the leaves. The air grows clear,
Until, with feathers sodden, he flies on ahead;
And as he flies, he does his best to dry the wet.
His eyes fall on a lonely field where wheat lies spread,
And where a pigeon pecks, his appetite to whet.
Alighting, he falls prisoner to a noose, await
    Beneath the wheat's delusive bait.
The noose was frayed, and so the bird with beating wing,
And busy feet and bill, at last has broken loose

With only feathers lost. But fate allows no truce: A certain
Sharp-clawed hawk, above him hovering,
Descries our luckless victim trailing bits of string
That as he flies he carries still about him draped,
        As might a convict just escaped.
The hawk being poised to strike, down out of clouds descended
Now an eagle with yet fiercer claws extended.
Profiting from this dispute of thief with thief,
The Pigeon flees, escapes, lands near a peasant's hut,
        And hopes that now perhaps his grief
        May end with this adventure. But
A vagrant boy (that age is heartless), with his sling
And pebblestones, came very near to murdering
        The hapless feathered flyer, who came,
With curses on himself for an idle fling,
        And one foot dragging, and one wing,
        Half dead and more than halfway lame,
        Back to his home, which he contrived
        Somehow to reach, and so arrived
        Secure at last from ill luck's aim;
And so the two unite. I leave it to be guessed
With what extreme delight their sorrows they allay.

O lovers, happy lovers, must you fly the nest?
        Fly, then, but never far away.
Fly to a world of beauty fixed between you two,
        Forever different and new.
Be all things each to each, what though all else default.
There was a time when I too loved; and when I did,
        For all the Louvre and all it hid,
And all the starry firmament and Heaven's vault,
        I'd not have given the woodland dell
Trod by the light step, and whereon the bright glance fell,
        Of that young shepherdess who'd won
        My heart—for whom, by Cythera's son
Commanded, I served out my youth's first vows. But when,
Alas, shall moments such as those return again?
Must objects so beguiling and so charming, then,
Abandon me a victim to my spirit's thirst?
Ah, that love's flame still flared within my heart! Must I
Be warmed no more by charms that kept me young at first?
        Can love perhaps have passed me by?

# CHAPTER 4

# King Lear, Edmund Burke, and the French Revolution

### DAVID BROMWICH

The little dogs and all,
Tray, Blanch, and Sweetheart, see, they bark at me.
—Burke, answering jeers by the Foxite whigs,
    in the debate on Quebec (6 May 1791)

I tax you not, you elements, with unkindness;
I never gave you kingdom, call'd you children,
You owe me no subscription: then let fall
Your horrible pleasure; here I stand, your slave,
A poor, infirm, weak, and despis'd old man.
But yet I call you servile ministers,
That will with two pernicious daughters join
Your high-engender'd battles against a head
So old and white as this.
—*King Lear*, 3.2.16–24

The storm has gone over me; and I lie like one of those old oaks
    which the late hurricane has scattered about me. I am stripped
of all my honors, I am torn up by the roots, and lie prostrate on
the earth. There, and prostrate there, I most unfeignedly recognize
    the Divine justice, and in some degree submit to it. But whilst
I humble myself before God, I do not know that it is forbidden to
    repel the attacks of unjust and inconsiderate men.
—Burke, *A Letter to a Noble Lord* (1796)

*T*hese pieces of extrinsic testimony are meant to suggest the depth of the contact between Burke's sense of his time and his interpretation of the story of *King Lear*. But I do not think that one needs these or any other circumstantial data to be persuaded by the argument that follows; and it has been my experience that the nature of the internal case is more than commonly intuitive. Either one hears or one does not hear Burke listening to Shakespeare think, as he himself thinks about the politics of revolution. The logic of his choice of a dramatic frame for reflecting on a real-life catastrophe is a good deal easier to trace. In a notebook that he kept between the ages of twenty-one and twenty-seven, he wrote this aphorism: "The Action of a play ought to be like a Rack to make Actors discover the bottom of their Souls, the most hidden part of their Characters. Else 'tis good for little."[1] Placed as it is in the 1750s, the sentiment feels anomalous and extreme, though Burke was not alone in his care for a passion that seemed to penetrate the actor and audience alike. An anecdote tells of Garrick as Lear kneeling once to deliver the terrible curse against Goneril, and how the front row of the pit rose to their feet to watch the utterance, and row after row stood up in silent homage. Criticism in that age appears to have lagged behind performance in its sense that a strong passion might work with reflex authority on the actor. But the reports of Garrick that I have read still lack the full force of Burke's words: that an experience of emotion, both inward and expressive, must cost the actor something too.

Turn to Johnson's *Dictionary of the English Language* and much of the interest of the aphorism may seem to dissipate. An actor, for Johnson, is one who performs an action—a personal or historical agent. A player on the stage is his second meaning. But taking that to be the order observed by Burke as well, the aphorism becomes striking in a new way: a tragedy, he must be saying, is a rack to make its fictive persons discover the bottom of their souls, the most hidden part of their characters. Even on the conventional reading, such intensity of psychological concern is rare among Burke's contemporaries. A tragedy was an imitation of an action that ought to be serious, complete, and of a certain magnitude. Character is then inferable from the action—it is to be witnessed and understood. Outside Burke, it is difficult to find a suggestion that the purpose of the drama is to force into view the conscience of a character as it comes to know itself, or that it comes to know itself most truly when in the extreme of a crisis.

Anyway I am not sure it is wrong to hear in his use of *actor* a strong implication that the effects are felt by the performer—that a character is resonant to the extent that all that he acts and suffers is proved on the pulses of the stage actor who portrays him. Burke elsewhere was in the habit of running together Johnson's first and second meanings: one who performs a real action, and one who performs a fictive action on which we will eventually model our responses to real actions. His first recorded response to the French Revolution, "What Spectators, and what actors,"[2] mixes the two kinds of reference. And the very image of the rack calls to mind a particular character, Lear, in passages where his ordeal is held up to view, both by himself and others, as an exemplary and harrowing spectacle. "O let him pass," says Kent near the end: "he hates him / That would upon the rack of this tough world / Stretch him out longer."

Burke was likely to have *King Lear* in mind whenever he wrote of the connection between catastrophe and character; the association underlies the motives that prompted him to write about the French Revolution as a tragedy. But in looking as I will at the play and the event together, there is some risk of a sliding comparison: one is placing, as if in natural conjunction, a fiction on one side and on the other an actual occurrence that has been woven by a historian into credible fictive shape. One ought to declare in advance what such an interpretative venture can and what it cannot accomplish. Many differences of period, and the vast and essential difference between the coherence of any story and the want of coherence in events as they happen, will be ignored in an account like mine—more so than even Burke, by his allegory and his echoes, can be supposed to give a warrant for ignoring them. And yet, too conscious an anxiety regarding the discreteness of fact and narrative would go against the grain of Burke's imagination; while to show how he imposes "literary form" on a political event would seem to me a dubious undertaking, even if one could be sure what it meant. I see neither an aesthetic nor a historical scandal in the fact that a memory of a play did evidently inform his narrative of actual events, with an effect that was characteristic in its distortion and in its revelation. All histories are informed by some preexisting narrative: we should get over the habit of celebrating ourselves on this discovery, or assuming it tells us something new about the contingent nature of either historical or aesthetic truth.

I try to avoid much eulogism toward Burke as a prophet. He knew that he was living in extraordinary times, and his way of registering that awareness was often extraordinarily acute; but by the broadcast of his fears he brought a human measure of mischief along with reflection, and it will not do to pretend that the imaginative energy of his writings renders them somehow akin to divination. Still, one of the ways in which he gains credence is to persuade us to regard the words of *King Lear* as a prophecy of the words of *Reflections on the Revolution in France*; and the change of perspective that occurs in consequence is a change in our sense of the play as much as in our sense of the revolution. In the light of his analysis, some archaic motives of disorder come to seem at issue in France in 1789, and a modern psychology of revolt appears to receive its first adequate description in *King Lear*.

*T*he immoderate originality of Burke on France may be harder to feel today than it was twenty or thirty years ago. Because his portrait of the revolution looked like an analysis of totalitarianism *avant la lettre*, his reputation prospered from the attention of ideologists; after 1989, the fall of the modern regimes founded on "armed doctrine" curiously levelled the force of his descriptions. His suspicion was proved so right that it could be assimilated as merely sound. With French historians above all, his reading of the revolution has won its way to something like normal acceptance, owing to the labors of François Furet and his school. The entry on Burke in Furet and Mona Ozouf's excellent *Critical Dictionary of the French Revolution* concludes with the judgment that his work "remains profitable for anyone who would understand what was truly at stake in a Revolution from which the whole modern French political tradition ultimately derives."[3] Undoubtedly, after years of being misprized this credit was owed to Burke. But the truth is that it was his democratic contemporaries—Price, Fox, Paine, and others—who possessed the normal vision of events. This revolution appeared to them to belong to the same family as the American: it was part of a movement for widening liberty and rationalizing commerce, to which the old regime in Europe could only present an obstacle—the last of a series of battles of republican principle against monarchy, reason against superstition, equality against privilege, publicity against secret corruption, and uniformity and decentralization against an increasingly unstable government which was seen as both centralized and arbitrary. When one reads Burke with these claims in mind, one sees how consistently his metaphors, personifications, and deliberate reductions are meant to parry, by anticipation, any ameliorative reading of the crisis. He writes, from early in the *Reflections*, as one familiar with "situations where those who appear the most stirring in the scene may possibly not be the real movers."[4]

By an act of abstraction Burke redescribed 1789. In his telling, it becomes the first of a series of unlimited wars, fought, on the question of generational succession, between the ambitious and enterprising young and the honorable but impotent old. He asks us to see that the survival of an ancient inheritance is threatened by the heat of innovation. The contrast of landed property with the mobility of "sudden fortunes" from commerce, accordingly makes a large and not an incidental element of his account;[5] and as we proceed, it will be useful to hold in mind Burke's short definition of Jacobinism in the *Letter to William Smith* of 1795: "What is Jacobinism? It is an attempt (hitherto but too successful) to eradicate prejudice out of the minds of men."[6] He expands it a little in the first *Letter on a Regicide Peace* of 1796: "Jacobinism is the revolt of the enterprising talents of a country against its property."[7] From these characterizations alone, one might predict an emphasis that has puzzled many readers of the *Reflections*, namely the amount of attention given in the second half of the book to the enactment of 2 November 1789, whereby all church lands were put at the disposal of the state. That law, more than any other, seems to have suggested to Burke that the agitations of France were not merely "an irregular, convulsive movement" such as might be necessary to cure "an irregular, convulsive disease." Rather, the revolution was a war of confiscation. Few who sympathized with the change would have disputed his judgment that it was effected by men of talent against men of unearned, and unearnable, status, though they might well dissent from his praise of the manners associated with established property as "the unbought grace of life, the cheap defense of nations." Advocates of the revolution believed that industry at last had found its proper reward in overthrowing idleness. From a rational understanding of merit and reward, of status as something that has somehow to be earned, it was possible to conclude that no confiscation the revolutionaries attempted could be illegitimate.

For a nation to belong to the system of modern Europe, it must, Burke believed, have incorporated in its mixed system of opinion and sentiment a respect for graciousness, quite distinct from respect for utility. At the same time, it could not persist as a nation without persons renowned for industry and energy. These are the men of merit; and the *Reflections* gives a carefully modulated view of their place in the establishment. Burke speaks of them as persons of actual, as distinct from presumptive, virtue:

There is no qualification for government, but virtue and wisdom, actual or presumptive. Wherever they are actually found, they have, in whatever state, condition, profession or trade, the passport of Heaven to human place and honour. Woe to the country which would madly and impiously reject the service of the talents and virtues, civil, military, or religious, that are given to grace and to serve it; and would condemn to obscurity everything formed to diffuse lustre and glory around a state. Woe to that country too, that passing into the opposite extreme, considers a low education, a mean contracted view of things, a sordid mercenary occupation, as a preferable title to command. Every thing ought to be open; but not indifferently to every man. No rotation; no appointment by lot; no mode of election operating in the spirit of sortition or rotation, can be generally good in a government conversant in extensive objects. Because they have no tendency, direct or indirect, to select the man with a view to the duty, or to accommodate the one to the other, I do not hesitate to say, that the road to eminence and power, from obscure condition, ought not to be made too easy, nor a thing too much of course. If rare merit be the rarest of all rare things, it ought to pass through some sort of probation. The temple of honour ought to be seated on an eminence. If it be opened through virtue, let it be remembered too, that virtue is never tried but by some difficulty, and some struggle.[8]

The temple ought to be seated on an eminence, visible to all, but not of easy access. And there ought to be some sort of probation, or proving time of salutary difficulty. If a nation owes a reward to such aspiring persons, the number rewarded cannot precisely correspond to the number whose claim is fair. Without men of talents in government, a nation will suffer disaster because it will fail of intelligence, or so Burke seems to say.

But there is an opposite current of feeling, just beneath the surface of the words. In a speech in the House of Commons in 1770, defending himself against an anti-Catholic slur by a lord, Burke had assigned a different possible cause of disaster to an established state. The sense of injured merit felt by excluded talents might dispose them to join the forces outside government clamoring for its destruction. He "took to himself," a report of the speech says, "the appellation of a *Novus Homo*. He knew the envy attending that character. *Novorum Hominum Industriam odisti*; but as he knew the envy, he knew the duty of *Novus Homo*. . . . He expatiated upon the Impropriety and danger of discouraging new Men. . . . If they are precluded the just and constitutional roads to Ambition, they will seek others."[9] That has a less conciliatory sound than the longer passage in the *Reflections*. Yet both trains of thought confess the same ambivalence of rising merit toward an establishment that at once shelters and restrains its growth. The ambivalence is sharpened by another phase of Burke's analysis of 1789, his linking of the French Revolution with the creation of a new social type: the revolutionist.

Cosmopolitan radicals like Thomas Paine and Anacharsis Cloots may have contributed something to Burke's idea of the type, but there had been usurpers before, subverters of the established order, systematic opponents of the authority of old governments; only never before a class of persons consistently and professionally sworn to the destruction of social order. Burke knew this class of persons well; you might say he knew them before they knew themselves. The significant part of their character was what he called their atheism. "These," he said once of atheists, distinguishing them from the Dissenters for whose rights of toleration he was then arguing,

> these are the wicked Dissenters whom you ought to fear; these are the people against whom you ought to aim the shaft of the law; these are the men to whom, arrayed in all the terrors of government, I would say, "You shall not degrade us into brutes!"

Genuine professions of conscience ought to be respected, but:

> The others, the infidels are outlaws of the constitution, not of this country, but of the human race. They are never, never to be supported, never to be tolerated. Under the systematic assaults of these people, I see some of the props of good government already begin to fall; I see propagated principles which will not leave to religion even a toleration. I see myself sinking every day under the attacks of these wretched people.[10]

A tone of vehemence appears to connect this utterance with the *Letters on a Regicide Peace*, the last, coldest, and most savage of Burke's anti-revolutionary writings; but in fact the speech in which the denunciation appears was made in 1773, and the common feature with his mood of two decades later is France. As he spoke, Burke had lately returned from a journey there—the same visit from which, in the *Reflections*, he would recall his first sight of Marie Antoinette. Something in the whisper or laughter of the salons did not agree with him.

Starting with Holbach's *System of Nature*, and in a vast pamphlet literature of eighteenth-century metaphysics and morals, Nature was a nickname for the only omnipotence recognized by atheism. The common marks of the theoretical naturalist were impiety, determinism, and in personal practice an extreme libertinism. Edmund in *King Lear* is not a determinist, but it may be said he freely adapts other people's conceptions of fate and fortune as the artistic medium in which to work his own effects. He describes his nature and his liberty in the soliloquy of Act 1, scene 2.

> Thou, Nature, art my goddess; to thy law
> My services are bound. Wherefore should I
> Stand in the plague of custom, and permit
> The curiosity of nations to deprive me,
> For that I am some twelve or fourteen moonshines
> Lag of a brother? Why bastard? Wherefore base?
> When my dimensions are as well compact,
> My mind as generous, and my shape as true,
> As honest madam's issue? Why brand they us
> With base? with baseness? bastardy? base, base?
> Who in the lusty stealth of nature take
> More composition and fierce quality
> Than doth, within a dull, stale, tired bed,
> Go to th'creating a whole tribe of fops,
> Got 'tween asleep and wake? Well then,
> Legitimate Edgar, I must have your land;
> Our father's love is to the bastard Edmund
> As to th' legitimate. Fine word, "legitimate"!
> Well, my legitimate, if this letter speed,
> And my invention thrive, Edmund the base
> Shall top th' legitimate—; I grow, I prosper;
> Now, gods, stand up for bastards![11]

He chooses his goddess more than she chooses him, and at the bottom of this, as of all his other choices, is the resolve that he alone shall say what he owes, and what is owed him by others. Enterprise marks Edmund, in his own eyes, as the natural superior of his legitimate brother; and his judgment is confirmed by Gloucester at the beginning of the play: "There was good sport at his making, and the whoreson must be acknowledged." Through Gloucester's opening jests, there runs another and less civil inference, namely that he might have chosen not to acknowledge Edmund. There is no justice in any of the crimes Edmund will commit, and yet there is justice in his ingratitude. All merit has a ground of resentment as soon as it knows its difference from others, sees that its difference might have been rewarded but has not been, and recognizes the unsteady footing on which authority rests in assigning for its preference any justification other than merit.

*H*azlitt said that Iago had the character of a Jacobin; but a separate pathology was involved there. Iago is a restless experimenter, whose coolness toward persons, and inside knowledge of society, help him to burn through the coat of convention while seeming to share the protection it affords. Iago's action terminates in itself—a dramatic trait consonant with the fact that *Othello*, of all the tragedies of Shakespeare, has the least to show of the pathos of strife between generations. By contrast, Edmund is an example of something: an aberration that may be repeated, the shadow of life without custom which "we who are young" may be destined to see more of. Burke's extended view of Jacobinism in the *Regicide Peace* seems much in accord with Edmund's opinion of himself:

> I have a good opinion of the general abilities of the Jacobins: not that I suppose them better born than others; but stronger passions awaken their faculties; they suffer not a particle of the man to be lost. The spirit of the enterprise gives to this description the full use of all their native energies.[12]

Enterprise, with Burke, is, like energy, a queasily ambiguous word. In the *Reflections* and again in the *Letter to a Member of the National Assembly*, he makes it a point against the members that, because they are active and energetic, they can never pause to see the effects of their policy. "You never give yourselves time to cool." An apparent contrast and an actual completion of this thought occurs in a famous passage of the *Reflections*, where the highest praise of chivalry turns out to be that it was "the nurse of manly sentiment and heroic enterprise." The Jacobin is a child of honest spirit and passion, monstrously inverted.

What did Burke mean in the *Letter to a Noble Lord* when he remarked that ingratitude was the first of revolutionary virtues? One might take him to imply only: these people should be more grateful than they are to the society that nurtured them. But *King Lear* creates a peculiar resonance for the idea of ingratitude: "How sharper than a serpent's tooth it is / To have a thankless child"; and "Ingratitude, thou marble-hearted fiend, / More hideous, when thou show'st thee in a child, / Than the sea-monster"; and again,

> She hath abated me of half my train;
> Look'd black upon me; struck me with her tongue,
> Most serpent-like, upon the very heart.
> All the stor'd vengeances of Heaven fall
> On her ingrateful top!

(2.4.160–164)

And finally in the scene on the heath: "Filial ingratitude! / Is it not as this mouth should tear this hand / For lifting food to't?" In all these speeches the motive is domestic: a scene of a tranquil offer of shelter or feeding is disrupted by a sudden withdrawal of charity. Sterility can become the curse of Goneril or Regan, and violence justly be visited upon them, because in the new scheme of things they have renounced piety and gentleness. They are mothers who are not mothers.

But Shakespeare's plot and Burke's are both working out a radically unfamiliar idea of gratitude, alongside this conventional one. Parents, who hope that their daughters will become mothers, think of gratitude as a habit that passes gradually into a reflex of remembering. But there is a naturally previous sense of gratitude, a sense Lear has in view when he says on the heath:

> O, I have ta'en
> Too little care of this. Take physic, Pomp;
> Expose thyself to feel what wretches feel,
> That thou mayst shake the superflux to them,
> And show the Heavens more just.

(3.4.32–36)

The lines describe a generosity proper to an aristocratic ethos, but they have a broader correlative in human experience. We create gratitude by enacting in ourselves the useless reality of a feeling. By contrast, the ethic of economic utility is grounded in use; and the more habitual sort of gratitude, with which that ethic is associated, implies, as Burke once observed, "an inert principle because it concerns only things done."[13] It has inevitably an element of I-give-you: you-give-me, the tropism of response that Adam Smith classed under the heading of "keeping time" with the feelings of another person.

Burke finally repudiates any idea of gratitude that entails such a necessary relation between giver and receiver. Gratitude in the sense he favors must belong to decency of manners, which has its own distant but deep utility for the survival of a civil order. That is why his defense of chivalry begins with an attack on "sophisters, oeconomists, and calculators"—people whose business it is to scour "care" from the face of the moral world. The sense of gratitude that Burke here evokes has nothing to do with counting. Its objects may be persons so old that nobody minds who takes care of them now, or so strange that people like me hardly look at them with recognition—objects so remote from myself that the act of gratitude looks radically unmotivated. The choice to defend an old order, even against its own loss of decency, is bound to appear mysterious because it is uncalculated: Cordelia, refusing the exchange of lands for her words of praise, is also refusing this moral arithmetic as a slander against the ideal gratitude that she honors. Ingratitude, on the other hand, is a useful vice, which the revolutionists have turned into a virtue. Through it, I identify advancing spirits like myself; by ingratitude to others, I know myself to belong. This intuition, that gratitude is subtly allied with the perpetuation of differences, and ingratitude with the cultivation of reflex similarity, runs so deep in Burke that he is often able to express it only by metaphor. He writes of the Jacobins in the *Letter to a Noble Lord*: "They have a means of compounding with their nature"—compounding, that is, conspiring to commit a crime; calculating the interest on the crime; and also doubling themselves, as they discover fellow criminals who by imitative action draw off the taint of criminality itself.

Ingratitude has to be two sisters conspiring: "I am made of that self mettle as my sister." Gratitude has to be one sister disarmed: "What shall

Cordelia speak? Love, and be silent." In the same way, for Burke, constitutional governments are tied to a past, and based on reasonless differences. Innovative governments are tied to a present that has been utterly rationalized by contract and uniformity: the imposed identity of place with place, of status with status, of oneself with one's political professions, of oneself with every other broker of such professions. The existence of a "mixed constitution" becomes at times, for him, a figure for any system made from elements that are stubbornly various. But with a government driven by innovation, one will look around oneself, and at oneself, and be reassured: there is no disturbing contrast to alarm the will into reflection, or retard the promotion of new projects. The *Letter to a Noble Lord* will round off the portrait of the political men of letters that began in the *Reflections*: "Naturally, men so formed and finished are the first gifts of Providence to the world. But when they have once thrown off the fear of God, which was in all ages too often the case, and the fear of man, which is now the case, and when in that state they come to understand one another, and to act in corps, a more dreadful calamity cannot arise out of hell to scourge mankind."[14] The exemplary scene in literature of such a coming to an understanding I take to be the dialogue between Regan and Goneril, at the end of Act I scene i, in which nothing is explicitly arranged yet everything is understood: "Such unconstant starts are we like to have of him. . . ." "Pray you, let us hit together; if our father carry authority with such disposition. . . ." "We shall further think of it." "We must do something, and i'the heat."

It is the avowed horror of the *Letter to a Noble Lord* that, if ever humankind were to give up the fear of man, they "(with Mr. Paine) would soon be taught that no one generation can bind another." Paine has for a long time been counted the winner in his contestation with Burke on the question of one generation binding another. We grant him the victory, I think, because we read the argument romantically, through the allegory of Prometheus bound on the rock, or we read it as if Burke were repeating the argument of Filmer's *Patriarcha* and Paine repeating Locke's reply in the *First Treatise* on government. But this view of the contest picks up different lights and shadows if we recollect that the binding of one generation by another is the subject of the first scene of *King Lear*: "'Tis our fast intent / To shake all cares and business from our age, / Conferring them on younger strengths, while we / Unburthen'd crawl towards death. . . . I do invest you jointly with my power, / Pre-eminence, and all the large effects / That troop with majesty. . . . Only we shall retain / The name and all th'addition to a king; the sway, / Revenue, execution of the rest, / Beloved sons, be yours." The bond is an implicit acceptance, by Lear's daughters and sons-in-law, of the honor of preserving one's duties toward someone who renounces every power to enforce them. The daughters, by despising such duties openly, and by rendering them void, show the liberating effects of refusing to allow their generation to be bound to another.

One may recall, in this connection, Burke's suspicion of lawyers as a class—a prejudice already plain in the 1770s, in his description of the social traits that pressed the American colonists to rebel. Lawyers, he speculated, form the group in a modern society most "alert, inquisitive, dexterous, prompt in attack, ready in defense, full of resources"; they are expert at proving every bond to be an extricable obligation rather than a duty, making every social relation depend on the contractual acknowledgement of reciprocal under-standings. One great change we see occur to society in the progress of *King Lear* is a passage from the fabulous acceptance of ritual to a demand for exacting legalism in all things; a situation that is bitterly alluded to by Albany, when he warns Regan to follow proper procedures in her negotiations with Edmund: "For your claim, fair sister, / I bar it in the interest of my wife; / 'Tis she is subcontracted to this lord, / And I, her husband, contradict your banes. / If you will marry, make your loves to me, / My lady is bespoke." Albany is ungentle, as he needs to be. He knows there is a sympathy approaching to identity between the creation of ingratitude and the creation of contract. One might say a contract is always an instrument for the disen-chantment of gratitude. What then becomes of the Burkean supposition that a decent political order must be able to inspire love simply by its loveliness? Under a rationalized legal order, that belief must pass into a discarded superstition. This is one reason, commonly neglected by critics, why Burke's attack on lawyers naturally occupies so large a share of his strictures against the new government of France.

He says near the start of the *Reflections* that the French is "one among the revolutions which have given splendour to obscurity, and distinction to undiscerned merit."[15] The obscurity of its leaders ought to create a legitimate presumption against them, on the Burkean logic that associates honor, as a motive of pride, with public reputation and recognition. Honor does not work like that among the obscure, who, having no previous public stake in character to defend, exhibit a shamelessness exactly proportioned to their anonymity. "Judge, Sir, of my surprize," he writes in a critical passage,

> when I found that a very great proportion of the Assembly (a majority, I believe, of the members who attended) was composed of practitioners in the law. It was composed not of distinguished magistrates, who had given pledges to their country of their science, prudence, and integrity; not of leading advocates, the glory of the bar; not of renowned pro-fessors in universities;—but for the far greater part, as it must in such a number, of the inferior, unlearned, mechanical, merely instrumental members of the profession. There were distinguished exceptions; but the general composition was of obscure provincial advocates, of stewards of petty local jurisdictions, country attornies, notaries, and the whole train of the ministers of municipal litigation, the fomentors and conductors of the petty war of village vexation. From the moment I read the list I saw distinctly, and very nearly as it has happened, all that was to follow.[16]

One ought to be wary of a style of praise that suggests Burke may have deserved Wilde's encomium on Carlyle: that he wrote the best kind of history because he kept facts in their proper subordinate position. But in matters in which fact and interpretation are really inseparable, one is surprised again and again to find how accurate Burke's information was. William Doyle remarks of the elected members of the assembly of 1789 that the third-estate deputies

> were remarkably homogeneous and united. . . . Two thirds of those elected had some form or other of legal qualifications. A quarter were advocates or notaries, among them people like Barnave and Robespierre. Forty three percent (278) were holders of venal offices, including many senior judges from *bailliage* and *sénéchaussée* courts who had been entrusted by electoral regulations with the organization of the third-estate assemblies. . . . Most of the deputies were unknown and untested outside their own localities.[17]

To form a mixture suitably volatile, there required, says Burke, in addition to the provincial mediocrities a smaller mass of "turbulent, discontented men of quality." It was these men, of the type of Mirabeau rather than Robespierre, whom he had in mind when he wrote: "Something they must destroy, or they seem to themselves to exist for no purpose."[18]

State policy under this kind of influence comes to be identified with the successive spasmodic reflexes of a popular will embodied by the club, the section, the commune, or the mob, reflexes which in their total mass are then projected as the will of the nation. The consequence is what Burke calls a "distemper of remedy": a thoughtless determination to enact measures of legislative and spontaneous violence which "temper and harden the breast, in order to prepare it for the desperate strokes which are sometimes used in extreme occasions." But, he adds, "as these occasions may never arrive, the mind receives a gratuitous taint."[19] It is a moral, I believe, of the subplot of *King Lear*, in which Edmund traduces Gloucester, that the descent of society into such giddy betrayals and tortures does not reflect the necessary nature of the persons who execute its will. These are prudent characters and most of what they do in the first two acts is defensible as prudent. A woman like Goneril for all we know becomes worse for the temptations to disorder that are scattered in her path. We know this to be a possibility from her husband Albany, who descends unthinking part way into the evil, but then, maybe in some measure because he sees himself as one of the betrayed, stops short of the worst of the violence.

*B*urke, supposing him to be theorist of any kind, is best thought of as a theorist of ceremony—an office whose knowledge differs not at all from that of the theatrical critic. And the most delicate of his maneuvers in the *Reflections* is the attempt to persuade us, on theatrical grounds, that the influence of a feminine nobility may constitute, for society, a ceremony of innocence. The degree of actual innocence in any person of majesty cherished for his or her manner is a consideration of very little interest to Burke. The carrying forward of state ceremonies, and of social rituals promoted by government, he regards as a way of leading a society back unendingly to a knowledge of the decency it lives by. Yet these are practices to which, except in enlarged or artificial settings, nobody gives much thought. We do become aware of them at moments of miscarried public authority, and that is why crooked or botched ceremonies have so singular an importance in all Burke's writings, starting with the *Speech on American Taxation*. The most familiar real-life example from modern France is the use of the captive King Louis XVI as a publicist for the will of the assembly, on the pretence of a perfect concurrence between old and new authorities.

*King Lear* opens with an aborted ceremonial recognition of authority. "He hath ever but slenderly known himself," we are told of Lear after it has misfired: "The best and soundest of his time hath been but rash." The scene of rejection exhibits to public view this monarch's fatal defect of self-knowledge; for Lear both desires and deplores the renunciation of power that he has declared: "I gave you all," he will say to Regan, still counting, where he has vowed never to count his powers again. "And in good time you gave it," she answers, fearing nothing. The scene of the division of the kingdom has of course been rigged, as all the observers know. Lear tells them outright that Cordelia is his favorite child. His startled rage at her refusal to comply with the trustless artifice of the ceremony—where, by one piece of formulaic flattery, she was meant to achieve an enviable reward—becomes the first of many anticlimaxes the king himself will execute. These are disappointments of a probable plot, which tend in their sum to illegitimate all authority. The same sort of misstep occurs in his response to the dry request of Goneril "a little to disquantity your train" and in his reversion to Regan and back again to Goneril.

The hazard of a king whose mind is, to adapt a phrase of Burke's, "not even dramatically right,"[20] is that, in crisis after crisis, the rhythm of failed assertion and half-hearted withdrawal will turn even his power into a source of instability. It is bad politics because it is bad theater; it frustrates our wish to see action along a continuous path. Here again, the career of Louis XVI offered a contemporary index of comparison. The years 1787–1792 would include, among their conspicuous anticlimaxes, his saying to the Parlement of Paris (after a labored discussion of the registering of loans), "It's law because I say so." Yet, at the earliest crisis of the revolution, he had granted the Estates General almost all they wanted, even before the Tennis Court Oath. Then, a master of punctilio, he ordered them to disperse and, on hearing their refusal, conceded it was all right for them to stay—a gesture by which, as Doyle remarks, "with one word a whole strategy was thrown away." His being led by the triumphant marchers from Versailles to Paris in October 1789, his flight to Varennes in June 1791 (leaving behind documents that confessed his service to the assembly a sham), followed by the official retraction extorted by his capture at Varennes: all these interludes belong to the same story. In appearance of policy, the French king was a greater democrat than Burke. But this in itself, on Burke's own analysis, damaged him less than his cooperation with the project of evacuating all ceremony from his office. It was only by virtue of that dignity that he had ever deserved to survive. The broad allowance Burke makes for the politically tolerable, provided it is dramatically right, can shock any reader of the *Reflections* who stops to ponder its recommendations of tactics. Burke imagines once the possibility that even regicide, if it were brought off with a solemn grandeur, might receive some extenuation from persons who would surely disapprove of it as a naked act. "If I were to punish a wicked king, I should regard the dignity in avenging the crime. Justice is grave and decorous, and in its punishments rather seems to submit to a necessity, than to make a choice."[21]

Weakened as Louis's rule has been by caprice and improbability, all the authority of monarchy seems to have grown idle. This brings out a subversive thought whose power one can learn from Edmund. "I begin," he says in his forgery of Edgar's letter, "to find an idle and fond bondage in the oppression of aged tyranny, who sways, not as it hath the power, but as it is suffer'd." The judgment and the word are echoed by Goneril: "Idle old man, / That still would manage those authorities / That he hath given away." But the tokens of chaos that Gloucester enumerates—"In cities mutinies, in countries discord, in palaces treason, and the bond crack'd twixt son and father"—are not merely the result of tyranny presenting itself as legitimate authority. Another cause of disorder is the meanness of the scrutiny to which authority—which ought always to be mainly reasonless—has now been reduced by enterprising spirits who require a reason for everything. A deeper chivalric sense of authority belongs to Kent, who, disguised as Caius, is asked by Lear why he would serve him and answers: "You have that in your countenance which I would fain call master." "What's that?" "Authority."

This encounter between an old and despised king bereft of his powers, and the unknown voice that asserts his legitimacy once again, seems as much a miracle of the moral world as the reversal in which Lear tells Cordelia he has given her cause to do him wrong, and she replies: "No cause, no cause." The final simplicity not of moral actions but of the declarable reasons for actions, suggests a difference between spontaneous gratitude, which must always look unmotivated, and the gratitude of exchange, which presupposes and can easily articulate a reason. To those captive to reason-giving, the sense of moral action as gratuitous, which *King Lear* and the *Reflections* alike insist on, must be as senseless as the idea of a partnership without a contract. Georg Simmel has an observation so acute on this point that it might have been written with either text in mind: "Gratitude, as it were, is the moral memory of mankind. . . . It is an ideal bridge which the soul comes across again and again, so to speak, and which, upon provocations too slight to throw a *new* bridge to the other person, it uses to come closer to him. . . . If every grateful action, which lingers on from good turns received in the past, were suddenly eliminated, society (at least as we know it) would break apart."[22] The speech by Lear beginning "Reason not the need" is directed against any calculation that would render this ideal bridge a thing of material dimensions. It is a lesson—on the limits of assigning reasons for an action—which he teaches without having understood.

Do not ask why some things are necessary, the speech is going to say; do not try to say which things are necessary and which not: that would be to inquire too closely into what constitutes us as human, and that is an inquiry whose end we ought to prefer never to see. The lines have a long foreground and many reverberations in the play; but, for Burke, a late reference was likely to be all-important: the moment when Lear on the heath says, "The art of our necessities is strange, / And can make vile things precious." The unexpected touch in the proverb is "art"; and one remembers that in Burke's judgment vice, under the chivalric code, lost half its evil by losing all its grossness—not vile things but vileness itself was made partly precious. "Coming as if from heaven," the words seem to say, "the artifice that protects us makes us grateful." Or again: "Right down to zero, the little that we have possesses a charm beyond measuring—we see the humanness of need when we ourselves are all need." This does not mean that a man is only an animal. The most falsifying part of the modern readings that descend from Jan Kott is the idea that this play is somehow a therapy, an iconoclastic reduction of nature to a truth about "the thing itself," the truth that "unaccommodated man is nothing but such a poor, bare, forked creature as thou art." But these are words Lear speaks to Edgar who, in disguise, is not what he seems, and is anything but unaccommodated man—he is making his accommodations with immense craft, and with a sense that even "true need" can be a kind of clothing. In this context, "Reason not the need" gives a warning, by anticipation, against any romance of mere instinctual or creaturely life.

The moral weight of the speech is brought home dramatically by its placement, after the auction-in-reverse at which the wicked sisters have pared down the permissible size of Lear's train of knights. "What need you five and twenty, ten or five?" "What need one?"

> O! reason not the need; our basest beggars
> Are in the poorest thing superfluous:
> Allow not nature more than nature needs,
> Man's life is cheap as beast's. Thou art a lady;
> If only to go warm were gorgeous,
> Why, nature needs not what thou gorgeous wear'st,
> Which scarcely keeps thee warm. But, for true need,—
> You Heavens, give me that patience, patience I need!
>
> (2.4.266–273)

There is an echo in this, surprising enough to make one to feel the point mattered greatly to Shakespeare, of the admonition by Hamlet to Polonius on the treatment of the players. "I will use them according to their desert," says Polonius, and Hamlet answers with his shaming correction: "Much better. Use every man after his desert, and who shall scape whipping? Use them after your own honor and dignity. The less they deserve, the more merit is in your bounty." Here again is the image of a necessary shelter as in *Lear*, and of a superfluous giving to those whose deserving we ought in honor never to measure—all this accompanied in *Hamlet*, just as in *Lear*, by the image of human beings reduced to accept punishment like beasts if the morality of deserving were to be strictly followed. We are not to deal with people at their estimated worth, or by reckoning their calculable wants, but from a gratuitous good in our idea of who we are. Followers of honor are not obeyers of rules. If they were, they could shave down every reward a degree or more.

The heart of the best known passage in Burke's *Reflections* seems to me to have been composed as an interpretation of Lear's speech:

> But now all is to be changed. All the pleasing illusions, which made power gentle, and obedience liberal, which harmonized the different shades of life, and which, by a bland assimilation, incorporated into politics the sentiments which beautify and soften private society, are to be dissolved by this new conquering empire of light and reason. All the decent drapery of life is to be rudely torn off. All the super-added ideas, furnished from the wardrobe of a moral imagination, which the heart owns, and the understanding ratifies, as necessary to cover the defects of our naked, shivering nature, and to raise it to dignity in our own estimation, are to be exploded as a ridiculous, absurd, and antiquated fashion.
>
> On this scheme of things, a king is but a man, a queen is but a woman; a woman is but an animal, and an animal not of the highest order. All homage paid to the sex in general as such, and without distinct views, is to be regarded as romance and folly. Regicide, and parricide, and sacrilege are but fictions of superstition, corrupting jurisprudence by destroying its simplicity.[23]

Clothing alone, whether as bodily garment or the wardrobe of a moral imagination: on Burke's reading of *Lear*, this and this only protects the artifice of humanity from the terrible possibility that, in revenge or bewilderment, at a chaotic time, any person could contribute his own derangement to the general terror. The theory that man is like a beast leads to the practice of making him as much like one as possible. We are shown an appropriate image of the end of humanity by the soldier who agrees to kill Cordelia, who says "I cannot draw a cart nor eat dried oats; / If it be man's work, I'll do it"—by which he means, "If it be a man's work . . . (and, of course, man is an animal)." This is unaccommodated man. For better or worse, the characters in this play become human only by their accommodation.

Let us follow a step further Hamlet's clue to the survival of nature in artificial society. "I did love you once," he says to Ophelia. "Indeed my lord you made me believe so." "You should not have believed me, for virtue cannot so inoculate our old stock but we shall relish of it." In the *Reflections*, Burke writes of 1689: "Upon that body and stock of inheritance we have taken care not to inoculate any cyon alien to the nature of the original plant." Hamlet is an ironist who believes in the persistence of nature under every circumstance, in spite of the "politic, well-wrought veil" of necessary artifice and hypocrisy that a stable society builds against it. Whereas, on Burke's reading of *King Lear*, nature is and can only be an understanding of artifice grown customary. This may be nothing but a difference of shading; yet Burke has pursued Hamlet's fears and guarded against the iconoclasm in which they might end, with a strange tenacity: he makes it the duty of all statesmanship to prevent a falling back from our second or social nature to the "old stock" of nature itself. "You began ill," he says to the revolutionists, "because you began by despising every thing that belonged to you."[24] Again, Hamlet says to Ophelia: "The power of beauty will sooner transform honesty from what it is to a bawd than the force of honesty can translate beauty into his likeness. This was sometime a paradox, but now the time gives it proof." This is the deepest foreshadowing in literature of Burke's perception that, in a system where beauty "ennobled whatever it touched," vice itself "lost half its evil, by losing all its grossness." Hamlet, melancholy naturalist, deplores the truth to human nature that the paradox expresses. Burke, the skeptical advocate of artificial society, holds the paradox close, as the best imaginable analysis of the way accommodation succeeds.

In *King Lear* it is Albany who takes up Hamlet's thought; and yet he speaks, like Burke, not of an involuntary recurrence to nature but a deliberate cleaving to a part of it chosen for preservation:

> *Alb.*                    O Goneril!
> You are not worth the dust which the rude wind
> Blows in your face. I fear your disposition:
> That nature, which contemns its origin,
> Cannot be border'd certain in itself;
> She that herself will sliver and disbranch
> From her material sap, perforce must wither
> And come to deadly use.
> *Gon.* No more; the text is foolish.
> *Alb.* Wisdom and goodness to the vile seem vile:
> Filths savor but themselves. What have you done?
> Tigers, not daughters, what have you perform'd?
>                              (4.2.29–40)

The great speech will conclude by linking an archaic retribution with the very possibility of justice: if these daughters are not punished, "It will come, / Humanity must perforce prey on itself, / Like monsters of the deep." One reason we accept that judgment is that it comes from Albany, a normative character even in his unimaginativeness, who feels bewilderment at Goneril's torment of Lear, then disgust, and only at last horror that the derogation of authority should have issued in a degeneration of human nature itself. The allegory here is still in Burke's mind when he comes to write the *Letter to a Noble Lord*. "They have tigers to fall upon animated strength"—"These obscene harpies, who deck themselves in I know not what divine attributes, but who in reality are foul and ravenous birds of prey, (both mothers and daughters,)"— "Their humanity is at their horizon—and, like the horizon, it always flies before them."[25]

*If* there is a character in *King Lear* with whom Burke by instinct must want to associate himself, it is certainly not Lear and, notwithstanding the accidents of rhetorical stance and texture, it is not Albany and not Edgar either, but Kent. A modern poet said that morals are the memory of success that no longer succeeds.[26] Honor, as Burke understands it, and as Kent does, is loyalty to the memory of a success that no longer can succeed; and in Kent one finds the survival of an idea of morality as a habit of action informed only by right prejudice. "In this enlightened age," as Burke explains the conception, we are still "generally men of untaught feelings":

> instead of casting away all our old prejudices, we cherish them to a
> very considerable degree, and, to take more shame to ourselves, we
> cherish them because they are prejudices; and the longer they have
> lasted, and the more generally they have prevailed, the more we
> cherish them.

We continue to do so in spite of our interest in enlightenment, because we are reluctant

> to cast away the coat of prejudice, and to leave nothing but the naked
> reason; because prejudice, with its reason, has a motive to give action
> to that reason, and an affection which will give it permanence.
> Prejudice is of ready application in the emergency; it previously
> engages the mind in a steady course of wisdom and virtue, and does
> not leave the man hesitating in the moment of decision, sceptical,
> puzzled, and unresolved. Prejudice renders a man's virtue his habit;
> and not a series of unconnected acts.[27]

Kent, never puzzled, skeptical, or unresolved in settings that find his master perplexed, thinks of Lear before the crisis and after as Royal Lear—"Whom I have ever honoured as my King, / Lov'd as my father, as my master follow'd,/ As my great patron thought on in my prayers." It approaches the justice Kent would desire to say of him that, though a truthful and observant man, he is also an unreflecting one. He acts from untaught feelings, or feelings rooted so deep in his past that they are beyond reflection. About only one other character in the play could we begin to say the same, but Cordelia does think once, beautifully and fatefully in the opening scene. It is the sort of choice that divides a life in two, and for us to see it creates her as a character, in a way that Kent in some sense does not emerge as a character. He is a virtuous man obedient to a duty that has become a habit.

This constancy of Kent's, bred of the idealism of chivalric honor, presents an inherited design of exemplary conduct that any revolution must deny. In the play, he makes the idealism most vivid in the final scene with Lear, where he reveals himself after having taken the name of Caius:

> *Lear.*              Are you not Kent?
> *Kent.*                              The same;
>   Your servant Kent. Where is your servant Caius?
> *Lear.* He's a good fellow; I can tell you that;
>   He'll strike, and quickly too. He's dead and rotten.
> *Kent.* No, my Lord; I am the very man,—
> *Lear.* I'll see that straight.
> *Kent.* That from the first of difference and decay,
>   Have follow'd your sad steps.
>                        (5.3.282–289)

The first of difference and decay: the words look a long way back, for, by the end, Lear and his world have been dying a long time. That world attains in retrospect some of the coherence it never had in fact, from our impression that Kent has watched over its vanishing. When he says "the best of me is diligence," he must mean that even in the shadow of so many deaths, if there should prove to be one man like Kent it would show that honor is real, that something in the old order was worthy of defense. He moves us because in the setting where we encounter him he appears an almost unintelligible remnant, a man of nobility cut off from the system of the court by every fact of his life except his chosen relation to Lear. He is the valiant guardian and counselor, childless and fatherless at the heart of an order that has suffered catastrophe.

The unhappiest circumstance of the French Revolution, for Burke, was that it brought forward no character resembling Kent. "I thought ten thousand swords must have leaped from their scabbards to avenge even a look that threatened her with insult," he said of the queen; but only two were raised by the palace guard, at the time of the march on Versailles, and they were killed and their heads put on pikes. Lafayette, who did finally rescue her, was a political trimmer who played soon after the equivocal part of escorting the royal couple to Paris, in the keeping of the same mob now triumphant and appeased. The astonishing fact was how the disturbance seemed to carry instantly everywhere. As Victor Hugo would describe it in *Ninety-Three*, from a different politics but a similarly chastened sense of the spectacle: "Mirabeau felt Robespierre stirring at some unknown depth below; Robespierre felt Marat stir; Marat felt Hébert stir; Hébert, Babeuf. As long as the layers underneath are still, the politician can advance; but under the most revolutionary there must be some subsoil, and the boldest stop in dismay when they feel under their feet the earthquake they have created."[28] No one could say to anyone, You have that which I would fain obey.

"The Action of a play ought to be like a rack to make Actors discover the bottom of their souls." Burke's dealings with the French Revolution through the medium of *King Lear* show this not to have been the maxim of a spectator whose thoughts about personal identity had ever grown fixed by sectarian attachment. In his celebration of the existing order, he is too violent and unaccepting for its good. In this, one may say, he partly does resemble Kent, but there remains in him a good deal of the New Man he had affirmed himself to be long before, someone who could have become Edmund but strangely did not. Burke, in his last phase, as Wollstonecraft among others noticed, has a pride in saying on behalf of the old order what it cannot say for itself, pitying it as it is incapable of pitying itself. He will write in a letter to a friend, on 14 November 1794, about the knighthood lately conferred on his relation Edmund Nagle: "These are the pleasant things of the old world—and let us take them whilst the old world continues. A worse is coming."[29] It is a tone one learns to appreciate in the later Burke, commanding because it is so much in character, and sufficiently Kent-like: "I am too old to learn." Yet if one were allowed to select a passage to represent faithfully Burke's final certainties along with his final doubts, I would choose one of a very different tenor from the *Regicide Peace*, where, speculating on the possible causes of salvage or calamity in war, he finds his thoughts turning to a power of human chance that persists beyond war: "A common soldier, a child, a girl at the door of an inn, have changed the face of fortune, and almost of Nature."[30] It is the voice of a historian for whom life must resemble art, but for whom nothing is so strange as life, and nothing so apt to create occasions for valor where all that is glimpsed by the spectators is a horror of unconnected acts.

### Notes

1. H.V.F. Somerset, ed., *A Note-book of Edmund Burke* (Cambridge: Cambridge University Press, 1957), 97.
2. "As to us here our thoughts of every thing at home are suspended, by our astonishment at the wonderful Spectacle which is exhibited in a Neighbouring and rival Country—what Spectators, and what actors! England gazing with astonishment at a French struggle for Liberty and not knowing whether to blame or to applaud!" Letter to the Earl of Charlemont, 9 August 1789, in Thomas Copeland, ed., *The Correspondence of Edmund Burke*, 10 vols. (Chicago: University of Chicago Press, 1958–1978), 6:10.
3. Gérard Gengembre, "Burke," in François Furet and Mona Ozouf, eds., *A Critical Dictionary of the French Revolution*, trans. Arthur Goldhammer (Cambridge: Harvard University Press, 1989), 922.
4. Edmund Burke, *Reflections on the Revolution in France*, ed. Conor Cruise O'Brien (Harmondsworth: Penguin, 1969), 91.

5. The phrase "sudden fortunes" appears in Burke's writings on India. He seems to have taken it from Smith's *Wealth of Nations*, where the distrust of such fortunes is almost as pronounced.

6. *The Works of Edmund Burke*, 12 vols. (Boston: Little, Brown, 1869), 6:367.

7. Burke, *Works*, 5:309.

8. Burke, *Reflections*, 139–140.

9. *Correspondence of Edmund Burke*, 2:128. The report of Burke's reply to Sir William Bagot is by his friend Will Burke, in a letter to William Dennis, dated by the volume's editor Lucy Sutherland 3, 6 April 1770. The Latin phrase from Cicero, *In Verrem* (3.4.7) is adapted by Sutherland to translate "novorum" as "self-made": "You hate the industry of self-made men." A fair adaptation of "industriam" is "energy"—the word Burke often employed in such contexts.

10. Burke, *Works*, 7:35–36.

11. *King Lear*, Arden Edition, ed. Kenneth Muir (London: Methuen, 1964), 2.2.1–22. Subsequent act, scene, and line references to this edition will be printed in the text.

12. Burke, *Works*, 5:287.

13. Somerset, *Note-book*, 70.

14. Burke, *Works*, 5:216.

15. Burke, *Reflections*, 87.

16. Burke, *Reflections*, 129–130.

17. William Doyle, *The Oxford History of the French Revolution* (Oxford: Oxford University Press, 1989), 101.

18. Burke, *Reflections*, 147.

19. Burke, *Reflections*, 156.

20. From Burke's letter to Philip Francis, 20 February 1790, replying to the criticism of his eulogy on the queen of France as "pure foppery": "What, are not high Rank, great Splendour of descent, great personal Elegance, and outward accomplishments ingredients of moment in forming the interest we take in the Misfortunes of Men? The minds of those who do not feel thus are not even Dramatically right." *Correspondence*, 6:90.

21. Burke, *Reflections*, 178.

22. Georg Simmel, "Faithfulness and Gratitude," in *The Sociology of Georg Simmel*, ed. Kurt H. Wolff (New York: Free Press, 1964), 388–389.

23. Burke, *Reflections*, 171.

24. Burke, *Reflections*, 117, 122.

25. Burke, *Works*, 5:175, 187, 216.

26. William Carlos Williams, *In the American Grain* (New York: New Directions, 1956), 67.

27. Burke, *Reflections*, 183.

28. Victor Hugo, *Ninety-Three*, trans. Frank Lee Benedict (New York: Carroll and Graf, 1988), 132–133.

29. Burke, *Correspondence*, ed. R. B. McDowell, 8:77.

30. Burke, *Works*, 5:236.

CHAPTER 5

# Listening to Words: David, St. Mark, Emily Brontë, and the Exorbitancies in Narrative

BARRY V. QUALLS

Civilization has been overgenerous to these novelists in providing designs for living and for writing, and to that very degree it has made life itself, and the life in language, increasingly difficult to come by.
—Richard Poirier, *The Performing Self* (1971), 26, on Pynchon

In being historical he [Pynchon] must also be marvelously exorbitant.
—Richard Poirier, "Rocket Power," *Saturday Review*, March, 1973, 59.

*R*ichard Poirier's interest in "the life in language" has always asserted itself against system-makers and theorists. The writers to whom Poirier responds—Emerson and the Beatles, Mailer and Pynchon, Henry James and Gertrude Stein, William James and Robert Frost—assert how much the work of civilization has in essential ways wanted to curtail, with insistent conventions and designs, "life itself." Poirier celebrates the pressures and chaos of historical moments and those writers who work exorbitantly amidst them—that is, whose language escapes the patterns dictated by tradition as it copes with the new and different.

In these pages, I want to consider three signally compelling illustrations in "historical" narrative of this inevitable conflict between civilization and "life": the David stories in the Hebrew scriptures, Mark's gospel in the Christian scriptures, and *Wuthering Heights*. I choose these narratives because they define for me what character and design in history mean in western narrative; they illustrate baldly the designs for living—that is, for writing narrative—that were a part of writing from "the beginning"; and they illuminate the conflicts between design and "life" inherent in storytelling. The Hebrew Bible and its most capacious progeny, the nineteenth-century English novel, have no hesitation that their subject is human life in all its complexity. Both revel in history; and they look to the representation of character in history, in all of its chaotic fullness, as the chief, perhaps the only, path to worlds elsewhere. Even that precursor of the novel Bunyan, who knew that there was no Christian without design, distracted his pilgrim repeatedly with the extravagances of worldly-wise people living gaily or woefully in history.

But of course Bunyan, and the nineteenth-century novel after him, organized this exuberant life into more than narrative—into a plot that exiles threatening desire and promises an ending in heaven or beside the domestic hearth that signifies the ontological topos of so many English novels. As Leo Bersani argues, literature's "nature is to coerce experience into making sense," to "fit deceptively random lines of action into a single structure."[1] D. A. Miller adds that "the tyranny of narrative control" expressed in closure defines most succinctly the traditional novel. Miller (here speaking of *Middlemarch*) traces how the novel's text bows to the community that articulates the conventions of realism even as it seems to celebrate its protagonists' wishes for worlds elsewhere. But in the end, the novel must "persecut[e] with clearheaded insight what it profoundly seems to cherish"—the stories of desire that give it life.[2]

This idea of literature differs profoundly from that of the great early Hebrew writers, the Yahwist J and the court historians of Saul and David. These writers organize reality into narrative that is exorbitant because so full of history and so unconcerned with design—even as it sees God's hand in everything. For them, there are no ends; God's work in and through history continues forever. Thus these writers make little of death, whether it be Saul's or David's or an enemy's (e.g., Jezebel's); their texts do not endlessly anticipate their end. But the later Hebrew and Jewish redactors, canonizers, and Jewish-Christians are uneasy with this ease, uncertain that promised covenants not yet realized *should* be so easily narrated. They thus theorize narrative into religion and turn life into design.[3]

In focusing my discussion of narrative on the Judaeo-Christian scriptures, I am saying that whatever the origins of the novel, its conventions for plot and for character in plot at once oppose the ease of the great Hebrew writers in narrative and long for it. The Hebrews, forbidden material representation of God, used the Word and its words—their origin and their life—to develop ways of representing the human in history that have changed little since Sarah laughed, Rebecca schemed, and David triumphed over God's prohibitions against his people being "like the nations."[4] Mark, in that gospel that the early saints thought barbaric and the twentieth century has thought sublime, found his narrative life in representing Jesus as God's son who never seems to fit the typological patterns so necessary to the other gospel narrators.

The great nineteenth-century novelists—Dickens and George Eliot, Hawthorne and Henry James—work continually to resecure, from the inherited modes of realism with its moral designs and expected endings, the freedom of the narrative implications of those original representations. They are forever seeking to resist, even to escape, the stunted life enforced by patterns that had their origins in biblical typologies—in the march towards settlements in the *new* Jerusalem—that the early Hebrew writers so easily ignored. Characters in their texts may sometimes hunger for the safety of predetermined patterns; the strongest writers know their costs.

Emily Brontë, from her parsonage on the moors, recognized that the exorbitancies of life and the language that produces it will allow narrative to escape design, even if her narrators crave it for their lives. As a coda to my discussion, I use Brontë as a representative of this latter-day resistance to pattern that characterizes the Judaeo-Christian narrative tradition's first story-tellers as well as the determination of strong writers to escape the expectations of narrative tradition and readers. Before Woolf and modernism, before Stein and Pynchon, Brontë read the progress of fiction in the fictions she read and the Bible she knew. *Wuthering Heights*, in saying "no" to, even as it used, the conventions that so animated, and limited, the nineteenth-century novel, affirms that life in language is supreme when it responds to the exorbitancies of life that defeat the designs of narrative.

# I

Thou shalt have none other gods before me. Thou shalt not make thee any graven image, or any likeness of any thing that is in heaven above, or that is in the earth beneath, or that is in the waters beneath the earth: thou shalt not bow down thyself unto them, nor serve them. . . . Neither shalt thou desire thy neighbor's wife. (Deut. 5:7–9, 21)[5]

Two of these commandments David easily negotiated on his way to being Israel's king; the third brought him disaster. No one in the Hebrew scriptures so listened to history and to God, and so understood how he himself caused that communication to sour. He was so successful because he knew how to read the self-generated designs that capture others—Saul and his children, especially—and how to use words—Psalms, the elegy on the death of Saul and Jonathan, the lament about his son Absalom—to free himself from his own political designs. His "author," as Harold Bloom has written, does not conduct David's life by the normative patterns we take to be the life of a hero. No birth scene; a death rendered in a verse or two; extended family scenes only when he betrays his God privately; no anxiety about whether he is virtuous. These signal events in the lives of *our* heroes and heroines do not interest David's author. History is too importunate for these narrators to stop time and exact significance. Religion is life, not a theory of life.[6]

Thus the narrative offers David *two* entrances into the text—two to illuminate, not explain, his complexity. And in both he enters in medias res, amidst the turmoil surrounding Saul, Israel's first King whom God chose reluctantly when the people pleaded to the prophet Samuel for a king so that they might be "like all the nations" (1 Sam. 8:20). David first enters when God urges Samuel to cease mourning for the rejected Saul and to seek a king among the sons of Jesse.

> And [Jesse] sent, and brought him in. Now he was ruddy, and withal
> of a beautiful countenance, and goodly to look to. And the Lord said,
> Arise, anoint him, for this is he. . . . and the Spirit of the Lord came
> upon David from that day forward. (1 Sam. 16:12–13)

Immediately thereafter he becomes the harp player to Saul who, troubled by "an evil spirit from the Lord," asks for someone to minister to him with music. A servant responds: "Behold, I have seen a son of Jesse the Bethlehemite, that is cunning in playing, and a mighty valiant man, and a man of war, and prudent in matters, and a comely person, and the Lord is with him" (16:14–18). And the king is "refreshed" by David's playing.

The second entrance is altogether different and provides the double perspective so crucial to these narratives. No God directs this script, only David himself, marching into battle as a brash youth certain he will slay Goliath. It is the stuff of tall tales, but the Hebrew narrators treat it no differently in tone from the God-directed entrance. So David's mighty actions in war refresh Israel—for life, as it were. As these mighty events occur, however, the reader keeps recalling the narrator's early words about David—"cunning" and "prudent in matters"—and the phrases of David's brother, appalled by the shepherd boy's arrogance in the face of the giant: "I know thy pride, and the naughtiness of thine heart" (17:28). Yet these words add to his thickness of character; they do not define him morally; they never detract from his magnificence, a specialness that wins the people, Saul's son Jonathan and daughter Michal, and even Saul. Whether in poetry or in dancing, in battle or in misery, in love or in politics, he sweeps all before him—except, finally, God.

David's lifelong seduction of Israel and of Israel's God enforces the ironies against a people whose God desires no kings and despairs that his chosen people want to be "like all the nations." They have repeatedly wanted to deny their chosenness, their godlike specialness. Samuel's choice of Saul because "he was higher than any of the people" (the only reason given; 1 Sam. 9:2) is a satire against the people's desire for less specialness, more designed order; they want the monarch, rituals, and the *visibly* ordered lives of their neighbors. They get a tall man. And yet David's beauty, not his intelligence or valor, is also the first thing reported about him when he enters the scriptures *and* when Goliath sees him: "Now he was ruddy, and withal of a beautiful countenance, and goodly to look to" (1 Sam. 16:12, 17:42; Goliath "disdained him" for his youth and fairness). God's ironies never cease.

Saul's tragedy is that he cannot follow God's way, cannot see God's perspective, but chooses his own and the people's—and thus his separation from God becomes the only meaning of his life. The issue here is the ease of Hebrews in history who acknowledge God's direction of it amidst their absolute freedom. Those who choose against God fall into the desperate metaphysical homelessness of a world without order because there is no "dialogue" with God within *their* history. Paradoxically, with this homelessness their freedom is gone and their end in human isolation certain. Whether it is Saul's pleas at Endor for Samuel to return from the grave and bring him God's words; or his tears before David who has spared his life (unaccountably, exorbitantly, from his perspective); or his anger towards David as his children choose the former shepherd boy; or the nobility of his "literary" death, this man who has lost God's favor is one of the few sublimely existential figures in the Hebrew or Christian scriptures—and existential precisely because we know his end before it arrives, as he does.[7]

David rarely has trouble choosing God's point of view, and we never anticipate his end. Much, perhaps all, of his extraordinariness from the reader's view resides in the commensurate nature of his desires and God's, until he covets another man's wife and "displeases the Lord." God and David want a united Israel; God and David want the ark in Jerusalem; and God and David want the people to know their holy city, the city that becomes forever the City of David. But this specialness in doing the Lord's commandments, which makes Israel superior to its neighbors—a great royal power—also makes the nation all too like them in ambition. David's certainty, even when battling Saul, that "the Lord's anointed," the King, must never be touched, prepares his people to treat their king as their neighbors treated theirs, with awe and reverence—though not as a god. David always recognizes this limit, even as he enforces the political exaltation of kingship which ambiguously places the king between the people and their God.

Even David's greatest lyric moment recalls the rich ambiguities of his life in narrative. The elegy on Saul and Jonathan proclaims palpable fictions: "In their death they were not divided" is poetry for public mourning by an inspired poet and politician; Saul and Jonathan *were* divided—and by David. Yet the poem becomes suddenly and unexpectedly personal (if still political):

> O Jonathan, thou wast slain in thine high places.
> I am distressed for thee, my brother Jonathan:
> very pleasant hast thou been unto me:
> thy love to me was wonderful,
> passing the love of women.
> How are the mighty fallen,
> and the weapons of war perished.
>
> (2 Sam. 1:25–27)

David is simply incommensurate: exorbitant because so profoundly personal in his first great ceremonial moment in the text, not trapped in the patterns of state and politics. The language and its rhythms obliterate for the moment the sordid bloody world of Hebrew history. Whatever the political demands of the moment, the personal here surprises by its intensity and by its utter irrelevance to the public (and political) occasion. The return to the poem's framing couplet—"How are the mighty fallen"—suddenly recalls David's audience to the public ceremony.

The narrative's refusal of design is compelled by its profound ease in representing man and God in the same space: history. At the pivotal private moment of David's life—when in desire of Bathsheba he has had Uriah slain and understood Nathan's parable of the ewe lamb from God's perspective—he sees himself clearly: "I have sinned against the Lord," he replies to Nathan's "Thou art the man" (2 Sam. 12:7–15). No terror of God in David; just the recognition of himself as one who has broken the law. What follows this scene spells out the ease of David's "author" with the king's exorbitancies:

> And the Lord struck the child that Uriah's wife bare unto David, and it was very sick. David therefore besought God for the child; and David fasted, and went in, and lay all night upon the earth. . . . And it came to pass on the seventh day, that the child died. And the servants feared of David to tell him that the child was dead: for they said, "Behold, while the child was yet alive, we spake unto him, and he would not hearken unto our voice: how will he then vex himself, if we tell him that the child is dead?" But when David saw that his servants whispered, David perceived that the child was dead. . . .
>
> Then said his servants unto him, "What thing is this that thou hast done? thou didst fast and weep for the child, while it was alive; but when the child was dead, thou didst rise, and eat bread." And he said, "While the child was yet alive, I fasted and wept: for I said, Who can tell whether God will be gracious to me, that the child may live? But now he is dead, and wherefore should I fast? can I bring him back again? I shall go to him, but he shall not return to me."
>
> And David comforted Bathsheba, his wife, and went unto her, and lay with her: and she bare a son, and he called his name Solomon, and the Lord loved him. (2 Sam. 12:15–24)

With its ellipses and refusals, this scene can well stand for what great Hebrew narrative is. There is no effort to explain David; no effort to defend him from calculation; no effort to defend God from inconsistency; no effort to moralize, to find religious meaning. The rapid entrance of Solomon into David's life comes so fast as to seem a reward . . . but for what? And why does the same God whose sword "shall never depart from thine own house" (2 Sam. 12:10) so readily love Solomon? The narrative lives in its compactness; its rapid movement through time, indeed the omnipresent sense that time will move onwards no matter what the human wills; its gaps that imply causality but never state it; its endless conjunctions of narrative bits that suggest even as they refuse to declare. In a novel, we would complain that such elliptical representation defeated the real through its very laziness. In these narratives, reality exists in such omissions and gaps, when human exorbitancies triumph over language's power to represent them.

David's death testifies yet again to his freedom within traditional narrative expectations. One verse removes him from life—if never from these scriptures:

> Now the days of David drew nigh that he should die; and he charged
> Solomon his son. . . . So David slept with his fathers, and was buried
> in the city of David. And the days that David reigned over Israel were
> forty years. (1 Kings 2:1, 10–11)

No novelist would dare this farewell; the deaths of kings demand realism's—and history's—attention. But not Israel's, nor Israel's narrators. Israel has as much time for deathbed scenes as it has for endings figured through marriage. They do not halt its progress in ritual or in tears. Indeed, David's "last words" have been given earlier, at the end of 2 Samuel, where "the sweet psalmist of Israel" says, simply:

> The Spirit of the Lord spake by me,
> and his word was in my tongue.
> The God of Israel said,
> the rock of Israel spake to me,
> He that ruleth over men must be just,
> ruling in the fear of God.
> And he shall be as the light of the morning,
>     when the sun riseth,
>     even a morning without clouds;
>     as the tender grass springing out of the earth
>     by clear shining after rain.
> Although my house be not so with God;
> yet he hath made with me an everlasting covenant,
> ordered in all things, and sure:
> for this is all my salvation, and all my desire,
> although he make it not to grow.
>                             (2 Sam. 23:1–5)

## II

"And his word was in my tongue," the tongue of him who was indeed "as the light of the morning." David has always been irresistible: his poetry, his murderous lust, his ease with God: these characteristics of one man—the stuff of Hebrew history and narrative, of Hebrew art—would burst the boundaries of a realist novel where some consistency of motivation and some moral scrutiny are required. Yet as the historians were writing of Abraham and Jacob, of Saul and David, the priests and redactors were also composing the laws and beginning to make religious meaning out of, and to find religious design in, history. When the writers of the Chronicles retell David's story, the same story is repeated, but its originality is omitted. David's sins vanish (along with Bathsheba), his glory remains (but not the poetry), and God is never inconsistent.

Gabriel Josipovici, in *The Book of God*, usefully charts this process, which begins in the symmetries of the opening verses of Genesis (not the older Eden story that is the J narrator's creation narrative). The Bible is founded, he argues, on the acknowledgment that we all need patterns of divine order to sustain us, and yet also on the recognition that for the early Hebrew writers life in history always escapes, or threatens to escape, those patterns. In this world, contingency never gives way to interpretation; even David acknowledges that his story is not the only one, perhaps not even the main one. As Josipovici says of him: "We can not 'make sense' of him; we can only repeat his story. . . . David lives for us much more immediately, much more fully, than figures far better attested to by history. . . . And he does so because we are made to sense at so many moments the way in which life always runs ahead of meaning" (209). According to this view, it is the power of language to establish dialogue with God that insures this sense of more life. It puts *his* words on our tongues. Josipovici writes: "The primary function of language, the Hebrew Bible shows, is not to convey information but to enable us to utter ourselves and thus come fully alive" (165).

Yet the danger in this is idolatry, that we will choose our image of ourselves, our own voice, as enough, and will not "trust dialogue to reveal to us our own potential" (175–176), will not see the limitations of our solipsism. The constant threat of this idolatry the Hebrews early on recognized as they composed their laws and compiled their sacred stories. Harold Bloom has noted that the refusal of the Yahwist J to feel awe, fear, or wonder before God frightened later redactors into turning God's "personality" into a concept.[8] They wanted to make writers and their "characters" religious when they are simply historical. Rebecca instructing Jacob how to use God's name as a trick to secure Isaac's blessing, and God's; Sarah laughing at God; Samson in Delilah's lap—like David these figures, as Robert Alter notes, derive from the work of "literary invention and religious imagination" and from the domain which for the Hebrew necessarily contains such work: history. As Alter demonstrated in *The Art of Biblical Narrative*, because of the "double dialectic" between "design and disorder, providence and freedom," meaning in these texts "was conceived as *process*, requiring continual revision. . . , continual suspension of judgment, weighing of multiple possibilities, brooding over gaps in the information provided."[9] The result is to make readers endlessly add, renarrate, revise. "The reader is implicitly summoned to take part, fill in," says Alan Lelchuk.[10]

As the histories proceed, as Israel moves farther and farther from the promises of the covenant and the anticipation of their fulfillment, "the stresses of reporting history overwhelm and reduce characters."[11] The need to make religious meaning, to theorize God in history, closes down the life in narrative. The more the Israelites are threatened as a people, the less does any sense of double perspective appear in their stories. By the time of the prophets, as Josipovici argues, "the weight of the dialogue has become too great for the nation of Israel. . . . Things no longer happen, they always *mean*" (177, 182).

In the prophets' need for allegory and emblem is a desperation for extracting meaning from the exorbitancies of life. Experience, the lifeblood of Hebrew narrative, becomes the captive of laws and rules, leading, in Leon Wieseltier's apt phrase, to the organization of "reality into religious order" and "to a reduction of divinity by textuality."[12] Redactors thus gave Job a "happy" ending and inserted sundry wisdom texts ("acceptable words") into Ecclesiastes that contradicted all this "preacher" had been saying: "Fear God, and keep his commandments; for this is the whole duty of man" (12:13). Yet Ecclesiastes found all Hebrew texts at best consoling fictions (*vanitas vanitatum*). For this writer, there is a time to be born and a time to die, and nothing beyond the cyclicity of history but language and the fictions it compiles. History—Hebrew life in history—is a sublime fiction.

This change in attitude towards language—when it becomes a shield against nothingness rather than the place of dialogue with God—is brought to crisis and promised resolution in the Christian scriptures, especially in Matthew, Luke, John, and Paul. In Josipovici's reading, "Moses showed the people signs; Isaiah, Jeremiah and Ezekiel presented *themselves* to the people as signs. But they were signs of something else. Jesus presents something else *as a sign of himself*" (185).[13] This emphasis on one person as fulfilling the scriptures acts to establish meaning, to "seal" interpretation, once and for all. No wonder the author of the Apocalypse threatens with plagues and fire anyone who would alter his words: "And if any man shall take away from the words of the book of this prophecy, God shall take away his part out of the book of life" (Revelation 22:19). Here is the imperial urge to control interpretation, to assert meaning, and it resides in the only book in the Christian scriptures that claims to be an inspired text. As Josipovici argues, the Christian writings present not questions but the answer, not ambiguities but certainty. The Hebrew "turning" towards the right path becomes for Paul and the Christians a "conversion" to the one way (242). The Blessing becomes Revelation. The command to Remember becomes the injunction to "See, know, understand" (275). The Jewish-Christians are choosing a world beyond history, a New Jerusalem, and a "Savior" whom they represent as "the Word made flesh," as the "fulfillment" of Hebrew scriptures (the word is everywhere in the Christian texts). "The darkness is past, and the true light now shineth" (1 John 2:8).

These efforts to control biblical interpretation find their first articulation in the gospel narratives of Jesus' life in history, with their appeal to typology and its clear certainties. In the gospels, typological readings of the Hebrew narratives are necessary and are indeed fully and self-consciously invoked because the gospel writers see the Hebrew texts as preparing the way for their texts, as indeed scripting them. Matthew's gospel is typology in excelsis. Christ's life from beginning to end is modeled on, determined by, the story of Israel. The genealogy of "the book of the generation of Jesus Christ, the son of David, the son of Abraham" (1:1) enforces at the outset what Matthew is interested in: the promises made to Israel are "fulfilled" in the Kingdom of

Christ (the word "kingdom" is used some eighty times), a kingdom that completes the historical progress of Israel. For Matthew, Jesus brings the light and, in the process, makes the scriptures "old."

The genealogy of Luke reveals the same strategy given an even larger context. Luke's Jesus finds his origin in Adam; he finds his narrative end when, risen, he sends his disciples to preach "among all nations." Luke's context is nothing less than the transformation of Hebrew and Jewish history into the world's *religious* history. Luke's style shows his imperial confidence; his opening verses need no gloss: "It seemed good to me, having had *perfect understanding* of all things from the very first, to write . . . that thou mightest know the *certainty* of those things wherein thou has been instructed" (1:3; my emphasis). Yet Luke's structuring of Jesus' life comes from his typologizing of the narrative methods of the Hebrews. The famous birth stories (Elizabeth and Mary), the shepherds, the parables of the good Samaritan and the Prodigal Son (itself a rewriting of the Joseph story), the cry of forgiveness from the cross—all show his interest in Jesus as a human life lived in history. But it is a life without the surprises that David's brings. This Jesus and his Father know their way—no mistakes or confusions here—and Luke understands them, perfectly.

If Matthew and Luke are at ease in their typological patterns, John goes further in announcing his certainties from the start: "In the beginning was the Word . . ." (1:1). Genesis has been replaced. And his Jesus speaks with these same certainties: "I am the bread," the fruit, the life, the light of the world, the Word. These metaphors construct a symbolic religious order of belief founded on such certainty about Jesus that history and narrative development are irrelevant.

The implications of this change are enormous, not least in the formation of Western ideas of the self, representation, narrative. God, or the dialogue between a people and their God, is being privatized, removed from life lived in community and history to an "inner self."[14] Living and believing—life in history—are becoming dissociated enterprises. Josipovici finds Saint Paul central to the novel's ideas about the self, and argues that these early Christian narratives have produced the patterns by which stories are told, in fictions and in history (252–253).[15]

## III

Yet the first narrator of Jesus resisted this determination to make meaning reside in the "I am . . ." of Christ rather than God. Mark sides always with the Yahwist J and with David's historians. He keeps refusing the typological patterns that his followers—his first critical readers Matthew and Luke—insisted were necessary for religious meaning. His text is thus an enigma from its first verse to its last. At the outset, Mark declares:

> The beginning of the gospel of Jesus Christ, the Son of God. As it is written in the prophets . . . .

At the end he narrates:

> And entering into the sepulchre, [the women] saw a young man sitting
> on the right side, clothed in a long white garment: and they were
> affrighted. And he saith unto them, "Ye seek Jesus of Nazareth . . .
> he is risen . . . go your way, tell his disciples and Peter that he goeth
> before you into Galilee; there shall ye see him, as he said unto you."
> And they went out quickly, and fled from the sepulchre; for they
> trembled and were amazed: neither said they anything to any man; for
> they were afraid. (16:5–8)

An author who is certain about Jesus as the Son of God and about what
transcends history paradoxically moves the reader into history. For a few verses
at the outset Mark places his reader within the Hebrew typology that later
gospel writers made so familiar (even as there is also something of the divine
fairy tale in this opening). But the typological pattern ceases to be insistent,
crowded out by the roar of the crowds and the rapidity of the movement; the
words "now" and "straightaway" appear repeatedly, all notes of time passing
quickly, of events seemingly out of control, beyond any (older) pattern of
understanding. Mark's Jesus, like David, enters his world in medias res. There
are no birth stories, no genealogies connecting him to the Hebrew historical past
(and Jesse) or to the mythic past (and Adam), and no effort to locate him in
some humanly conceivable, familiar context (the place surely of Luke's
triumph). Mark recognizes that for the reader of his world, God does not exist
within history. There is no "natural" dialogue with him. Indeed, God has
become supernatural, the deity of texts and rabbinic commentaries.

Mark's end is equally striking, and equally uninterested in any need for
pattern. He offers no resurrection, no praise of God and his son, no instructions
for the faithful men. Simply women, fear, and silence. He is the gospel writer
who is most at ease with gaps and who most fully comprehends the Yahwist's
willingness to entertain the contradictory and the ambiguous, the Hebrew
determination to summon the reader to take part in the story. Obsessed (in
Frank Kermode's words) with "mysteriousness, silence, and incomprehension,"
Mark "prefers the shadows."[16] He prefers to let his readers, like Jesus'
disciples, see, hear, possibly understand, and almost certainly doubt.

Mark's strategies of characterization show an author striving for the
contingent and the ambiguous. His "Son of God" is always in crowds and
always seeking an isolated place, always speaking and yet always urging
silence, always explaining and yet certain his words will not be understood. His
family, who enter the text without introduction, are amazed by his denial of
them (3:31-35); his friends are certain "he is beside himself" (3:21); his
enemies add new accusations after each public appearance. The disciples ask
"what manner of man is this" (4:41) from early on, and are repeatedly
"astonished at his words," questioning what such uses of familiar language

signify. Their idea of kingship involves which of them will "be greatest" in a humanly imaginable earthly kingdom; it seems incomprehensible that a kingdom might be compared, even in a parable, to a mustard seed (4:30–32). By the book's center these men are becoming the doubters precisely because they have listened so intently to his words. Jesus asks, "Whom say ye that I am?" "And Peter answereth and saith unto him, 'Thou art the Christ'" (8:29). Yet Peter then shows so little understanding of what his words mean that Jesus says to him, "Get thee behind me, Satan" (8:29, 33). It is a remarkable moment, placing Peter with the Satan who tempts Mark's Jesus "straightway" after "the Spirit" names him son (1:12–13). And it leads to another unpatterned moment when, in response to the high priest's question, "Art thou the Christ?", the captive Jesus asserts what he has never said before: "I am" (14:62).

At the end, when neither miracles nor words have produced disciples, Mark interweaves Jesus' unequivocal response with Peter's denial of him. This passage is surely one of the great narrative and dramatic moments in the gospels, and it is a scene that illuminates Mark's kinship with the Yahwist.[17] Peter experiences the endless contingencies of his humanity in conflict with Jesus' summons beyond history. His response is finally as simply human as Jacob's or David's. There he sits, "warming himself," outside the place where Jesus is questioned: warming himself, cursing, swearing, and denying; and then recalling "the word Jesus said unto him. . . . And when he thought thereon, he wept" (14:66–72).

Jesus' words produce silence and fear and foreshadow the close of Mark's narration. In the empty tomb the young man instructs the women to "tell his disciples and Peter"—not one of them now likely to believe—that they will see Jesus, "as he said" (16:7). The evocation of his words, like Peter's remembrance of them, provokes the fearful women to flee, silent and silenced. This silence is all the more ironic because Mark's Jesus has repeatedly urged those crowds who have witnessed his miraculous power to "tell no man"; and those witnesses have as repeatedly been unable not to "noise it abroad." Indeed, the only time when Jesus urges someone to tell—"tell them the great things the Lord has done for thee" (5:19)—the witness proclaims the great things *Jesus* has done for him. God has become so distant from man, so immaterial and supernatural, as to seem unnameable.

Mark further undercuts his "religious" authority at the end when he resists what must have been the great crisis of his narration, the representation of the resurrection and of Christ walking to Emmaus, then ascending to heaven. Mark's Jesus may speak of a world elsewhere; he may tell of his coming death and resurrection. But Mark leaves his reader with Peter and the women, with nothing beyond history to witness. His narrative's place, and his own, are within history—with the Yahwist. In the gaps and ambiguities, he states his own understanding, his refusal to materialize Jesus' words.

Even Mark's own initial identification, "Son of God," is repeated in such a way as to undercut its authority and surprise the reader. Its only appearances in the narrative, after that initial declaration (1:1), occur in the mouths of the demon-possessed, who have no trouble seeing Jesus' connection with God ("I know thee who thou art, the Holy One of God" [1:24; see also 5:7]), and at the end, in the words of the Roman centurion: "Truly this man was the Son of God" (15:39). Yet that only the demon-possessed and a Roman centurion see Jesus as the Son of God tells us how the gaps will be filled, the silences made meaningful. These figures are not confined to the patterns of believing, thinking, and witnessing of an inherited religious tradition.

Mark's parenthesis, "(Let him that readeth understand)" (13:14), is thus the central narrative statement that this artist of God's new ways offers. Words only indicate what remains unexpressed. They do not theorize religion; they point to its exorbitant life in human lives. When Mark writes (1:22), "they were astonished at his doctrine, for he taught as one that had authority, and not as the scribes" (who *had* authority), his irony about the conditions that contain, institutionalize, and domesticate faith and that seek to establish its human likeness is obvious. The real human likeness of this faith is in Peter's "warming himself," a detail of realism that comes at a sublimely inappropriate moment from the reader's perspective, and in the fearful women fleeing—that is, in the difficulties of belief. The rest is silence.

Thus what started out—"As it is written"—in the wilderness as yet one more journey to the promised land ends as . . . what? Mark's strategy is, at the outset, to announce that the story of Israel as God's chosen people provides the design governing the representation of this newer Son. Yet his most characteristic verbal feature, the repetition of "Who is this man?" that dominates every chapter, undercuts this design as it repeatedly announces how inadequate are typological narrative conventions for making sense of what is new, contingent. These words set aside tradition—the Hebrew tradition. The people call this Jesus the "Son of David" (e.g., 11:10); he calls himself "Son of Man." He emphasizes his common humanity and even mortality—his life in history; they emphasize the historical and heroic of (what has become for them) "religious" narrative. Miracles here do not produce disciples, any more than the miracles of Moses produced believers in God. The narrative begins as God's and ends as man's. Where is Jesus' supernatural power on Golgotha? Surely a miracle worker can do better than die on a blackguard's cross? In being historical, Mark knows he must be exorbitant.

## IV

As does Emily Brontë. No other nineteenth-century novelist offers so critical a reading of traditions of narration from the Yahwist and the gospel writers through Austen and Thackeray—and through those who follow her. By the time she began writing, the patterns of novels were firmly established; the marriage plot had taken hold in England, reproducing as the march towards the New Jerusalem a plot featuring representations of women as patrollers of the moral territories that men must leave when they go forth to make an imperial world and ending in domestic order and tranquility. This privatization of virtue and its removal to the home produced, and was produced by, what Victorian critic E. S. Dallas called "the increase of feminine influence in literature."

> Woman peculiarly represents the private life of the race. Her ascendancy in literature must mean the ascendancy of domestic ideas, and the assertion of the individual, not as a hero, but as a family man—not as a heroine, but an angel in the house. The individual as a great public character withers. The individual as a member of society in all his private relations grows in importance.[18]

Nothing could be farther from the Hebrews' notions of the autonomy of narrative; imagine David withering in his "private relations." Such privatization of life Israel's strongest writers resisted, as they resisted the melodrama that expressed ready-made notions of morality. Then the scribes and redactors installed into their scriptures those wisdom books that were intended to make life religious. It was redactors who added onto Job the "reward" for his patience, who theorized this drama's extraordinariness into a religious ideology of moral ledgers. In the original poem God does not even reply to Job, but simply points out what man cannot do: "Canst thou bind the sweet influences of Pleiades, / or loose the bands of Orion?"

Nothing farther from Emily Brontë's ideas of history and of representation can be imagined either. In Catherine Earnshaw and Heathcliff she produced something new indeed—or at least as new as the human beings in 1-2 Samuel, in 1 Kings, and in Mark. Catherine resists until her death being an angel in the house; Heathcliff rails against the "story" he inhabits. Yet in Nelly Dean and Lockwood, and in Catherine Linton and Hareton Earnshaw, Brontë constructed the narrators and characters who use, and live by, the design for living that characterizes the conventional Victorian novel. Nelly Dean belongs to Wuthering Heights by proximity of birth, and even more to the world of Thrushcross Grange by sympathies of class and culture, as well as by modes of storytelling. Yet in her desire for household and social order (she is, after all, a housekeeper) and for narrative order, she expresses Emily Brontë's genius for representing characters who escape the order of fiction so seemingly necessary to Victorian life. In *A Future for Astyanax*, Leo Bersani has said that Emily Brontë, in telling the love stories of two generations united by family ties and by the two women named Catherine, presents in the second story "a conventionalized replay" of the first. Until the death of the first Catherine, "the voices of Lockwood and of Nelly Dean have had to obey rhythms and tones with which they are deeply out of sympathy; indeed, they seem to be in the wrong novel, they are ludicrous vehicles for the story they tell. But gradually the story begins to obey them. . . . It's as if Emily Brontë were telling the same story twice, and eliminating its originality the second time."[19]

Brontë does tell the same story twice, and when its strangeness, its originality, is exiled from the novel, Nelly can live happily ever after at Thrushcross Grange and Lockwood can tour the moors. But before these storytellers cease speaking, the reader has discovered the real strangeness of the novel in its verbal surprises, in those moments where Lockwood, Nelly, and "their" characters forget their class positions, their moral disapprovals or hatreds, their domestic securities or prisons, and reveal more than themselves in the exorbitancies of their language and in the surprises of what they sometimes do against all (their) logic. Lockwood is so shallow as to misread the natures of everyone he encounters, yet he has a dream (chapter 3) whose violence is so seemingly unmotivated as to alert the reader to the kind of metaphysical universe Brontë has created. Bizarrely, it is also this dream that allows Catherine into the novel and again "into" Heathcliff's life. Equally unexpected, out of order, are the actions—not the words—of Edgar Linton. He marries Catherine. And though he may hide amongst his books to escape her insane need for Heathcliff, yet he refuses to have himself buried in Linton family vaults, choosing instead burial beside her on *her* moors.

Most astonishing of course are Heathcliff and the first Catherine. All of Nelly's sententious moralizing cannot "save" them. This is another universe indeed from that of Dickens's Esther Summerson or Paul Dombey, except from the perspectives of the narrators. Brontë unexpectedly allows Heathcliff, that urban orphan who enters the novel without Christian name or birth story to place him, to introduce Thrushcross Grange. Amidst his words of anger and hatred ("painting the house-front with Hindley's blood!") comes a spontaneous moment of awe in his description of the drawingroom at the Grange: "And we saw—ah! it was beautiful—a splendid place carpeted with crimson, . . . and a pure white ceiling bordered by gold, and a shower of glass-drops hanging in silver chains from the centre and shimmering with little soft tapers."[20] That "ah! it was beautiful" is no more expected than the surprises and contradictions of David's life. In Heathcliff, Brontë presents a lover whose feelings lie outside the tropes of language; his life is not in the patterns of experience that articulate, and control, desire: "The entire world is a dreadful collection of memoranda that she did exist, and that I have lost her!" (255). Signs, in his terms, may be readable but they offer no design for living.

Catherine Earnshaw also resists reading, and living in, the patterns indicated in the signs around her. She enters the novel in her words that Lockwood discovers in her diary, before she enters through his violent nightmare and then in Nelly's chronological narrative of the "cuckoo's" history. That diary—"Catherine Earnshaw, her book"—is scribbled in the margins of a Testament, but it rejects all biblical or religious inflections. "An awful Sunday . . . H. and I are going to rebel" (26). As Margaret Homans has noted, this writing is produced not simply in rebellion against the Heights and its restrictions. It is also against what writing signifies, against the designs for living that Catherine would escape.[21] She wants the moors and their distance from the inside world of the Heights and, later, the Grange; she wants a freedom beyond any of the conventions that collectively denominate the realist territories of domestic life and of nineteenth-century fiction. The exorbitancies of her desire continually threaten the domestic spaces she is expected to inhabit and adorn.

Her dream of going to heaven emphasizes this need to exist outside of social and cultural conventions and the narratives that give them power. For her, some dreams "have stayed with me ever after, and changed my ideas . . . altered the colour of my mind":

> Heaven did not seem to be my home; and I broke my heart with weeping to come back to earth; and the angels were so angry that they flung me out, into the middle of the heath on the top of Wuthering Heights; where I woke sobbing for joy. That will do to explain my secret. (72)

That of course does not "do" to explain anything. It simply adds life. No wonder she says, in a phrase indicating her self-consciousness and her elusiveness, "I cannot express it . . ." (73).

Expressing "it" has been, always, her problem and Heathcliff's, and the problem her readers—beginning with Nelly—have with her, Heathcliff, and *Wuthering Heights*. Yet when the narrative begins to obey Nelly Dean and Lockwood and their desires for domestic order, expressing "it" ceases to seem an issue. Catherine is dead, Heathcliff is a readily identifiable villain, and Nelly is anticipating the nuptial celebrations of the second Catherine. This cliched golden-haired heroine, the sign of her mother's domestication, brings language and book-learning to Hareton Earnshaw, the brutalized orphan whose property has been appropriated. Of course these two are rewarded for their restoration of domestic order; property, marriage, and a secured happy-ever-after prove their virtues. Throughout her life, this Catherine never imagines having problems finding language adequate to her needs. The point where she contrasts her "most perfect idea of heaven's happiness" with Linton Heathcliff's suggests Brontë's critique of the ways of representation in nineteenth-century fiction: "He wanted all to lie in an ecstasy of peace; I wanted all to sparkle, and dance in glorious jubilee" (199). The power of language to create and control, and to propose as models, worlds of domestic order and serenity resides with those satisfied with language's ability to express anything and easy in the life it creates.

But all this language, whether Catherine Linton's or the narrators', still does not explain "it." No wonder that Brontë chose the woman servant who loves the spatial and temporal world of Thrushcross Grange to tell the story of the woman who longed to escape: "What were the use of my creation if I were entirely contained here?" (74). Nelly, who early on tried to remove the boy Heathcliff from the Heights as an alien "it," sees in the deaths of Heathcliff and Catherine and in the marriage of the second Catherine a providential sign of the soundness of her interpretation ("I believe the dead are at peace") and of her social alignment. Narrative, the providential plot, and middle-class domestic order are indeed inextricably connected—and they have no space for the life of Catherine and Heathcliff.

Yet Brontë does not leave the reader at ease with Nelly at the Grange. After all, it is she who says, when Heathcliff re-enters the married Catherine's life: "Well, we *must* be for ourselves in the long run; the mild and generous are only more justly selfish than the domineering" (81). It is this obvious ethic of just selfishness—of protecting what is ours from those who are not like us—that makes Nelly (and the novel's totalizing plot) disturbing, and indicates the ways her narrative performs the cultural work of Victorian fiction. It also mirrors the work of those biblical redactors who found the early narratives' open-endedness too far from identifiably clear religious meaning. They too began to insist on laws and exclusions, on being separated from the foreign and other; they began to moralize.

The aptly named Lockwood is at ease only in a world of exclusions where he can confront the "other" as a tourist. He comes from the city to tour the country; he leaves the area with a benediction that is one of the most splendid paragraphs ever to close a novel, as gorgeous in its sounds as it is irrelevant in its meaning. Standing on the moors by three gravestones, he notes:

> I lingered round them, under that benign sky; watched the moths fluttering among the heath and hare-bells; listened to the soft wind breathing through the grass; and wondered how any one could ever imagine unquiet slumbers for the sleepers in that quiet earth. (266)

Lockwood's *pensées*. In his perfectly balanced periods and harmonically sounded vowels, no wayward human energies disrupt the storyteller's power or the listener's satisfaction. Who would think that his story is, in Dante Gabriel Rossetti's words, "a fiend of a book, an incredible monster. . . . The action is laid in Hell,—only it seems places and people have English names there"?[22]

The second time Brontë tells her story, she produces a Victorian family chronicle that theorizes life by designing it (and rewarding the "good"). She may offer her characters, through Nelly Dean and Lockwood, local habitations and English names. But for Catherine and Heathcliff, those names are simply words, not what one is. To Nelly Dean, that "cool spectator" whom Charlotte Brontë found a "specimen of true benevolence and homely fidelity," Catherine and Heathcliff make "a strange and fearful picture" and ruin a good love story. Yet the questions they repeatedly ask, because they focus the confinements of Victorian realism, haunt the history of the novel and of narrative, emphasizing how uneasy English fiction has been with what does not exist, metonymically, within the nation's homes.

Emily Brontë sees the limitation of this home and the patterns of living it endorses, and she understands the secure distance the conventional novel occupies away from the exorbitancies of life in language. "I cannot express it," says Catherine, "but surely you and everybody have a notion that there is, or should be, an existence of yours beyond you. What were the use of my creation if I were entirely contained here?" (74). Catherine and Heathcliff are indeed exiles from the patriarchal story of inclusion and exclusion, us and other, domestic love and social containment, that the realist novel, and the second half of *Wuthering Heights*, had to tell. They exist in inexpressible (and unrepresentable) freedom amidst a narrative of design.

## V

When Nelly Dean reports how Catherine first receives Edgar Linton at Wuthering Heights, she surprises the reader by the ways her language does the unexpected.

> "You've made me afraid, and ashamed of you," [Edgar] continued; "I'll not come here again!"
> Her eyes began to glisten and her lids to twinkle.
> "And you told a deliberate untruth!" he said.
> "I didn't!" she cried, recovering her speech. "I did nothing deliberately—Well, go, if you please, get away! And now I'll cry—I'll cry myself sick!"
> She dropped down on her knees by a chair and set to weeping in serious earnest.
> Edgar persevered in his resolution as far as the court; there he lingered. I resolved to encourage him.
> "Miss is dreadfully wayward, sir!" I called out. "As bad as any marred child—you'd better be riding home, or else she will be sick, only to grieve us."
> The soft thing looked askance through the window: he possessed the power to depart, as much as a cat possesses the power to leave a mouse half-killed, or a bird half eaten.
> Ah, I thought, there will be no saving him—He's doomed, and flies to his fate!
> And so it was. (66)

Here again Brontë asserts the life in language that makes her novel so probing a critique of the history of representation, from the work of her contemporaries back to the narratives of the Hebrew redactors. Brontë's "cool spectator" who has so few doubts about her understanding, of course calls Catherine a "marred" child, of course urges Edgar to flee her, of course knows he is "doomed": "And so it was." But amidst Nelly's easy certainties are those moments that challenge them. Edgar as "soft thing" does not surprise us; Edgar as a preying cat does, in the figure's terrible implications that he will secure the prey he desires, in the implications that Catherine is that prey (and already "half killed"), in the suggestion that this finely civilized man is a natural predator (and that we people of books are all Lintons).[23] Nelly here tells more about this "doomed" man than she knows, or wants to know, and reveals the dark implications of the cultural and ideological work of realist narration—that is: narration that serves the needs of ideology against the exorbitancies of life in language.

### Notes

I thank Bridget Gellert Lyons, Larry B. Qualls, and Carolyn Williams for their clarifying questions about this essay.

1. Leo Bersani, *A Future for Astyanax: Character and Desire in Literature* (New York: Little Brown, 1976), 65.
2. D. A. Miller, *Narrative and Its Discontents: Problems of Closure in the Traditional Novel* (Princeton: Princeton University Press, 1981), xv, 130.
3. See Gabriel Josipovici's discussion of this crucial characteristic of Hebrew narrative in *The Book of God: A Response to the Bible* (New Haven: Yale University Press, 1988). Subsequent references will be indicated by parenthetical page numbers in the text.
4. As Owen Barfield noted in *Saving the Appearances* (New York: Harcourt, n.d.), 109, God's injunction against making images of one's god "is perhaps the *unlikeliest* thing that ever happened": "The children of Israel became a nation and began their history in the moment when Moses, in the very heart of the ancient Egyptian civilization, delivered to them those ten commandments."
5. Throughout I have used the King James version of the Bible, the edition published by the American Bible Society (New York, 1982), which prints the original poetry in verse form.
6. Harold Bloom, *The Book of J* (New York: Grove Weidenfeld, 1990). In Josipovici's formulations, "no character in the Hebrew Bible looks back over his or her life from a vantage point from which he or she can say with certainty: till now I have been blind, but now I can see. . . . Nor does any character in the Hebrew Bible struggle with conflicting desires" (252).
7. Saul is so appealing because his end, like his life after God deserts him, recalls the ends of Shakespeare's noble defeated monarchs—that is, his life is obviously "literary" in conventional ways: "Then said Saul unto his armor-bearer, 'Draw thy sword, and thrust me through therewith; lest these uncircumcised come and thrust me through, and abuse me.' But his armor-bearer would not; for he was sore afraid. Therefore Saul took a sword, and fell upon it. And when his armor-bearer saw that Saul was dead, he fell likewise upon his sword, and died with him" (1 Sam. 31:4–5).
8. See Bloom, *The Book of J*. David Damrosch, in *The Literary Guide to the Bible*, ed. Robert Alter and Frank Kermode (Cambridge: Harvard University Press, 1987), 72–73, observes that in Leviticus "narrative order is subordinated to conceptual order." This book of the laws set out "to subsume narrative within a larger symbolic order." Indeed, it is "*anti*narrative"; it seeks "the transformation of history," seeks to turn it into rule and ritual and thus to sacralize the wayward histories that surround it. "Thou shalt not" may bring David face to face with his own humanness amidst his god*like*ness; but the tension between his way and the law amplifies his largeness.

9. Robert Alter, *The Art of Biblical Narrative* (New York: Basic Books, 1981), 12.

10. Alan Lelchuk in *Congregation: Contemporary Jewish Writers Read the Jewish Bible*, ed. David Rosenberg (San Diego: Harcourt, 1987), 143.

11. Lelchuk, *Congregation*, 139.

12. Wieseltier, in *Congregation*, 33, 30. Wieseltier notes that the activity in Leviticus and in the canonizers shows chosenness becoming an elaboration of exclusion, an assertion of difference that is more than human, until separation becomes "the instrument of containment, of order, social stability, continuity, coherence, tradition" (36).

13. The Epistle to the Hebrews marks for Josipovici the endpoint of the process of ending interpretation, of establishing *the* meaning. For him, the Hebrew scriptures constantly command us to ask questions, to wonder "How can this be?"—how can God support David, or choose Jacob and Abel and not Esau and Cain? The epistle, in contrast, "by providing an interpretation, removes the question." The "fruitful dialogue" among the Hebrew texts is obscured in the "single-minded" reading we are allowed. Hebrew heroes are no longer richly conceived complex human beings but "moral exemplars." See *The Book of God*, 257-275.

14. The moment in 2 Kings 19:9-13 when Elijah finds God not in wind, earthquake, or fire but in "a still small voice" marks in the Jewish scriptures the beginning of this privatization.

15. Frank Kermode, in *The Literary Guide to the Bible*, notes that Paul is signally the antinarrative Christian writer; he cared little for Jesus' life in history; with him "narratives beget not more narratives but theology" (384).

16. Frank Kermode, *The Genesis of Secrecy* (Cambridge: Harvard University Press, 1979), 132. Kermode argues that successive retellings of the story set out to fill in the gaps: "Explanations are ways of filling gaps in the causal sequence established by the narrative, a kind of modern midrash" (117).

17. See Kermode's discussion of this interweaving in *Genesis of Secrecy*, 114-116.

18. E. S. Dallas, *The Gay Science* (London: Chapman and Hall, 1866), 298-299.

19. Bersani, *A Future for Astyanax*, 222.

20. Emily Brontë, *Wuthering Heights*, ed. William M. Sale, Jr. (New York: Norton, 1963), 47. All subsequent page numbers in the text refer to this edition.

21. Margaret Homans, "Repression and the Sublimation of Nature in *Wuthering Heights*, *PMLA* 93 (1978), 9-19.

22. *Letters of Dante Gabriel Rossetti*, ed. Oswald Doughty and John Robert Wahl (Oxford: Clarendon Press, 1965), 1:224.

23. Q. D. Leavis, in *Lectures in America* (New York: Pantheon, 1969), 115-118, discusses this chapter at length. The figure of Edgar as "cat," she writes, "makes us realize a new truth, that a cat is really a victim of drives it can't resist too."

# CHAPTER 6

# The Morning Twilight of Intimacy: "The Pupil" and What Maisie Knew

MARGERY SABIN

$\mathcal{H}$enry James's intense absorption in the personal has always put off critics in a hurry to move from the personal to the social, the private to the public, domestic to historical crises. Raymond Williams identified James's "preoccupied rendering" of the personal as itself the sign of cultural "crisis" at the turn of the century:

> It is from that time on and especially in the novel that people tried to talk of "social" and "personal" as separable processes, separate realms. "Social" . . . became the pejorative "sociological," and a "sociological" interest was in "something other than human life," in classes, statistics, abstract ideas, systems. "Personal"—we may have noticed this less—became the whole of "human"; the recommending, ratifying "human"—love, friendship, marriage, death. And you can now very quickly start a fight anywhere between the claims of the definitions. . . . "Sociological" is a sneer you may think the last word until you hear "literary" from the other side of the fence.[1]

In the generation since Williams himself leaned so hard against the fence separating literature from sociology, its dramatic collapse has meant that sociological terms of analysis now dominate both criticism and praise of Henry James. Marxist sociology governs Fredric Jameson's indictment of the "powerful ideological instrument" concealed in Jamesian "point of view." In line with the notion that ideological clearance requires a style void of literary grace, Jameson clumsily scolds James for "perpetuation of an increasingly subjectivized and psychologized world, a world whose social vision is one of a thoroughgoing relativity of monads in coexistence."[2] A younger generation of

American critics, tired of Marxist orthodoxy, yet still intimidated by its strictures against the personal, has begun to defend James on the very grounds of his social vision.

Ross Posnock, for example, in *The Trial of Curiosity*, ambitiously mounts his defense of James as a "formidable cultural analyst" by calling upon the Frankfurt social theorists Max Horkheimer, Theodor Adorno, Walter Benjamin, as well as such American social thinkers as John Dewey, George Santayana, and (within the family) James's own brother William.[3] These American pragmatists and European post-Marxians seem to offer terms for reconciliation between the literary and the sociological, in part because they are themselves readers of literature and non-systematic writers who humanize the face of social theory. In addition, they seem to transpose key aesthetic values of modern literary criticism—indeterminacy, for example, and immersion in the particular—into terms of social value. John Carlos Rowe also enlists Max Hork- heimer. The epigraph to Rowe's "Henry James and Critical Theory" in the new *Companion to Henry James Studies* sets out to socialize James, as well as the term "critical theory," by way of Horkheimer's emancipatory formula: "Theory never aims simply at an increase of knowledge as such. Its goal is man's emancipation from slavery."[4]

I appreciate this revisionary social effort on James's behalf, especially as it recognizes Richard Poirier's important contribution to the study of American pragmatism, as well as of Henry James.[5] Without knowing in detail Poirier's own views of the great variety of new work indebted to his, I only trust to the model of his generous and affectionate skepticism in venturing my own skeptical reluctance to follow down some new turns of the paths opened by him. For me, Poirier's most inspiriting influence has come from his undefensive refusal to submit literary reading to the sole authority of social theory.

Fear of the sociological sneer has so suppressed words like "aesthetic," and "formal," as well as "personal," in our critical vocabulary that the fictions of a literary artist such as James have now to be coerced into nonliterary definitions of "intellectual" before they are deemed worthy of contemporary regard. Posnock defines an "intellectual" as "a writer who critically examines contemporary cultural, social, and political issues,"[6] and is at pains to justify the "intellectual" claims of fiction as a "mediated" form of the same analysis that "public intellectuals" formulate directly.[7] By this definition, James's fiction becomes secondary to what may seem the less mediated versions of the same ideas, while those characteristics of the fiction unamenable to the so-called intellectual project drop out of view altogether. The great body of fiction at the center of James's reputation has to ride on the ticket purchased by the peripheral, if also interesting, autobiographical and critical prose.

By way of two narratives from the 1890s, "The Pupil" and *What Maisie Knew* (texts especially crucial to Rowe's argument, though absent from Posnock's), I want to think anew about James's distinctly *novelistic* way of entangling the personal in the social. The current prestige of social theory within literary study promotes more restrictive formulations of what humanly matters than was the case when literature and sociology suspiciously competed with each other. William and Henry James may have gained more than they lost by communicating across the fence between them.

Antipathy to generic and national as well as disciplinary boundaries has all but erased certain elementary meanings of the term "social" in the Anglo-American literary tradition of fiction. Most baldly stated, fictional narratives in this tradition affirm the sociable dimensions of the "social"; they involve the unfolding complications of characters in intimate relation to each other. James subjects this sociability to the most subtle critical probing, but he never discards it as unworthy of serious attention. In James's fiction everything, from speech to meditation to walks in the city, is embedded in the intensities of interpersonal desires and disappointments. His social analysis therefore always comes *through* the dense medium of particular human relationships rather than in the singular form that Continental social theory and critique give even to the experience of being caught up in a crowd.[8]

A more restricted and specialized definition of intimacy emerges from aligning James with Walter Benjamin. "Urban *flânerie*," Posnock argues, is a form of social inquiry that links James to Benjamin on the basis of their analogous self-surrender to the modern city, as when James phrases his relation to New York in *An American Scene* as "inexpressibly intimate" or describes his "intimate surrender" to the city's immigrant population.[9] In James's fiction, however, urban strolling is most often the favorite activity of lovers and other irregular couples for whom the city offers first of all the pleasure of intimate companionship away from constraining domestic arrangements.

William Empson helps here more than Walter Benjamin, for James creates a version of urban pastoral.[10] The strolling Jamesian couple surrender not so much to the city itself as to the opportunity for intimacy with each other. Pemberton in "The Pupil," exploring Paris with Morgan Moreen; Maisie and Sir Claude out for the day in London, in *What Maisie Knew*; Charlotte and Amerigo in *The Golden Bowl*, roaming London on the pretext of shopping for Maggie's wedding gift—these are only a few of the interesting Jamesian couples who are more intimately involved with each other than with the city that stimulates and shelters their adventures.

Walter Benjamin's Parisian *flâneur* evokes by way of Baudelaire an entirely different sense of the personal and draws on different conventions of urban pleasure and pain. Isolation in the modern city attains virtually supernatural prestige when Benjamin describes "the stigmata which life in a metropolis inflicts upon love."[11] The mysterious veiled figure of Baudelaire's "A une Passante"—a woman seen, adored, and forever lost all in a moment—embodies for Benjamin the transient ecstasy of urban love: "The delight of the urban poet is love—not at first sight, but at last sight." This thrill—both its sudden joy and its pathos—derives from an avant-garde French poetry set against the hypocrisy and boredom of the bourgeois family. Benjamin follows

Baudelaire through the city in flight from what Posnock terms the "bourgeois bias for a privatized mode of living."[12]

James, for all his cosmopolitanism, does not adopt this chic but easily stereotyped contempt for private, personal relationships. Not that he falls into some equally clichéd version of bourgeois "family values." What is most daring in "The Pupil" and *What Maisie Knew* is the imaginative exploration of intimacies that take to the streets precisely because they do not fit prevailing conventions of domestic order (or even disorder). The failure of these exper- imental intimacies, however, does not displace the desire and disappointment of private love from the center of James's art. Even the smallest gestures of social speech in James have the same primary reference to interpersonal experience as the major movements of the plots. Abstractions that sever connection to this sense of the personal in James socialize his art only by dis- carding what is most distinctive about it. The ostensibly emancipatory impulse of critical theory ends up coercing literature into conformity with current intellectual biases against private relationships, rather than allowing James to resist, oppose, or simply snub prevailing fashions, as he freely did in his own day.

Thus Rowe, citing Horkheimer, misleadingly identifies in James an eman- cipatory interest in "democratic speech" by focussing on the American slang sentence uttered by little Morgan Moreen in "The Pupil."[13] In order to escape together into a better life away from the oppressive Moreen family, Pemberton will (Morgan insists) have to find paying work. And he will work also. "Why shouldn't *I* work? I ain't such a beastly little muff as *that* comes to" (545).[14]

Rowe is right to notice the oddity of this American slang in the story, but standard oppositions between the "democratic" and the genteel (or any other ruling class) go only a short way to account for James's verbal design in "The Pupil." The idiom of the whole Moreen family, like the rest of their expatriate cosmopolitan life, conspicuously evades categorization by social class. Their speech is an "ingenious dialect" of its own; Pemberton learns from Morgan the drollery of calling it "Ultramoreen": "They could imitate Venetian and sing Neapolitan, and when they wanted to say something very particular communicated with each other in an ingenious dialect of their own, an elastic spoken cipher which Pemberton at first took for some *patois* of one of their countries" (520). The drama of language in "The Pupil" represents not so much class struggle as more particularized personal troubles within the already emancipated category of the cosmopolitan.

"The Pupil" quite simply follows the troubles of the impoverished young American, Pemberton, whose European misadventures land him as tutor in the Moreen family in Nice. The Moreens handle their own financial problems ingeniously, as by their method of exploiting attachment to their precocious, invalid son, Morgan, in order to avoid paying his caretakers. While Pemberton (with Morgan's encouragement) eventually extricates himself from their hold by taking remunerated if less absorbing employment with another family in

England, he returns to Paris at their summons to find them in financial crisis, preparing to unload entire responsibility for the very sick boy on him. Although this ultimate liberation from the family has been precisely what Pemberton and Morgan have presumably desired all along, the story abruptly ends with the tutor's bewildered reluctance and the boy's sudden fatal collapse in heart failure. In the end, the resilient Moreens predictably recover from what is surely not the last of their crises, while Pemberton fades into the bewilderment of loss that James adopts from the start as the story's tone.

Even brief summary should make clear that the Moreen family already embodies a kind of emancipation from social order. James presents their freedom through Pemberton's own mixed reaction of appreciation and dismay: they are like "a band of gipsies" (519), everything topsy-turvy and phantasmagoric. Yet it is precisely the Moreen system of liberated worldliness that is exploiting the boy and tutor and from which they want to escape. Morgan and, eventually, Pemberton recognize the Moreens' cosmopolitanism as a system of lying and cheating; most specifically, the family is cheating the tutor by not paying him. That is why escape requires them to find other paid work. The sentimental drama cannot go forward without a material basis for survival. In this simple way, the personal is intimately entangled with the social in "The Pupil." The story's center is the bewildered failure, at once personal and social, to establish a more viable relationship between work and love than what the Moreens propose. What Pemberton and Morgan need is a rectified cosmopolitanism that would support their intimacy apart from the falsity and exploitation of the Moreen system.

The ambiguous class implications of this predicament come up explicitly in Paris, where the Moreens' neglect has released Pemberton and Morgan to the free pleasures of the city: "Visiting the Invalides and Notre Dame, the Concièrgerie and all the museums, [they] took a hundred remunerative rambles. They learned to know their Paris" (528). James infuses the "free" pleasures of Paris with the romance of shared connoisseurship. Charlotte and Amerigo are similarly remunerated in London, and so are Maisie and Sir Claude "in a wonderful month of May," when they "rambled the great town together": "They rode on the top of 'buses; they visited outlying parks; they went to cricket-matches where Maisie fell asleep; they tried a hundred places for the best one to have tea" (109). In such wonderful passages of Jamesian urban pastoral, the great city liberates singular intimacies from conventional strictures. The whole great city becomes a seemingly free and private space.

In "The Pupil," Pemberton's strained joke about where he and Morgan stand in relation to the city's "multitude" calls attention to the self-conscious boundary between the private and the public as the location of personal anxiety as well as pleasure:

Wandering languidly through the Jardin des Plantes as if they had nowhere to go, sitting on the winter days in the galleries of the

Louvre, so splendidly ironical to the homeless, as if for the advantage of the *calorifère*. They joked about it sometimes: it was the sort of joke that was perfectly within the boy's compass. They figured themselves as part of the vast vague hand-to-mouth multitude of the enormous city and pretended they were proud of their position in it—it showed them "such a lot of life" and made them conscious of a democratic brotherhood. (530)

James's language differentiates a number of mental states within the private joke that Pemberton and Morgan share. Although their poverty entitles them to class identification with the poor, the Jamesian language of "figuring" and "as if" also separates them from the multitude. Even though they are (almost) really living hand-to-mouth, not merely pretending, an air of playful pretense is crucial to their intimacy. Their indolent indifference to money stops well short of gusto for the "democratic brotherhood" of the poor. The "such a lot of life" they observe in the warm shelter of the Louvre is somehow not *their* life, any more than the tending of flocks is the real life of pastoral lovers who watch it for their amusement:

Now and then [Morgan] had a five-franc piece, and except once, when they bought a couple of lovely neckties, one of which he made Pemberton accept, they laid it out scientifically in old books. This was sure to be a great day, always spent on the quays, in a rummage of the dusty boxes that garnish the parapets. Such occasions helped them to live, for their books ran low very soon after the beginning of their acquaintance. Pemberton had a good many in England, but he was obliged to write to a friend and ask him kindly to get some fellow to give him something for them. (530–531)

For the two of *them*, James's language insists, it is the books they manage to stock up on from the quay, if not also Morgan's extravagant gift of "lovely neckties," that "helps them to live." The meaningful terms of life for Morgan and Pemberton are private, intimate, decorative, and cultivated, even though Pemberton's vagueness about the material underpinnings of such a life makes their enjoyment of it so insecure.

The ambiguity of this intimacy in personal terms adds to Pemberton's social uneasiness. He wonders how his relation to the boy looks in public:

He used sometimes to wonder what people would think they were—to fancy they were looked askance at, as if it might be a suspected case of kidnapping. Morgan wouldn't be taken for a young patrician with a preceptor—he wasn't smart enough; though he might pass for his companion's sickly little brother. (530)

The homosexual displacement that many readers see in Pemberton's fantasies, as in the whole story, intensifies the effect of privacy, for there is no Whitmanesque intimation in "The Pupil" that homoerotic brotherhood opens fuller democratic participation.[15] Separated by tastes as well as by consciousness from the multitude, Pemberton feels his ambiguous relation to Morgan just as exposed to public scrutiny in the museum as he does in the house.

In a way, the Moreen household arouses less anxiety about the personal relationship, for it is the Moreens who fostered the intimacy in the first place so that they could keep the tutor without paying him. The entire intimacy is the family's ingenious creation, rather than a rebellion against them. Mrs. Moreen keeps up the "joke" of it with insinuating hilarity every time Pemberton braves her with threats to leave:

> "You won't, you *know* you won't—you're too interested," she said. "You *are* interested, you know you are, you dear kind man!" She laughed with almost condemnatory archness, as if it were a reproach—though she wouldn't insist; and flirted a soiled pocket-handkerchief at him. (533)

Whether Pemberton's "interest" in Morgan is condemned to Mrs. Moreen's soiled terms of control is another way of formulating the story's probing of cosmopolitan intimacy. Morgan is braver than Pemberton in pressing for escape. He voices his irreverent judgments from the beginning, with his first mockery of his mother's elaborate assurance about payment: "A pledge definite enough to elicit from the child a strange little comment in the shape of the mocking foreign ejaculation 'Oh la-la!'" (513).

As a sociable speech gesture, "Oh la-la" initiates mocking detachment as a basis for friendship, but it is hardly enough to live on. Nor is Pemberton capable of more substantial terms. The story begins by identifying precisely this weakness as Pemberton's problem: "It cost him such an effort to broach the subject of terms, to speak of money to a person who spoke only of feelings and, as it were, of the aristocracy" (511). When Morgan brings up the prospect of going to work later in the story, he has taken upon himself the burden of establishing a material basis for escape from the Moreen system. The problem is that his proposal to go to work may seem no less of an amusing foreign ejaculation than "Oh la-la."

Something awkward and artificial in the idiom, "beastly little muff," is suggested even by Rowe's need to gloss "muff" as baseball slang. Morgan speaks in more forceful common idiom when he remarks how his parents won't "fork out" money for Pemberton any more than they did, earlier, for his former nurse. Morgan is also capable of much plainer directness in standard English, as when he says, "I won't stand it any longer. You must get some occupation that pays" (545). But the crucial effect of Morgan's speech is that none of it—not the standard nor the common nor the slang—seems quite "natural" in his voice. James makes it hard to hear the separate pieces of Morgan's changeable speech as even coming from a single voice at all. This instability might be counted as another cost of the Moreen system of expatriate wandering, but it is also the main source of the boy's precocious seductiveness. All his gestures of speech seem flirtatious propositions; the provisional "figurings" have even more charm because they can always be jokingly set aside. For example, when Morgan appeals to Pemberton about all they have already "been through together," the exaggerated cliché of romantic suffering—"Our privations—our dark days"—raises the emotional temperature of the scene while allowing Pemberton to cool it down again through drollery: "Oh our days have been bright enough" (545). Banter between Pemberton and Morgan both masks and exposes the troubled uncertainty of the real terms of their relationship.

While intense and genuine feelings do come through some notes of Morgan's speech, as through his occasional tears, the effect is like singing in that the tone is always slightly independent of the words. Talking about Pemberton needing pay, for example, his voice rises to passion, "like some high silver note from a small cathedral chorister" (545). Morgan moves up and down the musical scale of speech—American slang is only one of the amusing low notes he sounds. It is the quality of mobility itself that astonishes and charms the constricted Pemberton, who figures it through the memorable image of the boy in "the morning twilight of childhood," with a precious delicacy, "never fixed, never arrested" (547).

The charm of this protean sexuality is evident in "The Pupil," but James also toughly exposes the weakness of its offering in social terms. For one thing, only the precarious sincerity of love differentiates Morgan's expressiveness from the equal mobility of Ultramoreen. And while James does not make the genuineness of the boy's love suspect, the verbal performances turn the feeling he offers into something as insubstantial as a child's game: "'We must be frank, at the last; we *must* come to an understanding,' said Morgan with the importance of the small boy who lets himself think he is arranging great affairs—almost playing at shipwreck or at Indians" (548). Although at the beginning of "The Pupil" Morgan is presented by his mother as a boy incapable of "play," his speech is all game and make-believe. The "play" of his language foreshadows the real impossibility of his whole fantasy of escape. An alternative to the down-at-heels cosmopolitanism of the Moreens requires something more than what may end up seeming only another version of Ultramoreen.

In "The Pupil," James envisions no terms that could translate—verbally or economically—the "morning twilight" of intimacy between boy and man into a viable social relationship. The personal idyll remains only a memory of play. At the end, Pemberton returns to his impoverished starting-point: a dislocated American who cannot bring the social, emotional, and economic terms of his life into any coherent relation.

When Horace Scudder of the *Atlantic Monthly* brashly rejected "The Pupil" in 1891, he complained in his letter to James that "the structure is so weak for carrying the sentiment."[16] James was traumatically aggrieved and for the first time consulted a literary agent. He had been confident of the "*one* long rhythm of the story."[17] In the New York edition, however, where "The Pupil" is placed at the end of the volume that begins with the later *What Maisie Knew,* the firmer structure of the novel gives additional support to the sentiment of the earlier story.[18] The two works have in common not only their abusive cosmopolitan families, but also the figuring, through the children, of doomed, tender, irregular intimacies. Maisie in relation to Sir Claude resembles Morgan in relation to Pemberton in that both children have the emotional freedom to give and desire love in social situations which systematically degrade and exploit the terms of feeling. But whereas the impasse of love in "The Pupil" ends in Morgan's abrupt collapse, Maisie survives her loss, as well as the couplings and uncouplings of her real and surrogate parents. Her disappointment of desire is no less decisive than Morgan's, but in her case the loss of intimacy is absorbed into a life that we are to suppose continuing, however mutedly, without that joy.

Maisie's strength is not only her capacity to recover from violently dashed hopes and fears, but to remain flexible enough to move with the continuing and quieter rise and fall of emotion that becomes the mark of her voyage back to England at the end, when her feeling of loss "slowly and imperceptibly drops" during the calm Channel crossing. In *What Maisie Knew*, the mobile, shimmering receptivity of childhood matures beyond a quality of charm to become a more sober attribute of Maisie's consciousness on the verge of adulthood. The structure of "The Pupil" excludes this development because the precocious boy, Morgan, dies and the tutor, Pemberton, lacks the capacity to absorb loss into fuller growth. There is a tremendous gap, however, between the promise of Maisie's renewed vitality and the accomplished "paradigm of cultural renovation" that Posnock wants to extract from James's art.[19] James's tone is more tender than celebratory in *What Maisie Knew*. Maisie's disappointed yearning for intimacy with her step-father and dearest friend, Sir Claude, remains the crisis of the novel and its emotional center.

The specialness of this love emerges at the start in the context of the novel's brilliant wit about the adults' dizzying sexual exchanges and heartless shuttling of Maisie between them. Most of the women in the book at one time or another fall "under the spell" of the charming Sir Claude, but only Maisie's cameraderie with him has the freedom and freshness that are reserved for non-sexual attachments in this novel's world. In the last third of the novel, however, the adventure of Sir Claude and Maisie becomes more ambiguous. Their move to separate from the disintegrating family system takes over the plot, deepening the tonality of its wit with more intense anxieties and pleasures.

Sir Claude's impulsive flight with Maisie to Folkestone, accompanied by only an insignificant servant, enacts the storybook kidnapping that Pemberton worries about and Morgan desires in "The Pupil." In both narratives, the image of flight extends the romantic spirit embodied earlier in the idyllic urban rambles. Thus Maisie connects the excitement of being in Folkestone with Sir Claude to their London outings: "The spirit of their old happy times, their rambles and expeditions in the easier better days of their first acquaintance" (206). Although the mood quickly darkens in the great scene when her mother, Ida, turns up in Folkestone to perform her definitive "bolting" from maternal responsibility, Ida's departure further liberates Maisie to enjoy the "bliss" of a new freedom with her stepfather, Sir Claude.

Once across the Channel in France, the idyllic possibilities multiply:

> She was "abroad" and she gave herself up to it, responded to it, in the bright air, before the pink houses, among the bare-legged fishwives and the red-legged soldiers, with the instant certitude of a vocation. Her vocation was to see the world and to thrill with enjoyment of the picture. (231)

Maisie's ecstatic initiation into the bright and free world initially represented by France at first appears an extension of her intimacy with Sir Claude. The arrival of Mrs. Wix, however, with her "straighteners" and over-eloquent "moral sense," and then Maisie's other step-parent, the formidable Mrs. Beale (who has now become Sir Claude's mistress), soon refocuses the picture into a complex familial struggle. Maisie has to "see" the world not merely through natural light, as in an Impressionist painting, but through the thick, humanly polluted atmosphere of her entangled and conflicting intimacies. She comes to see, for example, that Mrs. Beale (whom she loves) is her rival for Sir Claude, that her loyal governess, Mrs. Wix, is corruptible, for all her moral righteousness, and that Sir Claude himself is both weak and false. In the scene where her after-breakfast stroll with Sir Claude lands them at the train station, she doesn't need to know exactly how he is lying to her in order to sense all the differences from their earlier rambles.

It is in the context of this vision that Maisie seems impulsively ready to breach the "natural divisions" between "lovers and little girls" (204) and to propose that she and Sir Claude together board the train to Paris. Maisie's romantic impulse to escape, to be kidnapped, is the crisis of her "morning twilight" of childhood. Its ambiguity and elusiveness correspond to the pink and yellow covers of the French books they have bought at the station—the two in children's pink meant for her, and the yellow grownup one for Mrs. Beale. At this moment, Maisie clutches them both for herself. While the porter urges haste, and Sir Claude hesitates, Maisie's desire generates desperate verbal inspirations. This is the famous moment in the story when "in the intensity of her excitement" she becomes miraculously fluent in French: "She addressed herself straight to the porter. '*Prenny, prenny. Oh prenny!*'" (345). But Maisie cannot obtain the tickets by herself because the porter won't act until he is paid. "He waited there for the money." And while Sir Claude stares at her in silent terror, the train goes. Then comes the moment of her collapse, her fall "back to earth."

There has been much speculation on exactly how much sexual meaning to ascribe to Maisie's desire. Does her French proposal belong to the pink or to the yellow books? As in "The Pupil," it is the ambiguous hovering just at the edge of sexual passion that interests James. The sexual indeterminacy of Morgan's and Maisie's desires is crucial to the charm of the intimate relationships, but also to their insubstantiality. James does not offer indeterminacy of sexual, social, and even linguistic identity as an unambiguous value, no less as a "politics of nonidentity," to invoke a current phrase in fashion.[20] The delicate fleetingness of the scene intensifies the poignancy of desires so indeterminate that they would elude actualization even if Sir Claude were a better man than he is.

By making Maisie's best language for her crisis out of her childlike French mimicry of the porter's question about taking the tickets, James brilliantly concentrates a cluster of distinct social as well as psychological ironies. Like Morgan Moreen's interesting foreign ejaculations, Maisie's "*Prenny*," is a touching but impotent makeshift of language.[21] James delicately balances Maisie's success and failure through the peculiarity of her French improvisation. By shifting between the couple and the stolid train porter, for example, he amusingly specifies the same absence of material backing for desire that undermined Morgan Moreen. Maisie's "*Prenny*" mimics a bureaucratic French that she lacks the money to control. In these narratives of the 1890s, James's social vision is tough in its refusal to separate the fate of personal desire from seemingly immutable realities of money as well as sex.

Maisie's poignancy, moreover, borders on the melodrama that the book has been teaching us to mock. "*Prenny*" can be heard as an echo (in French) of Mrs. Wix's grotesque eloquence in the preceding scene, when after recovering from a collapse into "helplessness and woe," she rises to her own sublime expressiveness: "'I'll return to you and we'll go off together—we'll live together without a cloud. Take me, take me,' she went on and on—the tide of her eloquence was high" (262).

No matter how delicate Maisie's appeal, James suggests how her passion brings her close to the ludicrous Mrs. Wix, as when, Cleopatra-like in her own "infinite variety" (256), the governess also finds the voice of her desire: "'Here I am, here I am!'—she spread herself into an exhibition that, combined with her intensity and her decorations, appeared to suggest her for strange offices and devotions, for ridiculous replacements and substitutions" (263). Maisie's liberation from what may be regarded as a demeaning love has therefore seemed to some readers more gain than loss.[22] Yet her new autonomy costs her the loss of her chief "joy of life" (228). What differentiates the sentiment of loss in the novel from "The Pupil," however, is James's richer vision of how Maisie can sublimate disappointment into other less intimate but also intense joys that are beyond both Pemberton and Morgan Moreen.

James presents a rich and intricate imagining of survival in *What Maisie Knew*. The subtlety is that while her future will be without her beloved, Sir Claude, the feeling of this lost intimacy remains the creative source of her best scene at the end of the book: the beautiful, long interlude of Maisie and Mrs. Wix left alone when Sir Claude makes his dash back from France to England to deal (so ineffectually) with Mrs. Beale.

He leaves his forlorn admirers bribed into compliance by resources for a "lark" in his absence. They recognize their pleasures as a bribe. Still, when the weather clears, "the joy of the world so waylaid the steps of his friends, that little by little the spirit of hope filled the air and finally took possession of the scene" (266). James's language distinguishes between the complex "joy of the world" that almost surreptitiously waylays the abandoned women and Maisie's simpler "joy of life" in the sweet silence of intimacy with Sir Claude on the hotel terrace at Folkestone. Then, everything was immediately and fully attuned to her bliss: "There were a sense and a sound in everything to which words had nothing to add" (229). This later, less romantic spirit of hope only gradually steals upon an air permeated with anxiety.

Although Maisie and Mrs. Wix are united by their shared preoccupation with the absent Sir Claude, what James calls Maisie's "personal relation to her knowledge" significantly separates her from Mrs. Wix. The governess has become obsessed with the "crime," "immorality," and "impropriety" of their situation, especially insofar as it neglects her. For Maisie, the somnolent air of the ramparts induces a momentary fantasy of all four—Sir Claude, Mrs. Wix, herself, and Mrs. Beale—joining together in a Utopian community of generous courtesy and love. But her mere mention of such a resolution "jerks" Mrs. Wix into an outrage that spreads new violence over the ancient ramparts. The "lark" ends in Maisie's sobs, not only for her crushed vision of harmony, but also because her newly lucid critical judgment finds the governess unfit to be the arbiter of social morality. Maisie's recognition of how they are all (including Mrs. Wix) implicated in the "badness" of being "bought off" ends the chapter with a reminder that even the modest comforts of this French day are not "free" from worldly corruption. Somebody always has to pay and everybody (including Mrs. Wix) always takes bribes. That is one of the social truths Maisie comes to know beyond Mrs. Wix's moral sense.

James's remarkable blend of lyricism and irony manages to hold all the impurities of the situation together within the great range of Maisie's feelings and half-formed thoughts. Her intense mood makes her sensitive to "the brown old women" who "sat and knitted or snoozed" (270) on the benches of the ramparts, as well as to the "great golden Madonna" of the Church, who figures in this perspective not so much as the invitation to Catholic conversion that Mrs. Wix earlier felt, but rather as a mutely appealing memorial to other, far-off female suffering in courtesy. Maisie's private sorrow thus opens her to quiet communion with other great and humble sorrows, as they are evoked by the medieval church, the Virgin, the ramparts, and even the old French women on the bench. The rich beauty of the scene has no direct relation to Sir Claude, yet is infused by the "constant implication" of Maisie's longing for him. The beauty is all in the key of that feeling, even as James follows the development of a consciousness in Maisie already learning in advance of loss how to absorb private sorrow into larger responsiveness to the world.

Is Maisie's quiet knowingness at the end to be dismissed as nothing but "sterile negativity of knowing," in Terry Eagleton's often-quoted phrase of disparagement for James?[23] Posnock counters Eagleton's Marxist sneer by defending Jamesian "sublimation" as the basis for a vigorous social and cultural project.[24] My reading of *What Maisie Knew* suggests how Maisie might be recruited for this line of defense, but only by imposing on her a uniform so heavy as to make her (and the novella) almost unrecognizable. James's own "personal relation" to his knowledge, in the stories I have chosen, seems quieter, sadder, more modest. Desire and disappointment in this fiction are certainly social, as well as psychological, but not so easily generalizable into a model for the social collectivity. James's art draws us into intimate relation to situations as singular and elusive as "morning twilight." The stories also suggest how James was attracted by light that is evanescent, except when caught in the language and structure of art. Raymond Williams's protest against an earlier generation's inflated claims for the literary is correct in that such a light is certainly not "the whole of human life." In our own aggressively anti-aesthetic age, however, the challenge for readers is how to defend the distinctive human color and depth that James offers in his fiction without deferring too much to what the social theorists across the (invaluable) fence may pronounce.

### Notes

1. Raymond Williams, *The English Novel from Dickens to Lawrence* (London: Chatto and Windus, 1970), 132.
2. Fredric Jameson, *The Political Unconscious: Narrative as a Socially Symbolic Act* (Ithaca: Cornell University Press, 1981), 221–222.
3. Ross Posnock, *The Trial of Curiosity: Henry James, William James, and the Challenge of Modernity* (New York: Oxford University Press, 1991), ix and passim.
4. John Carlos Rowe, "Henry James and Critical Theory," in *A Companion to Henry James Studies*, ed. Daniel Mark Fogel (Westport, Conn.: Greenwood Press, 1993), 73–92. Citation from Max Horkheimer, "Postscript" to "Traditional and Critical Theory" (1937), in *Critical Theory: Selected Essays*, trans. Matthew J. O'Connell et al. (New York: Seabury Press, 1982).
5. Poirier's influence on Henry James criticism began with *The Comic Sense of Henry James: A Study of the Early Novels* (New York: Oxford University Press, 1960); his inquiries into the relationship between literature and the tradition of American pragmatism are known through numerous essays, reviews, and lectures, as well as *The Renewal of Literature: Emersonian Reflections* (New York: Random House, 1987) and *Poetry and Pragmatism* (Cambridge: Harvard University Press, 1992).
6. Posnock, *Trial of Curiosity*, 293 n. 1. Posnock summarizes the phases of critical debate in James criticism that motivate the terms of his defense on 59–70.
7. Poirier's comment on Jamesian interpretation at the start of his first book still seems timely: "Readers of his books sometimes act as if they are obliged to get beyond everything that is obvious, including their 'merely' personal reactions to it, so as to reach the supposedly deeper realms of meaning." *The Comic Sense of Henry James*, 9.
8. Laurence Holland similarly emphasizes James's form as involving him "intimately" with characters who are intimately involved with each other. See *The Expense of Vision: Essays on the Craft of Henry James* (Princeton: Princeton University Press, 1964), x-xi.

9. Posnock, *Trial of Curiosity*, 155.
10. Empson's speculations about the varieties of tone, situations, and social relationships that may be understood as "pastoral" appear in *Some Versions of Pastoral* (London: Chatto and Windus, 1935).
11. Walter Benjamin, "On Some Motifs in Baudelaire," in *Illuminations*, ed. Hannah Arendt, trans. Harry Zohn (New York: Schocken Books, 1969), 169.
12. Posnock, *Trial of Curiosity*, 187.
13. Rowe, "James and Critical Theory," 85, 92.
14. Quotations from "The Pupil" and to *What Maisie Knew* refer by page number in the text to the New York edition of Henry James, *What Maisie Knew, In the Cage, The Pupil* (New York: Scribner's, 1908), vol. 11.
15. Helen Hoy offers an astute analysis of homosexual displacement in "The Pupil" in "Homotextual Duplicity in 'The Pupil,'" *The Henry James Review* 14, no. 1 (1993), 34–42.
16. George Monteiro, "The *Atlantic Monthly's* Rejection of 'The Pupil': An Exchange of Letters Between Henry James and Horace Scudder," in *American Literary Realism: 1870-1910* 23, no. 1 (1990), 79.
17. James to Horace Scudder, London, 5 October 1890, and 4 March 1891, *Henry James Letters*, ed. Leon Edel (Cambridge: 1980), 3:301–302, 338–339; see also 194. Edel comments on the publishing episode in *Henry James: The Treacherous Years, 1895-1901* (London: Hart-Davis, 1969), 92–93.
18. "The Pupil" was initially published in *Longman's Magazine* in 1891; *What Maisie Knew* first appeared in 1897.
19. Posnock, *Trial of Curiosity*, 76.
20. See Posnock's "Coda: the Politics of Nonidentity," 285–291 as well as 334 n. 1 for citation of such writers as Adorno, Derrida, Nancy Chodorow, and Leslie Rabine, who have popularized "nonidentity" as an emancipatory political principle.
21. Randall Craig argues that Maisie's French reaches "the height of interpretive and communicative proficiency" in "'Reading the unspoken into the spoken': Interpreting *What Maisie Knew*," *The Henry James Review* 2, no. 3 (1981), 208. Carrie Kaston acknowledges but subordinates Maisie's failure to what she too sees here as the free expressiveness of Maisie's "personally desiring self." See *Imagination and Desire in the Novels of Henry James* (New Brunswick: Rutgers University Press, 1984), 128–129.
22. See Kaston, *Imagination and Desire*, 129.
23. Terry Eagleton, *Criticism and Ideology: A Study in Marxist Literary Theory* (London: Verso, 1980), 142.
24. Posnock, *Trial of Curiosity*, 45–50.

CHAPTER 7

# James and "Ideas": "Madame de Mauves"

MILLICENT BELL

$\mathcal{N}$o critical summation of Henry James has been more persistently famous or infamous than T. S. Eliot's in 1918 that he had a mind so fine that no idea could violate it. At the worst the statement suggests a certain anti-intellectualism on James's part, if not a stupidity about abstractions. But, of course, Eliot's comment was meant positively. Eliot said that James's "escape" from ideas was "the last test of a superior intelligence."[1] James, Eliot seems to have meant, was so committed to a vision of life as it is experienced directly that he distrusted the intervention of abstractions—or, perhaps, of that separation of thought from sensation and emotion, that famous "dissociation of sensibility" which had set in, it was Eliot's odd theory, after the seventeenth century. James, then, was a sort of metaphysical poet—as Eliot defined metaphysical poets—whose ideas existed only in indissoluble union with the concrete experiences and emotional facts he rendered in his fictions.

Eliot's tribute makes sense when taken in conjunction with Richard Poirier's demonstration in his remarkable early book, *The Comic Sense of Henry James*, that James's art bends itself constantly to deny the truth to life of purely theoretic notions. Poirier studied the role of characters like Rowland Mallet in *Roderick Hudson* who represent a commensensical view of life, and whose vision tends consequently to be open and sometimes comic. Such characters are set in contrast with others whose view of life is essentially melodramatic. These latter are obsessed with dreams out of the well-worn album of convention, romantic ideals of selfhood, pre-visions of their own histories borrowed from the traditions of literary story—and are consequently closed off from the fullest sense of either their own or others' potentialities. Such a tension of opposed attitudes towards life seems of central importance in James's fiction; it emerges as a deeply humane theme based on a respect for the unpredictable and unmeasurable in experience. But it is also expressed in his narrative method, which privileges presentation above analysis and finds a drama in the contest between the story-teller's own drive towards allegory and the resistance of reality to interpretation. It is this very tension that makes the particularities of James's own story-telling of such importance—so that no abstract summary of a tale does justice to the living experience of reading—and this experience is one that justifies the close-reading critic in an attentiveness which does not lapse in the excitement of discovering an intellectual subject that governs all.

The tension I speak of has been little noted in comparison with contests in James that run the danger of being themselves thematic abstractions—the most familiar of which, probably, is the opposition of cultural viewpoints and manners in situations in which his American characters encounter Europeans. James acknowledged the predominance of this interest in his work. "The reader of these volumes," he wrote in one of the prefaces to the New York Edition, would be likely to see in the collected stories and novels no issue "so salient as that of the opposition of aspects from country to country. Their author, I am quite aware, would seem struck with no possibility of contrast in the human lot so great as that encountered as we turn back and forth between the distinctively American and the distinctively European outlook. He might even perhaps on such a showing be represented as scarce aware, before the human scene, of any other sharp antithesis at all." Yet he seems to have anticipated with some apprehension the rush of criticism to this discovery. He pleads: "There are cases in which, however obvious and however contributive, its office for the particular demonstration, has been quite secondary, and in which the work is by no means merely addressed to the illustration of it." He wants recognition that in such late works as *The Wings of the Dove* and *The Golden Bowl* an "emphasized internationalism has either quite dropped or is well on its way to drop," and the subject of these works, though it "subsists of course on contrast . . . could in each case have been perfectly expressed had *all* the persons concerned been only American or only English or only Roman or whatever."

Looking back at some of his earlier stories, like "Lady Barberina," James still felt obliged to acknowledge that they could not have been conceived "without the narrower application of international terms."[2] In these stories, he had dealt repeatedly with a particular phenomenon of international life, the marriage of a young American woman to a "European of position." It was a phenomenon that had struck him in the seventies and eighties when, as a young traveler and soon a transplanted American he actually observed the successful landing of those female "buccaneers,"as Edith Wharton would later call them, upon the shores of the French and English aristocracy. But even in these stories, as too few of James's critics—and not even James himself—noted, the international theme is not as essential as one might think.

"Madame de Mauves" is certainly a challenge to this suspicion, for it is almost invariably dismissed as James's most formulaic example of the problems discovered in an international marriage. Looking again at the story after many years, James himself saw it as limited to the theme he had come to find so tiresome. When, in 1905, Auguste Monod proposed to translate it along with another tale of an American woman abroad, "The Siege of London," James was not encouraging; they were both, he said, "primitive cases." He did not intend, he told Monod, to republish these stories in the collected edition of his works then being planned.[3] Nevertheless, when the edition appeared, they were included. "Madame de Mauves" found a place among "early brevities" in the volume that also contained the oldest item in the New York Edition, "A Passionate Pilgrim," a story which shows the young James pondering, dividedly, the seductions of Europe.[4] But James's misgivings about "Madame de Mauves" had persisted. His 1908 preface refers to it slightingly, along with some of its companions in the volume, as "sops instinctively thrown to the international Cerberus . . . from whose capacity to loom larger and larger with the years there must already have sprung some chilling portent."[5] He also declares that he is unable to remember anything about how he had come to write the tale in the first place except that it was in an old inn at Bad-Homburg that "the gentle Euphemia" visited his imagination. "She again, after her fashion, was what I might have called experimentally international: she muffled her charming head in the lightest, finest, vaguest tissue of romance and put twenty questions by."[6]

But perhaps he condescends too much to his early self and misjudges his own story. Perhaps he has forgotten that, despite the pat situation of wicked foreign husband and innocent American wife in his story, it had once raised for him questions that transcend the international theme. Published in the *Galaxy* in 1874, the year before he produced *Roderick Hudson*, thirty-one-year-old James already shows himself concerned, as he was to be in the novel, with the danger of simplistic ideas.

It is no accident that the story's observing intelligence, the young American who falls in love, after a fashion, with Madame de Mauves, is a man who has not exhausted his curiosity about Paris but realizes how little he has come to know the city in a visit of six months. He finds himself a "disappointed observer" who has missed discovering any "thrilling chapter of experience"— missed, that is, the episode promised by his reading of novels. He is no Rastignac vowing to know and to make his mark upon Paris when he gazes at the city from the heights of Saint-Germain-en-Laye; he is ready to "close the book almost with a yawn."[7] The adventure he does find is hardly one. It takes place not only on the periphery of the great foreign capital but also on the border—never to be passed—of sentimental adventure.

Madame de Mauves, however, is someone who has already suffered the consequences of a too sentimental view of life. As her friend Mrs. Draper tells Longmore, "She was romantic and perverse—she thought the world she had been brought up in too vulgar or at least too prosaic." She had gone in too "desperately for thrills" (222). At the Parisian convent where her widowed American mother sent her for the acquisition of refined manners and accomplishments she acquired "a certain turn of the imagination" and dreamt of marrying a titled French husband. "She had a romantic belief that the enjoyment of inherited and transmitted consideration, consideration attached to the fact of birth, would be the direct guarantee of an ideal delicacy of feeling." It was a view not easily shaken; she "found it easier to believe in fables, when they had a certain nobleness of meaning, than in well-attested but sordid facts" (224–225).

"Various Ultramontane works of fiction" which she found in the convent library had implanted these notions—the abstract conventions of romance and melodrama. In such literature, "the hero was always a Legitimist vicomte who fought duels by the dozen but went twice a month to confession." Her school-mates contributed further by depicting their own brothers as "Prince Charmings or young Paladins" (225). One of these schoolmates was Mademoiselle de Mauves, a shrewd young woman who even at seventeen must have understood the uses of a rich and naive young American. In a move that belongs in a gothic novel—being the single-minded initiation of a wicked plot against the innocent heroine—she invited Euphemia to visit her family's ancient castle in Auvergne. There Euphemia did, indeed, meet the charming brother who seems to conform to her own novelistic expectations.

But James is not writing a simple romantic tale of innocence entrapped by selfish guile—of American idealism and wicked European greed—even though his heroine is a "pure" young woman quite unaware of how much her money attracts the interest of the titled but impoverished Mauves family. The error Euphemia falls into is of her own making. Richard de Mauves seems "the hero of the young girl's romance made real" (232), and while he imposes himself falsely upon her, she connives at the imposition by her own romantic expectations. By letting us see this, James criticizes romance while writing it.

The Count de Mauves is, indeed, handsome and ingratiating. But he is a thirty-three-year-old veteran of a decade devoted to pleasure and the running up of debts—experience which had "pretty well stifled the natural lad whose violent will and generous temper might have been shaped by a different pressure to some such showing as would have justified a romantic faith" (234). There is an interesting indulgence of sympathy in James's description here, a suggestion of potentiality not allowed for in the villain type. For a moment, we glimpse something quite outside the viewpoint of melodrama, a realistic insight into the history of the count's character. "He had formed himself, as the phrase was," James goes on, "and the form prescribed to him by the society into which his birth and his tastes had introduced him [included] the classification of the fairer half of humanity as objects not essentially different—say from those very lavender gloves that are soiled in an evening and thrown away" (235).

It is his attitude towards others—particularly women—that James identifies as a characteristic "prescribed" by his social world—and even peculiarly European, if we are to contrast it as we shortly will with the tender, unselfish solicitude of the American Longmore. But James again introduces a note of something else. He says that the Count's "imagination was touched" as he spends some weeks at home convalescing after an accident and observing his sister's visitor. He "seemed to give easy ear to some of the sweetest [music] he had ever heard" (236). We are permitted to guess that sentiment has, even if only momentarily, supplanted his opportunism when he proposes to her in a blossoming bosquet with a nightingale singing nearby. It is "like Jeannot and Jeannette," and his grandmother, the old Madame de Mauves, remarks, "the first marriage ever made in our family in this way" (239).

Some time before, this clever but "very honest old woman," had been stirred to give Euphemia good advice which she did not understand—not to trouble herself too much about "conscience," since that won't help her "case," and if not to cheat, not, at least, to be surprised that others do, and, above all, not to "lose at the game of life" (230). Now that she is to marry her grandson, the old lady warns that "there never was a man in the world—among the saints themselves—as good as [Euphemia] believes" him to be. But her grandson is a "*galant homme* and a gentleman." If she will just be her own serious, sincere self, in spite of "bad precepts and bad examples, bad fortune and even bad usage . . . even one of us—and one of those who is most what we *are*—will do you justice" (239–240). It remains to be seen if this prediction of the eventual outcome to the marriage will be fulfilled—and if it is fulfilled, to see whether Euphemia will value the arrival of this end as compensation and opportunity.

After her marriage we see Madame de Mauves chiefly through the eyes of Longmore, whose story this becomes when he encounters her several years later. He wonders that she has chosen to live a European life. As though romantic illusion no longer operates with her, she explains, "My imagination perhaps—I had a little when I was younger—helped me to think I should find happiness here." But it signifies nothing now that she is an American in France. "France is in the town and the forest; but here, close about me, in my room and in my mind, it's a nameless, and doubtless not at all remarkable, little country of my own. It's not her country that makes a woman happy or un-happy" (247–248). She herself rejects the importance of the international theme. Her chosen country has become a moral idea, a realm of the abstract spirit which denies a reference to any local conditions or traditions.

Perhaps to illustrate the fact that the distinction between Madame de Mauves and her husband is not necessarily one of nationality, James includes, as a sort of footnote, the further history of the Count's sister. Madame Clairin's marriage had also been made across boundaries, but of class rather than nation, for she married a rich wholesale druggist who craved elevation to higher circles, an aspiration comparable to Euphemia's youthful worship of the aris-tocracy. Monsieur Clairin had been ruined by his dreams, too; he had adopted aristocratic vice and gambled at the Bourse and lost his fortune, and ended by blowing out his brains. His practical widow then turns to the idea of an international replacement, Longmore himself, though she overestimates, we are told, his American wealth and complaisance, and underestimates the extent to which she is repellent to his "Puritanic soul."

Longmore is the instrument of an increasingly typological view as his admiration of Madame de Mauves grows and his dislike for her husband and sister-in-law becomes more intense, throwing the woman he admires "into radiant relief." There may have been times when he was "almost persuaded against his finer judgment that [the Count de Mauves] was really the most considerate of husbands and that it was not a man's fault if his wife's love of life had pitched itself once for all in a minor key" (253). But he is convinced of the man's "essential grossness" (255), his inability to appreciate a nature like hers. Longmore perceives that what he admires is precisely what bores her husband: "She was too dim, too delicate, too modest." The Count is "by race and instinct a *grand seigneur*" who holds himself free to "take his amusement where he finds it, and [be] . . . quite at liberty not to find it at home" (255–256). Later Madame Clairin will emphasize this racial-cultural measure by saying "There has never been a *galant homme* among us, I fear, who has not given his wife, even when she was very charming, the right to be jealous" (289).

And yet, James permits, again, a half-glimpse of the Count's own point of view. When Longmore tells the latter—who has been deploring her withdrawal from society—that Euphemia has intelligence and beauty and "many virtues," the husband pulls him up sharply: "I suspect you of thinking that I don't do my wife justice. Take care—take care, young man; that's a dangerous assumption. In general a man does his wife justice. More than justice—that we keep for the wives of other men!" (266). We are compelled to acknowledge qualities in the Count's personality not entirely accounted for by Longmore's dismissal:

> Something he had . . . that his critic vaguely envied, something in his address, splendidly positive, a manner rounded and polished by the habit of conversation and the friction of full experience, an urbanity exercised for his own sake, not for his neighbor's, which seemed the fruit of one of those strong temperaments that rule the inward scene better than the best conscience. The Count plainly had no sense for morals, and poor Longmore, who had the finest, would have been glad to borrow his recipe for appearing then so to range the whole scale of the senses. (254–255)

"Poor Longmore" is by no means convinced—nor are we—that the possession of a good conscience is all that the fully developed man requires.

Longmore suspects rightly, nonetheless, that the Count has his own reasons for encouraging him to divert Euphemia, and his suspicion is confirmed when he sees him entertaining a pretty companion in a Paris restaurant. It is the American's signal to return to Madame de Mauves with a more intense appeal for her confidence, a more urgent offer of his understanding. But when he blurts out that she is truth surrounded by falsehood she rebukes his poetic simplification, recalling her own, now rejected: "I believe I once supposed all the prose to be in America, which was very foolish. What I thought, what I believed, what I expected, when I was an ignorant girl fatally addicted to falling in love with my own theories is more than I can tell you now" (277–278). As Longmore had realized earlier, "She believed her husband to be a hero of rose-colored romance, and he turns out to be not even a hero of very sad-coloured reality" (268). Her marriage into the aristocracy had shown her a reality of corruption and betrayal from which she had chosen to retreat, but when Longmore tells her she deserves "a husband of your own faith and race and spiritual substance," she does not respond beyond saying, "Visions are vain things; we must make the best of the reality we happen to be in for" (280–281).

Does she, in fact, do this? Madame Clairin complains that her brother's wife has not lived up to the tradition of the wives of the family who were "dear brave women of wit. When they had a head-ache they put on a little rouge and came to supper as usual, and when they had a heart-ache they touched up that quarter with just such another brush." Madame de Mauves has failed to "keep up the tone" (289) by shutting herself away and, worse, by making a scene when she discovers her husband's most recent infidelity. And when his utter immorality stands further revealed, when he urges her to console herself with Longmore—and this recommendation is revealed to him by Madame Clairin—she takes another line altogether.

James is really playing with his "international theme" in this story, testing it for its self-contradictions. After Longmore learns from Madame Clairin how the Count has urged his wife to console herself, he wanders in the beautiful, "characteristically French" (297) countryside pondering the renunciation his sentimental moral code enjoins. "Sacrifice? The word was a trap for minds muddled with fear, an ignoble refuge of weakness" (299), he reflects. He observes a pretty young woman accompanying a young artist, and envies the happy couple until he hears from the innkeeper at the inn where they are staying that they are not married—nor will be—that being the usual way with artists. He then ponders the young woman's willingness to renounce her own future happiness in this case, and envies the young man again. And he goes again to see Madame de Mauves.

What she tells him is simply this: "Don't disappoint me" (312). He must reward her admiration by declining to be selfish, vulgar—to resolvedly leave her forever, "out of the fullness of [his] own wisdom" (314). "Was it strength, was it weakness, was it a vulgar fear, was it conviction, conscience, constancy?" (317–318) he asks himself. He decides that it is the last—she loved once, and will not love again—and he assents to this romantic interpretation, seeing that he must obey also so that his own character may stand unblemished in the story memory will tell. And once again he is in Paris, and once again he runs into M. de Mauves, who seems to have parted from his mistress there, and to be passing on to other light interests. But Longmore's last visit to Madame de Mauves only confirms the pact between them.

Does Madame de Mauves really make the best of her lot? It will be remembered that the Count's grandmother had recommended that in the face of revealed badness she should simply be her own serious, sincere self, and the wise old lady had promised that if she did so her husband would finally do her justice. This is exactly what happens. Euphemia's mute suffering and withdrawal has its effect. Longmore hears, much later, that the Count came to repent of "quelques folies which his wife had taken absurdly to heart [and] asked her forgiveness." But this she had "inexorably refused." De Mauves then fell more in love with her than he had been before—"madly in love with her. . . . He had begged her on his knees to take him back." He had finally done her justice, but "she was stone, she was ice, she was outraged virtue" (331), Longmore is told. The Count de Mauves finally blew his brains out—the second person in the story to do so, not, like M. Clairin because his romantic dreams have tumbled into dust but because he had discovered, too late, his own capacity for romance. This extraordinary dénouement, related in a few sentences on the last page of "Madame de Mauves," is not entirely believable—and James distances himself artistically from his ending by making us learn about it at third- or even fourth-hand—as a piece of news, no longer fresh, that Longmore heard from his friend Mrs. Draper who heard it from a Frenchman she met at Vichy who heard it from Madame Clairin.

Mrs. Draper's informant had referred to Longmore's admirable Euphemia as "the terrible little woman who killed her husband" (331). When James in his preface calls her "the gentle Euphemia," he seems to have forgotten the capacity to be stone or ice she revealed in the end. The truly terrifying virtuous woman kills by her virtue. Is it her puritan American rectitude that explains her stand against the humbled and infatuated Count? Perhaps, and so, also, can her previous rejection of Longmore's offered love be explained. But her difference from the husband who shoots himself, having abandoned his own irredeemable cynicism, is no longer the international difference originally posed by the story. James's small, hardly noticeable hints of the vulnerable side of this complete cynic may recur to our minds now.

But perhaps Madame de Mauves is not so much, or not merely, a representative of her own native culture as she is of a more general mode of response to life that James ultimately distrusts. As she herself had told Longmore, she inhabits a country of her own, neither France or America. From the beginning, she has shown most strongly that she was inclined to attach herself to abstract ideas. It had been her fantastic idea of a foreign nobleman that made her want to marry the Count in the first place. But in surrendering the poetry of such a conception for prose, as Mrs. Draper put it, she had only substituted another "poetic" notion—that he was an unforgivable scoundrel incapable of love. Equally the fruit of a poetic notion is her rejection of Longmore. In this second case in which love is offered we realize that her passion for thinking well of a possible lover and even more, probably, of herself, is stronger than passion itself.

Longmore may seem, perhaps, one of those weak Jamesian demi-heroes who suffer from a failure of resolution and passion. He is more a watcher than a doer; he waits for a long time before letting Madame de Mauves know his feelings. Even when he is provoked to expression at last by his knowledge about the Count's Parisian liaison, his love for Madame de Mauves is too diffident; he fails to press her to surrender her absolutism and to release her own feelings, and he is further dissuaded by the realization that to do so would be to enact the role that seemed so "prevu" to the vulgar Madame Clairin.

But Longmore should be defended from the general dismissal of most critics of the story. The resistance of Madame de Mauves to what he offers, permits, in fact, no argument. For an instant, after he has returned to her after his walk in the country, he wonders what her attitude really signifies: "Did [her] eyes warn him, did they plead, or did they confess to a sense of provocation?" (309). He almost makes a physical advance at last—"to stride forward and fold her in his arms" to make things clear. But he fails to move, and a moment later her attitude is made clear: "He couldn't clasp her to his arms now, any more than some antique worshipper could have clasped the marble statue in his temple" (310). The description of her as a woman of stone, which he thus makes for himself, is one he will later hear again when Mrs. Draper repeats the comment of her French informant concerning the end of the Count de Mauves.

In response to Madame de Mauves's fixed view of the "wisdom and taste" he must exercise by renouncing her, Longmore exclaims against her "horrible and unnatural lucidity" (314). It is a final condemnation of her unyielding attachment to ideas, though he goes again to make his farewell, and asks her to think of him "as a man who has felt much and claimed little" (325). Before returning to America he tells Mrs. Draper that he could not have "consoled" this friend who dispenses with anything that might alter her idea of herself: "She has her consolation in herself. She needs none that anyone else can offer her" (329).

Longmore is not quite the balanced, rational observer of the folly of romantic egoism that Roland Mallet is. But he learns to take the measure and reject the egoism of Madame de Mauves's fidelity to abstraction. After he hears Mrs. Draper's news he is tempted to return to France to see the interesting widow, but rejects the idea. The last sentence of the story tells all: "The truth is that, in the midst of all the ardent tenderness of his memory of Madame de Mauves, he has become conscious of a singular feeling—a feeling of wonder, of uncertainty, of awe" (331).

"Madame de Mauves" is not a perfectly realized fiction, and James later probably saw its defects. But it is fascinating to discover that it does not "put by" all of the questions that transcended its theme of international comparisons. Already evident, indeed, is his deeper theme of the deficiencies of a viewpoint dominated by ideas alone. Madame de Mauves's head may have seemed, to an admirer, "veiled in the lightest, finest, vaguest tissue of romance"—but James, like Longmore at the last, had ceased to be a complete admirer.

## Notes

1. T. S. Eliot, "On Henry James," in *The Question of Henry James*, ed. F. W. Dupee (New York: Henry Holt and Company, 1945), 110.
2. Henry James, *Literary Criticism: French Writers, Other European Writers, The Prefaces to the New York Edition*, ed. Leon Edel (New York: The Library of America), 1208–1209.
3. Henry James, *Letter to A. C. Benson and Auguste Monod*, ed. E. F. Benson (New York: Charles Scribner's Sons, 1930), 97.
4. James, *Literary Criticism*, 1192.
5. James, *Literary Criticism*, 1204.
6. James, *Literary Criticism*, 1206-1207.
7. *The Novels and Tales of Henry James: The New York Edition* (New York: Charles Scribner's Sons, 1908), 13:215. All subsequent quotations from "Madame de Mauves" will be from this edition, noted parenthetically.

CHAPTER 8

# Persuasion and the Life of Feeling

THOMAS R. EDWARDS

*R*ichard Poirier's "Mark Twain, Jane Austen, and the Imagination of Society" quotes some unenthusiastic remarks on Austen's fiction by three American masters:

> To me [Poe's] prose is unreadable. Like Jane Austin's [sic]. No, there is a difference. I could read his prose on salary, but not Jane's. Jane is entirely impossible. It seems a great pity that they allowed her to die a natural death.
>
> (Twain, letter to W.D. Howells, January 18, 1909)

> . . . vulgar in tone, sterile in invention, imprisoned in the wretched conventions of English society, without genius, wit, or knowledge of the world. Never was life so pinched and narrow. . . . [Her main subject,] marriageableness [is] the "nympholepsy of a fond despair," say, rather, of an English boarding house. Suicide is more respectable.
>
> (Emerson, *Journal*, August 5, 1861)

> The key to Jane Austen's fortune with posterity has been in part the extraordinary grace of her facility, in fact of her unconsciousness; as if, at the most, for difficulty, for embarrassment, she sometimes, over her work-basket, her tapestry flowers, in the spare, cool drawing-room of other days, fell a-musing, lapsed too metaphorically, as one may say, into wool gathering, and her dropped stitches, of these pardonable, of these precious moments, were afterwards picked up as little touches of human truth, little glimpses of steady vision, little master strokes of imagination.
>
> (Henry James, "The Lesson of Balzac," 1905)[1]

We may presume that she touched a different soreness in each of them: Twain's dread of feminized high culture, Emerson's scorn for old-world insularity and primness, James's exasperation at how readily "unconscious" art finds an audience. Nor was there much solidarity within this critical bloc; Twain said he would rather be "damned to John Bunyan's heaven" than read *The Bostonians*, and some of James's comments on Twain and Emerson, if slyer, were no less funny.[2]

Poirier sees these dissimilar readers agreeing about Austen because each knew in his own way that the American self was divided, into a part amenable to social system and another "more admirable, even if impractical part, that exists in imagination only, or in a vocabulary of abstractions, or in relationships to landscape." Emerson's idea (in "The Transcendentalist") of an inescapable "double consciousness" helps explain why Huck Finn, Isabel Archer, and Lambert Strether fail to achieve, or refuse, the kind of social and psychological self-definition that Emma and Elizabeth Bennet acquire painfully but in the end accept happily. Social fiction, bent on the "beguilement" of readers, is at odds with American writers' fear that society is (in Emerson's words) "a conspiracy against the manhood of every one of its members," which suggests why American novels have such trouble with endings. "The illusion that society might someday, somehow be transformed by the vision and sacrifice of an Isabel Archer or the needs of a Huck Finn is necessarily among the things that their creators try to make us believe even when they themselves are skeptical," Poirier says. "Emerson's 'I' could not exist in a novel at all—he simply would not be interested in social dialogue for a sufficient length of time."[3]

On the other hand, Austen is "fully aware of the dangers *in* society which for [James and Twain] are the dangers *of* it."[4] In *Emma* we find an effort to "prevent society from *becoming* what it is condemned for *being* in *Huckleberry Finn*": a set of habits and affectations that impedes any wise choice of social forms—the choice, for Emma, of what Mr. Knightley calls "the simple and natural" over the artifice and conformity that Mrs. Elton calls "the natural." The ending of *Huckleberry Finn* shows a collapse of "the dramatic organization of the novel, which depends on the social audibility of Huck's voice," a voice fated never fully to embody the understandings that created it; but *Emma* ends with the heroine assuming the social directness, and its speaking style, of both Mr. Knightley and the author herself.

In such comparisons Poirier was of course continuing the critical project begun in *The Comic Sense of Henry James* and later advanced so powerfully in *A World Elsewhere* and in his writings on Frost, Emerson, and American pragmatism. His subject was, and is, the behavior of American literary language as it both observes and resists European antecedents and analogues, and *Emma* convincingly supports his point about *Huckleberry Finn*. So too, I think, do most of Austen's other novels. But her last, *Persuasion*, seems strikingly less intent on showing how the best possibilities of society may be realized by those who bring good sense and good will to the demands of human community.

Readers often find *Persuasion* insufficiently "finished." Some important secondary figures, like Mr. Elliot and Mrs. Smith, may seem incomplete or confusingly drawn; some of the satiric asides, like the notorious one about Mrs. Musgrove's "large fat sighings," may seem gratuitous; there may be too much narration and too little dramatizing of issues. Still, nearly everyone loves Anne Elliot and finds the book's new interest in the emotional life appealing. So do I, but without wanting to treat Anne's feelings as the beauties of a novel with more than its share of defects. One of Austen's most rigorous critics, Marvin Mudrick, sensed the dangers of that sort of balancing act: "The new element in *Persuasion* is personal feeling. It pervades the characters and settings, it complicates the moral climate. Further revision would—we may surmise—have altered the book for the better, but only by refining and proportioning its novelty."[5] Keeping in mind Poirier's discussion of Austen and her American belittlers, I want to look at a certain way of describing personal feeling that pervades and complicates *Persuasion*, before asking what it suggests about Anne's social condition and fate.

Anne's happy marriage to the man she rejected eight years earlier lies close to the stuff of popular romances, and like all good romance it at least touches on real life. Her deferred union with Captain Frederick Wentworth has, for example, some intriguing parallels to the marriage, in 1805, of the future Duke of Wellington.[6] Her earlier persuasion by her dear friend Lady Russell that it would be disastrous for a penniless young sailor to marry the second daughter of a "foolish spendthrift baronet" (24:248) keeps the fiscal realities in view. And where hyper-romance has little use for clocks and calendars—"I cannot be dictated to by a watch," says Mary Crawford, the *faux*-romanticist of *Mansfield Park*—*Persuasion*, as R. W. Chapman noted seventy-three years ago, is uncommonly exact about temporality. We know, for example, the birthdates of all the Elliots; we know that the lovers first met in the summer of 1806, when Anne was nineteen, and that the book begins in the autumn of 1814 and ends the next February. Temporal exactness clears space in which to ponder the emotional and moral consequences of living in time, or of trying not to live in it.

Sir Walter Elliot, Anne's father and Austen's supreme egotist and snob, raises the matter of time in the opening paragraphs. In his pride in his undimmed handsomeness and distinction he fills his house with mirrors and admires himself endlessly in the Baronetage, where he finds unfailing assurance that, among "the limited remnants of the earliest patents" and "the almost endless creations of the last century," he is still and always "Elliot of Kellynch-hall" (1:3). As he smugly pictures himself and his favorite daughter, Elizabeth, to be "blooming as ever, amidst the wreck of the good looks of everybody else," the narrator concedes that Anne's own "bloom had vanished early" (1:6). The floral metaphor calls the effect of time natural even as it withholds that comfort—an *early* loss of bloom is as unnatural as none at all. Even so, at twenty-seven, Anne at first seems to have recovered well enough: "Time had softened down much, perhaps nearly all of peculiar attachment to [Wentworth]" (4:28).

When Sir Walter's improvidence forces him to let out Kellynch and move with Elizabeth to Bath, Anne stays on in Somerset to help with the children of her self-centered sister Mary, who has married into the neighboring Musgrove family.[7] And the advent of the new tenants, Admiral and Mrs. Croft, threatens her tranquillity, since Mrs. Croft is a Wentworth:

> She could not hear that Captain Wentworth's sister was likely to live at Kellynch, without a revival of former pain; and many a stroll and many a sigh were necessary to dispel the agitation of the idea. She often told herself it was folly, before she could harden her nerves sufficiently to feel the continual discussion of the Crofts and their business no evil. (4:30)

This quasi-clinical vocabulary—agitation, revival of pain, harden the nerves—will figure often in Anne's experience, and its effect is complex. For pain to revive is hurtful, yet revival is a return to *life*; to dispel the agitation of an idea, to harden the nerves, sounds both curative and ominously anaesthetic, a resistance to a future more open to feeling than her vulnerability can afford.

In volume one, as Anne struggles to "teach herself to be insensible" (6:52) even to memory, time perceptibly passes all around her. Her proud father has to make way for a sailor, one of a rising professional class, of questionable gentility, enriched by the prize-money of the French and American wars. (Sir Walter's solace is that sailors "are all knocked about, and exposed to every climate, and every weather, till they are not fit to be seen" [3:20].) The prosperous, affably vulgar Musgroves are, "like their houses . . . in a state of alteration, perhaps improvement" (5:40); Anne sees Mary "lying on the faded sofa of the pretty little drawing-room" at Uppercross Cottage, "the once elegant furniture of which had been gradually growing shabby, under the influence of four summers and two children" (5:37). Wentworth's first command, the *Asp*, is no longer in the Navy List, being now "quite worn out and broken up" (8:64). And something like historical or even geological time-keeping colors the observation, near Lyme, of "green chasms between romantic rocks, where the scattered forest trees and orchards . . . declare that many a generation must have passed away since the first partial falling of the cliff prepared the ground for such a state" (11:95–96). "Prepared the ground" puns on painting or engraving, and "romantic"[8] reflects the period's love of pastness, memories softened and safely distanced from the viewer as "picturesque" scenes, in art or nature, were felt to be.[9]

Anne's famous taste for the autumnal—"the last smiles of the year upon the tawny leaves and withered hedges" (10:84)—shows her finding in nature a tranquilized image of her own condition. Remembering lost romance while figuring herself as faded greenery may at least assure her that she's now safe, unlikely to inspire any painful renewal of love, even as the reader reflects that trees and hedges do not die in autumn but only go dormant. (The mood grows almost elegiac later: "She was the last . . . the very last, the only remaining one of all that filled and animated both houses" [13:123].) But her first new encounter with Wentworth is jarring:

A thousand feelings rushed on Anne, of which this was the most consoling, that it would soon be over. And it was soon over. . . . [T]he room seemed full—full of persons and voices—but a few minutes ended it. . . .

"It is over! it is over!" she repeated to herself again, and again, in nervous gratitude. "The worst is over!". . . .

Soon, however, she began to reason with herself, and try to be feeling less. Eight years, almost eight years had passed, since all had been given up. How absurd to be resuming the agitation which such an interval had banished into distance and indistinctness! What might not eight years do? Events of every description, changes, alienations, removals—all, all must be comprised in it; and oblivion of the past—how natural, how certain too! It included nearly a third part of her own life. (7:59-60)

Austen's writing had not previously entered so sympathetically and deeply into personal emotion. The "thousand feelings" that rushed on Anne figure as a kind of attacking army and then dissolve into a literal invasive host—the roomful of persons and voices suggests how menacing "society" feels to a wounded, reclusive heroine. In the prayer-like iterations of "over," "eight years," and "all" she tries to be feeling less by stressing pastness, converting both present and remembered pain into aestheticized "distance and indistinctness." But the peril of such comfort asserts itself in "how natural, how certain too!," as if to say that the oblivion she craves is troublingly like death.

Fortunately, oblivion is not all she wants, and the passage finds a new turn that points the book toward its proper outcome:

Alas! with all her reasonings, she found, that to retentive feelings eight years may be little more than nothing.

Now, how were his sentiments to be read? Was this like wishing to avoid her? And the next moment she was hating herself for the folly which asked the question. (7:60)

It's surely folly if feelings and reasonings are firm opposites. But Anne's great virtue is that, with all her talent for feeling, she is—as that rather brisk "Now" suggests—quite reasonable and businesslike too. The good sense that once made her persuadable now encourages her to "read" Wentworth like a text, employ her sense of metaphor ("Was this like . . . ?") in the service of present understanding and possible future benefit.

Mary's heartless report of his response to seeing Anne—"'he said, "You were so altered he should not have known you again"'" (7:60)—is a blow, especially since to her eyes, "he was not altered, or not for the worse" (7:61). She uses his words to persuade herself that the past *is* safely past: "They allayed agitation; they composed, and consequently must make her happier" (7:61). But composure is not life, and it is not exactly happiness that her ensuing meetings with him bring. When, literally behind her back, he frees her from the grasp of her naughty nephew Walter (as he later frees her from the figurative clutches of other bad Walters, her father and cousin), learning who has so obliged her leaves her speechless:

> She could not even thank him. She could only hang over little Charles, with most disordered feelings. His kindness . . . produced such a confusion of varying, but very painful agitation, as she could not recover from. . . . [N]either Charles Hayter's feelings, nor any body's feelings, could interest her, till she had a little better arranged her own. She was ashamed of herself, quite ashamed of being so nervous, so overcome by such a trifle; but so it was; and it required a long application of solitude and reflection to recover her. (9:80–81)

The jocularly medical "application" and "recover," with the lightened narrative tone of "nor any body's feelings," invite an affectionate smile at Anne here, with a hope that she won't recover if that means substituting memory for immediate feeling.

Indeed, *Persuasion* is full of real illness and pain: Anne's headaches and fatigue, Charles Musgrove's broken collar-bone, Admiral Croft's gout, Mary's sore throat, Louisa Musgrove's awful fall at Lyme, Captain Harville's severe wound, Captain Benwick's melancholia, Mrs. Smith's crippling rheumatic fever. And a lot of deaths are reported—Lady Russell, Mrs. Clay, Mrs. Smith, and Lady Dalrymple have lost their husbands, Sir Walter and Mr. Elliot their wives, the Byronic Benwick his fiancée (who was also Harville's sister), and the senior Musgroves their scapegrace sailor son Dick. This high casualty rate may owe something to the onset of Austen's fatal illness as she was writing the book, but it also overshadows Anne's early loss of bloom and then makes her recovery of vigor and beauty seem even more remarkable.

Her looks, in fact, recuperate rather quickly. When Mr. Elliot sees her at Lyme, he admires her "exceedingly," as Wentworth notices: "He gave her a momentary glance,—a glance of brightness, which seemed to say, 'That man is struck with you,—and even I, at this moment, see something like Anne Elliot again' " (12:104). As she reads him the past begins to be something not simply remembered but more actively "recalled," "recollected," or "restored," as when he praises her effective conduct after Louisa's accident:

> She paused a moment to recover from the emotion of hearing herself so spoken of. . . . "You will stay, I am sure; you will stay and nurse her;" cried he, turning to her and speaking with a glow, and yet a gentleness, which seemed almost restoring the past.—She coloured deeply. (12:114)

His vocal glow seems almost to create her blush, the emblem of both returning beauty and returning life.

Though in some ways the gentlest of Austen's heroines, Anne is not at all soft. Unlike her father, she faces up to the fiscal crisis that requires Kellynch to be rented; it was "not regret," the narrator says dryly, that made her "heart beat" and "brought colour into her cheeks" at the news that Louisa is betrothed not to Wentworth but to Benwick (18:167); when she meets Wentworth unexpectedly in Bath, she takes satisfaction in seeing *him* blush: "For the first time, since their renewed acquaintance, she felt that she was betraying the least sensibility of the two. She had the advantage. . . . Still, however, she had enough to feel! It was agitation, pain, pleasure, a something between delight and misery" (19:175). And a moment later she thinks of him as he earlier spoke of her: "Time had changed him" (19:176). "[S]ick of knowing nothing, and fancying herself stronger because her strength was not tried (19:180)," she looks forward to seeing him again; and when they next meet, at the concert rooms, she made "a little advance [and] instantly spoke," feeling "equal to everything which she believed right to be done" (20:181).

As he criticizes Benwick's over-rapid recovery from his loss of Fanny Harville, Anne can tune out social intrusions—"the various noises of the room, the almost ceaseless slam of the door, and ceaseless buzz of persons walking through" (20:193)—to hear his every word and have another complex reaction: she "was struck, gratified, confused, and beginning to breathe very quick, and feel an hundred things in a moment" (20:193). The language recalls their earlier encounter, but the "hundred things" she feels are not like the hostile "thousand feelings" that rushed on her then; now she tries, not to repress feeling but to welcome the quick breath of new life and, within the bounds of propriety and public visibility, tell him something of what she feels. "The last few hours were certainly very painful," she says of their visit to Lyme, before adding a lovely Virgilian qualification: "But when pain is over, the remembrance of it often becomes a pleasure. One does not love a place the less for having suffered in it" (20:183–184).[10]

After this moment she reads his behavior confidently, as saying "that he had a heart returning to her at least; that anger, resentment, avoidance, were no more; and that they were succeeded, not merely by friendship and regard, but by the tenderness of the past. . . . She could not contemplate the change as implying less.—He must love her" (20:185–186). For all their intelligence, neither Emma nor Elizabeth Bennet sees so quickly and unerringly into her lover's heart. The rule that a lady must seem, and somehow *be*, surprised by a marriage offer is relaxed in *Persuasion*, and Anne is not just Austen's most sensitive heroine but her most forward and least self-deceiving one too.

In volume two Anne learns to live in the present and believe that Wentworth loves her *now*; she also tries to shape the future to fit her desires, at whatever risk of indecorum. When, just after she finds that Wentworth must still love her, her scheming cousin sits down beside her at the concert and begins to ingratiate himself, she sees Wentworth watching and wishes Mr. Elliot were "not so near her" (20:188). She keeps her seat at intermission, hoping Wentworth will approach her; when he doesn't, "a little scheming of her own" allows her to "place herself much nearer the end of the bench. . . , much more within reach of a passer-by" (20:189). This endearing stratagem fails, but when he abruptly "accost[s]" her to take his leave, saying "there is nothing worth my staying for," she is delighted by his mood and turns to practical thoughts: "how was such jealousy to be quieted? How was the truth to reach him? How, in all the peculiar disadvantages of their respective situations, would he ever learn her real sentiments?" (20:191).

These disadvantages are of course mainly social ones. Anne is staying with Sir Walter and Elizabeth, who opposed her earlier involvement with him and who, though now not unreceptive to a handsome man with £25,000, still are a problem—could any sensible suitor stomach such in-laws? The conventions of their class, and the public conviviality of a popular resort like Bath, almost rule out the privacy that lovers need for settling things. And they both are reticent people, whose good breeding, self-respect, and past hurts discourage impetuous avowals of love. But Anne finds acceptable ways, at least, of putting herself more within reach. When she calls on the newly arrived Musgroves at their hotel, another visitor, Wentworth, contrives to approach her without quite seeming to, and she responds warmly:

> Captain Wentworth left his seat, and walked to the fire-place; probably for the sake of walking away from it soon afterwards, and taking a station, with less bare-faced design, by Anne.
>
> "You have not been long enough in Bath," said he, to enjoy the evening parties of the place."
>
> "Oh! no. The usual character of them has nothing for me. I am no card-player."
>
> "You were not formerly, I know. You did not use to like cards; but time makes many changes."
>
> "I am not yet so much changed," cried Anne, and stopped, fearing she hardly knew what misconstruction. After waiting a few moments he said—and as if it were the result of immediate feeling—"It is a period, indeed! Eight years and a half is a period!" (22:225)

Probably she fears both misconstruction and accurate construal—her words are inviting even if her motive is not to invite—but her great answer to "so altered he should not have known you" lets him show that he knows exactly how long ago they first met.

The romance plot conquers its social impediments in the brilliant chapter 23 of *Persuasion*, the genesis of which is suggestive. The published chapters 22 and 23 replaced a single, much briefer one which survives in a manuscript first printed in the *Memoir* by Austen's nephew J. E. Leigh-Austen (1871). There, after hearing Mrs. Smith's revelations about Mr. Elliot, Anne meets Admiral

Croft in the street, is brought home by him on a pretext, and finds Wentworth there. When his wily in-law leaves them alone, Wentworth determines that Anne is not engaged to her cousin, avows his love, and is instantly accepted. Austen radically reworked this clumsy dénouement for publication. In the wholly new chapter 22 the Musgroves arrive with word of Louisa's unexpected betrothal to Benwick, and Anne makes her great declaration that she is not yet so much changed; in chapter 23 Wentworth proposes in a different place and a way much better in tune with the book as a whole, before the manuscript version resumes with the lovers' exquisite "re-union"—now playfully set in Bath's Union-street—which fuses past, present, and future by preparing for "the present hour . . . all the immortality which the happiest recollections of their own future lives could bestow" (23:240).

As chapter 23 begins, Anne arrives at the White Hart to find two conversations in progress, Mrs. Musgrove with Mrs. Croft and Wentworth with Harville. Though "outwardly composed," she again feels herself "plunged at once in . . . agitations" (23:229). Wentworth ends his conversation and begins to write a letter, "nearly turning his back on them all"; but the sociability he spurns is vigorously sustained by Mrs. Musgrove, who tells Mrs. Croft of Louisa's betrothal "in that inconvenient tone of voice which was perfectly audible while it pretended to be a whisper," so that Anne (and others) "could not avoid hearing" (23:230). And what follows hinges on the question of who hears what. Mrs. Musgrove's "powerful whisper" (23:230) is mentioned again, and both Anne and Wentworth hear Mrs. Croft's words about the unwisdom of marrying without an assured income:

> Anne found an unexpected interest here. She felt its application to herself . . . in a nervous thrill all over her, and at the same moment that her eyes instinctively glanced toward the distant table, Captain Wentworth's pen ceased to move, his head was raised, pausing, listening, and he turned round the next instant to give a look—one quick, conscious look at her. (23:231)

Though the women go on chatting, Anne once again reduces social sound to mere noise: she "heard nothing distinctly; it was only a buzz of words in her ear, her mind was in confusion" (23:231).

This aural rejection of the social is made physical when Harville beckons and she joins him "at the other end of the room from where the two ladies were sitting, and though nearer to Captain Wentworth's table, not very near" (23:231–232). This last seems to be her own estimate of a distance she's acutely aware of, and one that soon becomes crucial. She is now closer to him than were the women he just overheard, but her chat with Harville begins quietly, and she may reasonably suppose that it will carry less far than a powerful whisper does. They soon turn from Benwick's recovery from grief to the larger topic of the relative constancy of men's and women's love. Anne claims greater durability for the latter in a "low" (23:232) voice, but when "a slight noise called their attention to Captain Wentworth's hitherto perfectly quiet division of the room" and she sees that "his pen had fallen down," she's "startled at finding him nearer than she had supposed" and half suspects that he has been "striving to catch sounds, which yet she did not think he could have caught" (23:233–234).

The writing makes it impossible to impute a clear motive to Anne here, and for good reason. No woman of her delicacy could intend to be overheard in such a situation; yet friendship requires her to speak candidly to Harville, and her growing readiness to act in her own interest allows at least a suspicion that, if she doesn't exactly mean to be overheard, she may not mind if she is. Harville lowers his own voice as he half-teasingly mentions literature's near unanimity about women's fickleness, though admitting that the books were "all written by men." Her response points inescapably toward the present figure of Wentworth: "Men have had every advantage of us in telling their own story. . . . [The] pen has been in their hands" (23:234). And Austen clearly is amusing herself with what has not yet been revealed to Anne and the reader, that Wentworth is indeed writing his own story, his avowal of restored love; and of course what she, the author, is writing is a book, for once by a woman, about female constancy.

Anne and Harville go on more loudly—thrice we hear that one of them "cried" rather than spoke—and she again risks impropriety in "eagerly" allowing that men too may be constant, while adding that "All the privilege I claim for my own sex (it is not a very enviable one, you need not covet it) is that of loving longest, when existence or when hope is gone" (23:235). At this point Wentworth seals up his letter with a "hurried, agitated air," abruptly goes out, returns to draw another letter from the papers on his table, and covertly hands it to Anne "with eyes of glowing entreaty" (23:236).

This is, of course, his renewed offer of himself, encouraged by what he has heard: "I can listen no longer in silence," writes the captain of HMS *Laconia*, "I must speak to you by such means as are within my reach. You pierce my soul. I am half agony, half hope" (23:237). The problem of means is important, as the manuscript proposal scene made almost melodramatically clear: "the door was closed, and the moment arrived in which Anne was alone with Capt. W——" (23:261). The plain fact is that they have never been alone together since his return. Their every encounter has been in the company, usually intrusive or distracting, of others; if they have sometimes spoken briefly out of the hearing of observers, they have always been observed. Mr. Darcy's proposal to Elizabeth astonishes everyone; Emma and Fanny Price have been intimate friends of their eventual husbands for so long that romance comes almost unnoticed, at least by others. But Wentworth's earlier offer was known to Sir Walter, Elizabeth, and Lady Russell, if seldom discussed. "Society" impedes these lovers; in the name of prudence it blocked their first romance, and now it hems them in with other people's purposes.

Society in *Persuasion*, while an obstacle to love, does remain a (possible) medium for its (oblique) expression. Unspoken feeling gets a conventionally sentimental primacy over language in the manuscript, where betrothal requires only a private exchange of looks—"It was a silent, but a very powerful Dialogue;—on his side, Supplication, on her's acceptance"—before he takes her hand and descends into the banality of spoken love: "'Anne, my own dear Anne!'" (23:263). They only need to *be* there—in no sense do they make their happiness by what they do or say. In the richly dramatized new Chapter 23, however, even movement—Wentworth away from Harville and Anne from the older women—shows feeling keeping its distance from what is merely social. Or at best, society inadvertently provides feeling with communicative materials. Mrs. Musgrove in her gracelessness finds just the right topic for the lovers to listen in on, and Harville's grief for his sister offers language Anne can use, consciously or not, to tell Wentworth most of what he needs to know about her feelings.

But the social medium loses its importance once she can literally read his sentiments, and the letter she reads them in identifies reading as what is needed: "Have you not seen this? Can you fail to have understood my wishes?—I had not waited even these ten days, could I have read your feelings, as I think you must have penetrated mine. I can hardly write. I am every instant hearing something which overpowers me" (23:237). He calls her the better reader, and "overpowers" must make gratifying reading, remembering what his words so often did to her earlier. And her reading finally resolves the issues the book's language of feeling has raised:

> Such a letter was not to be soon recovered from. Half an hour's solitude and reflection might have tranquillized her; but the ten minutes only, which now passed before she was interrupted, with all the restraints of her situation, could do nothing towards tranquillity. Every moment rather brought fresh agitation. It was an overpowering happiness. (23:238)

The terms of illness and infirmity—"recovered," "tranquillized"—are put aside; social "restraints" remain but are not decisive; if he was overpowered by her words to Harville, she is now overpowered by what his words bring her, an "agitation" that no longer resists happiness but becomes its synonym.

What happiness has overpowered is, I suppose, the socially-born idea that *not* to trust and express one's deepest feelings makes things more comfortable for everyone, oneself included. Words like "solitude and reflection" and "tranquillity" look back both sympathetically and teasingly to Anne's old emotional habits, and their cause. A. Walton Litz observes that in *Persuasion* "the sense of community has disappeared, and the heroine finds herself terribly alone."[11] This should not be overstated: Anne's is not the radical isolation of Huck Finn ("I felt so lonesome I most wished I was dead"), and in her new happiness she is in a way *less* autonomous than she was in her insulated spinsterhood, before Wentworth's return. At the end Austen devises a new society for Anne, composed of her husband, his naval friends, Lady Russell, and Mrs. Smith. But it's a pitifully small and narrow one, as societies go; of its members only Wentworth seems humanly complete, and, considering his vocation, Anne has in store the protracted loneliness and anxiety that navy families like the Austens knew all about.

Traditional society itself seems to be dissolving in the book. The coherence of family and inherited privilege are dying out: Sir Walter's descendants will be Musgroves and (one hopes) Wentworths, and even should his name and title survive, in the fruits of some possible union of unworthies like Mr. Elliot and Mrs. Clay, no later Elliot of Kellynch-hall will carry Sir Walter's blood. However little we or Austen may regret the passing of Sir Walter and his ilk, the regulative and instructive powers of tradition do have their value, and Anne, unlike Austen's other heroines, learns little about style or social sympathy from her experiences, if only because she has so little left to learn. She finds her happiness at the White Hart by venturing into areas of consciousness where desire may be gratified without clear reference to what society calls proper. Austen will not tell us how to respond, and the effect is to enlarge and mystify ethical and moral issues that seem clear enough in *Pride and Prejudice* and *Emma*, and perhaps too clear in *Mansfield Park*. The "message" of *Persuasion* may be only that it is good to have feelings and obey most of them, especially as you grow older and the options narrow.

Part of Anne's fate, finally, is to have no natural family and few friends outside marriage, but there are compensations. The Wentworths will be quite well off, certainly.[12] As a post captain he will (if he survives) become an admiral through mere seniority, with no damned nonsense about merit; and his abilities, with luck and political interest, could bring a title —Austen's sailor brothers both became admirals, and one, Sir Francis, died (at ninety-three) as Senior Admiral of the Fleet. But money and honors are not everything, as Mary Musgrove reflects with her usual ruthlessness: "Anne had no Uppercross-hall before her, no landed estate, no headship of a family; and if they could but keep Captain Wentworth from being made a baronet, she would not change situations with Anne" (24:250). The other Austen heroines find love and security within the established order, marrying rich landowners of old stock and clerics from prosperous families. Though Anne gets love and money, she has literally no place to *go* at the end—no Pemberley or Donwell or Delaford, no Woodston or Mansfield Parsonage. The good life of personal happiness is now unlocated, without communal or institutional authentication.[13]

If Anne doesn't exactly light out for the Territory, she does escape from something inimical to life that infects most other people in the book, even the good ones. This menace emerges strikingly toward the end, when Lady Russell urges her to consider marrying Mr. Elliot, for practical reasons resembling those with which she once persuaded her to refuse Wentworth. Anne's brief but strong attraction to the idea takes the eerie imaginative form of becoming her own dead mother, who, we remember, was "not the very happiest being in the world" (1:4) in her own marriage:

> Anne was obliged to turn away, to rise, to walk to a distant table, and,
> leaning there in pretended employment, try to subdue the feelings this
> picture excited. For a few moments her imagination and her heart were
> bewitched. The idea of becoming what her mother had been; of having
> the precious name of "Lady Elliot" first revived in herself; of being
> restored to Kellynch, calling it her home again, her home for ever,
> was a charm which she could not immediately resist. (17:160)

With "her home *for ever*" romance turns just a little sinister and Gothic, but the point is subtler. She has been learning to trust feeling, but "revived" and "restored" here imply something like black magic, a deadly pseudo-life and not a vital happiness. To regain Kellynch, to become Lady Elliot, would again trap her in the past, in a social destiny antipathetic to life, even if the life she gains brings its own kind of risks.

Austen's language for Anne Elliot's sense of things shows that in *Persuasion* "society" is not some ponderous, empty abstraction but a complex apprehension of what—in traditional institutions, the wills of other people, or one's own unexamined hopes for comfort and safety—impedes the admittedly dangerous choice of freedom. The distaste of Emerson, James, and Twain for Austen's novels in general may need answering in other terms, but they might at least have noticed that her last one sees society in ways that surprisingly resemble their own.

### Notes

I owe thanks to William Dowling, William Galperin, and Bridget Gellert Lyons for comments on my essay that helped improve it.

1. Reuben A. Brower and Richard Poirier, eds., *In Defense of Reading* (New York: Dutton, 1962), 282–309; an expanded version appears as chapter 4 of *A World Elsewhere*. Quotations from *Persuasion*, identified in the text by chapter and page number, are from *The Novels of Jane Austen*, ed. R. W. Chapman, 3rd ed., rev. (Oxford: Oxford University Press, 1969), vol. 5. In identifying chapters I follow the modern practice of consecutive numbering, without regard to the original two-volume format, which Chapman preserves; thus my chapter 13 = the first chapter of Chapman's second volume, and so on.

2. These, for example: "In the day of Mark of Twain there is no harm in being reminded that the absence of drollery may, at a stretch, be compensated by the presence of sublimity" (review of David Masson, *Three Devils*, 1875); "The confession of an insensibility ranging from Shelley to Dickens and from Dante to Miss Austen and taking Don Quixote and Aristophanes on the way, is a large allowance to have to make for a man of letters. . . . The truth was that, sparely constructed as he was and formed not wastefully, not with material left over, as it were, for a special function, there were certain chords in Emerson that did not vibrate at all" (review of J. E. Cabot, *Life of Emerson*, 1887). Both reviews are in Henry James, *Literary Criticism: Essays, American and English Writers*, ed. Leon Edel (New York: The Library of America, 1984).

3. Brower and Poirier, eds., *In Defense of Reading*, 285.

4. Brower and Poirier, eds., *In Defense of Reading*, 287.

5. Marvin Mudrick, *Jane Austen: Irony as Defense and Discovery* (Princeton: Princeton University Press, 1952), 218.

6. In 1793 Arthur Wesley, age twenty-four, a well-born but impecunious soldier, offered marriage to Kitty Pakenham, twenty, the second daughter of an Irish baron, Lord Longford. She was pretty, bookish, retiring, and sweet-tempered; her family's doubts about his prospects led her to refuse him, but she married no one else. On his return to England in 1805, now Major-General Sir Arthur Wellesley, KB, MP, and enriched by his great victories in India, friends of Kitty's urged him to try again, which he did, by letter. She hesitantly accepted, also by letter, warning that "in so many years I may be much more changed than I myself am conscious of." (When he finally saw her, shortly before the wedding, he whispered to his brother: "She has grown ugly, by Jove!")

   Their story was widely known and relished; Queen Charlotte questioned Kitty about it when she was presented at Court, and it was thought to have inspired Tom Moore's "Believe me, if all those endearing young charms." I feel sure that Austen remembered it when writing *Persuasion*, in the year after Waterloo. Sadly, the marriage was a disaster, with Kitty's social and domestic incompetence and the Duke's womanizing endlessly nourishing each other. See Elizabeth Longford, *Wellington: The Years of the Sword* (New York: Harper and Row, 1969), 28–34, 103–124.

7. It seems very like Sir Walter to have named his daughters after the (then) most recent Queens Regnant; his still-born son (1:3), however, would doubtless have been called "Walter" had he survived.

8. The newer sense of "romance" as "love affair"—so new as to have been ignored by the *OED* as late as 1909—seems to stir in Austen's remark that Anne, having "been forced into prudence in her youth, . . . learned romance as she grew older" (4:30), as it does in *Pride and Prejudice* when Charlotte Lucas explains why she will marry Mr. Collins: "'I am not romantic, you know.'"

9. The unsigned "Biographical Notice of the Author" (by her brother Henry) in the posthumous first edition of *Northanger Abbey* and *Persuasion* (1818) observed that "At a very early age she was enamoured of Gilpin on the Picturesque."

10. Compare Aeneas's encouragement of his dejected comrades, *Aeneid* 1.203: *forsan et haec olim meminisse iuvabit* ("Perhaps even this will some day give pleasure to remember"). Writing to James Stanier Clarke (11 Dec 1815) Austen called herself "a woman who . . . knows only her mother tongue, and has read very little in that." But Clarke was a pompous ass, and she was surely putting him on; it would be very surprising if she had not read at least the first book of the *Aeneid* in translation.

11. A. Walton Litz, *Jane Austen* (New York: Oxford University Press, 1965), 153.

12. Wentworth's prize-money, his pay, and the £10,000 due to Anne from her mother's marriage settlement should yield about £2000 a year, or what the Bennet family in *Pride and Prejudice* lives on very nicely indeed.

13. See Alistair Duckworth, *The Improvement of the Estate* (Baltimore: Johns Hopkins Press, 1971) for conclusions about the book similar to mine, though quite differently reached.

# CHAPTER 9

# Robert Frost and the Renewal of Birds

## JOHN HOLLANDER

*M*ythologizing a construction of nature's—an animal, plant, geological formation, moment of process—could be seen both as a desecration and a celebration of pragmatically considered fact. When this goes on in poetry—what Frost called "the renewal of words for ever and ever"—it is accompanied and invigorated by a reciprocal mythologizing, as it were, of the very words used in the poetic process.[1] Literature is full of purely mythological, mostly composite, creatures—phoenix, unicorn, basilisk, chimera, hydra, centaur—as nature is even more full of creatures totally innocent of interpretation—woodchuck, anteater, turbot, Shetland pony, jellyfish, quail.

But then there are the fallen creatures—lion, eagle, ant, grasshopper, barracuda, fox, hyena—who have been infected with signification from Aesop on. It is one of the tasks of poetry to keep renewing the taxonomic class of such creatures, by luring them, unwittingly, into a cage of trope (which of course, they are not aware of inhabiting). Such new reconstructions of animals are almost a post-romantic cottage industry, even as the rehearsal again and again of the traditional ones characterized pre-romantic emblematic poetry. Significant emblematic readings of previously unread creatures can do the work of reinventing them—I think of Oliver Wendell Holmes's chambered nautilus, for example, as well as animals of Baudelaire and Rilke. I want to reconsider in these pages a well-known instance of such reconstruction in the case of Frost's oven bird. And it is in no way to compromise the kind of somewhat old-fashioned reading of the poem I intend to give (in the words of Reuben Brower quoted by Poirier, "what is it like to read 'The Oven Bird'") that I shall explore the literary environment of poetic ornithology which Frost's poem partly exemplifies and partly rejects.[2]

North American poetry has no living nightingales or skylarks upon which to descant, observe, meditate, or preach. Our literature inherited a museum of textual ones, from Ovid's Philomela through Milton's almost personally emblematic nightingale, through the more naturalized bird of Coleridge's conversation poem, "The Nightingale," and on to Keats's.[3] John Crowe Ransom's account is more mythographic than ornithological:

> Not to these shores she came! this other Thrace,
> Environ barbarous to the royal Attic;
> How could her delicate dirge run democratic,
> Delivered in a cloudless, boundless public place
> To an inordinate race?[4]

And for the younger T. S. Eliot, the fallen form of the nightingale singing in the royal Attic ("once within the bloody wood / When Agamemnon cried aloud") in modernity can only shit on an allusively invoked sequence of American failures, letting "their liquid siftings fall / To stain the stiff, dishonored shroud," and thereby not only on the "dim, dishonored brow" of Whittier's treacherous "Ichabod," but on morally purposeful poetry itself.

A glance at the aetiology of the poetic bird would certainly take in the old, blind Milton's later nightingale (not his youthful question-raiser, of whom more later on), who "sings darkling" at the beginning of the third book of *Paradise Lost*. It is answered by Keats ("darkling, I listen") in his nightingale poem. Shelley's skylark, Blake's lark, George Meredith's wonderful "The Lark Ascending" are all daylight's reciprocal poetical birds and poetical surrogates. Even Yeats's aggressively unnatural clockwork golden bird in "Sailing to Byzantium" partakes of the lark-nightingale tradition. But in the transatlantic new world, skylarkless and unnightingaled, another mythologized bird replaced them. There is a sequence of poems—from Richard Lewis's remarkable poem of the 1740s, through those of Joseph Rodman Drake, Sidney Lanier and Walt Whitman—which re-trope the skylark-nightingale for American poetry as the mockingbird.

Lewis's "A Journey from Patapsko to Annapolis," telling in Augustan couplets, but from a Thomsonian perspective, of a trip along the Maryland coast in the 1730s, describes an encounter with a mockingbird. It so allegorizes the creature as the voice of the new-old American Imagination that—regardless of the poem itself remaining largely in oblivion until this century—never again would mockingbirds' song be the same. The passage is splendid enough to quote entire here:

> But what is *He* who, perched above the rest
> Pours out such various Music from his Breast!
> His Breast whose Plumes a cheerful white display,
> His quiv'ring Wings are dress'd in sober Grey.
> Sure, all the *Muses,* this their Bird inspire!
> And *He*, alone is equal to the Choir

Of warbling Songsters who around him play,
While, Echo like, *He* answers every lay.
The chirping *Lark* now sings with sprightly Note,
Responsive to her Strain *He* shapes his Throat:
Now the poor widow'd *Turtle* wails her Mate,
While in soft Sounds he cooes to mourn his Fate.
O sweet Musician, thou dost far excell
The soothing Song of pleasing *Philomel*;
Sweet is her Song, but in few Notes confin'd
But thine, thou *Mimic* of the feath'ry Kind,
Runs through all Notes!—*Thou* only knowst them *All*,
At once the *Copy,—and th'Original.*[5]

It is not only the anticipation both of Thoreau's echo that is "to some extent, an original sound" and of Frost's "counter-love, original response" in "The Most of It" that is slightly uncanny here.[6] It is almost as if a transcendence of limitation in genres, modes, conventions, styles—the belated not as incapacitated but inspired by its knowledge of what preceded it—were being embodied in an attendant of the Muse of the New.

Lewis's poem lays the ground for what will be a subsequent tradition. Joseph Rodman Drake's claim in "The Mocking-Bird" (published 1812) for the bird as poet is a bit more plonkingly expository. Twenty-three octosyllabic couplets of description catalogue—with less poetic glossing than Lewis—the repertoire (the voices of jay, quail, sparrow, cat-bird, red-bird, robin, black-bird, blue-bird, swallow, lark) of a mockingbird encountered on a May morning walk he admittedly moralizes:

In this bird can fancy trace
An emblem of the rhyming race.
Ere with heaven's immortal fire
Loud they strike the quivering wire . . .
Soft and low each note they sing,
Soft they try each varied string . . .[7]

Virgil, Milton, Shakespeare, Scott, Pope, Homer and—last and surely least—Campbell, are catalogued in that order as reciprocals of the birds: as Mockingbird sums up over these, so Poet sums up over those.

The interesting southern poet, Richard Henry Wilde (1789–1847), refigures the mockingbird in his sonnet, not as the fruitfully problematic American Originality, like Lewis, but as a kind of composite clown, sometimes a fellow of infinite jest, sometimes "the melancholy Jaques":

Wit, sophist, songster, Yorick of thy tribe,
Thou sportive satirist of Nature's school,
To thee the palm of scoffing we ascribe,
Arch mocker and mad abbot of misrule![8]

In effect, the bird's "mocking" has been construed not in its proper (but today, less common) sense of imitating, but as deriding: he is a satirist, rather than an allusive singer. But by and large, the mockingbird of subsequent southern tradition partakes of the sentimental souvenir in the refrain of Stephen Foster's song (*"Listen to the mock-ing-bird, Listen to the mock-ing-bird"*). Sidney Lanier's elevated singer perches "Superb and sole upon a plumèd spray"; his range is more than, in previous instances, summary, for "Whate'er birds did or dreamed, this bird could say." But Lanier's "The Mocking Bird" ends with a pseudo-riddle; the bird having gobbled up a grasshopper, the sonnet weakly inquires "How may the death of that dull insect be / The life of yon trim Shakspere on the tree?"[9] While Shakespeare can be considered as being legitimately adduced (given that the bird can say what was both done and dreamed), the fairly empty question embraces what isn't much of a paradox after all.

The greatest and most poetically powerful mockingbird, the male of the pair of "feather'd guests from Alabama," is Whitman's "singer solitary, projecting me," the bird singing of its loss to the "outsetting bard," to the "undertone" of the sea, "the savage old mother incessantly crying." The transumption, in "Out of the Cradle Endlessly Rocking," of Keatsian and Shelleyan nightingale and skylark, and of earlier poetic mockingbird alike, is a far more profound matter than the mere Americanization of English poetic tradition. The bird is shaken loose from even contingent personification, and extended another, a new, kind of personhood, in the first place. And given the role of the sea ("the savage old mother incessantly crying") in this great exemplar of what Harold Bloom has called Whitman's "shore odes," the relations of bird, boy, and their crucial occasions (of personal loss and poetic translation of birdsong) are determined by the liminal condition of the sea-shore. "Darkling," says Keats of his nightingale's song, "I listen"; we might paraphrase Whitman's remembered boy as implying that "Sea-ing, I listened." The mockingbird here is a truly "original response" to a convention which it outdoes as it seems to ignore. Like Whitman's self-portrait in *Song of Myself* 4, his fiction is "Both in and out of the game [of convention], and watching and wondering at it."

On the other hand, Richard Hovey's revisionist mockingbird (1896) is well on his way to modernist demystification; he promises to *"make it all clear"* saying *"I will let you know / Where the footfalls go / That through the thicket and over the hill / Allure, allure."* But the proto-modern bird—for whom, probably, the creature of nineteenth-century tradition might as well be a troped-out European nightingale—never delivers on this, as the speaker of this brief lyric concludes "But he will not tell, he will not tell, / For all he promises so well."[10]

It was to the received avian agenda in general that modern poetry felt unable to subscribe. Richard Wilbur spoke for all his twentieth-century precursors in the early 1950s, I believe, in "All These Birds" that

> Hawk or heavenly lark or heard-of nightingale
> Perform upon the kitestrings of our sight
> In a false distance . . . the day and night
> Are full of winged words
>                     gone rather stale
>     That nothing is so worn
>     As Philomel's bosom-thorn . . .

But Wilbur's late-modernist plea for a powerful ornithology to replace empty mythological clichés goes beyond its own strong demands for a demythologizing of what are, imaginatively speaking, stuffed owls. It pleads for new tropes of birdhood and avian particularity by showing both the limits and the consequent utility of a biological reductionism:

>     Let us, with glass or gun,
> Watch (from our clever blinds) the monsters of the sky
>     Dwindle to habit, habitat and song,
>     And tell the imagination it is wrong
>     Till, lest it be undone
>                     it spin a lie
>     So fresh, so pure, so rare
>     As to possess the air.[11]

For modernity, thrushes are previously unmystified songbirds that can be more than part of what Wordsworth in the famous lines from *The Recluse* calls "A history only of departed things / Or a mere fiction of what never was" (803–804), and Thomas Hardy's great poem of half-hearted—but at least, half-hearted—hurrah for the commencement of the twentieth century propounds a scruffy old thrush as prophetic singer. The adjective in the title of the "The Darkling Thrush" manifests the revisionary relation of the bird in the poem to the "darkling" poet-nightingales of Milton and Keats.

Then, too, there is Whitman's other singer, the hermit-thrush of "When Lilacs Last in the Door-Yard Bloom'd," who, along with those same lilacs, flies into *The Waste Land* to provide that dread vision's one moment of unironized melodic surcease. Whitman had not heard a hermit-thrush (a somewhat rare bird), but learned of it from John Burroughs. Moreover, he mistakenly put him among conifers (where the bird will not be found in the eastern United States), singing "Limitless out of the dusk, out of the cedars and pines." Eliot, whose hermit-thrush clearly sang to him from Whitman's pages, has him singing "in the pine trees."

I should guess that Robert Frost, knowing well of *The Waste Land* in 1941, and in better knowledge of thrushes and where and when they sing, sets up in "Come In" a literary thrush singing out of the pillared, dark wood. This is a wood possibly of classical tragedy, possibly even—as we shall see—of high modernism; but the "thrush music" is a call that must be evaded, even by acknowledging that a bird can be said to "sing" perhaps, yet not legitimately to

invite (or, one supposes, to promise, swear, or to commit any illocutionary act).
By suggesting that the darkening of evening is more than merely diurnal—and,
consequently, that the "west" is something like a Spenglerian Abendland—the
stakes are made rather high:

> The last of the light of the sun
> That had died in the west
> Still lived for one song more
> In a thrush's breast.

> Far in the pillared dark
> Thrush music went—
> Almost like a call to come in
> To the dark and lament.[12]

In Frost's poem, the seemingly audible vocation from the wood is rejected
in favor of a higher, totally silent call:

> But no, I was out for stars:
> I would not come in.
> I meant not even if asked,
> And I hadn't been.

(There is a price to be paid for the coyness of the acknowledgment in the last
two lines—I can almost hear Emerson retorting, from one part of his page, "Of
course you'd been asked! And you won't be again!" and, from another part of
that same page, "Of course you hadn't, and don't make such a fuss about it!")

But perhaps the essential modern rejection of a trope of birdsong is
Wallace Stevens's, in "Autumn Refrain," his near-sonnet of 1931—ten years
earlier than "Come In." In this poem (about not being able to write anything
for two years), grackles lately blattering recall to him the whole avian tradition,
and its perhaps empty literariness:

> The yellow moon of words about the nightingale
> In measureless measures, not a bird for me
> But the name of a bird and the name of a nameless air
> I have never—shall never hear . . .[13]

and he opts out of all of it: the typically bivalent phrase "the evasions of the nightingale" refers both to evading the poetic nightingale issue and what said
nightingale issue itself evades.

The poem ultimately finds, as Harold Bloom suggests, some difficult but
important "residuum" in the desolate sound of the grackles. There is a great
deal to be said of the Stevensian distrust of bird-song, but it is now time to turn
to my central text, Frost's powerful and problematic contribution to poetic
ornithology, the—in this case, accepted—thrush of "The Oven Bird." The poem
invoking it negotiates a remarkable course between a rhetoric of certainty about
what a bird is singing/saying/doing, and a strong inner sense of its "evasions."

And it maintains a very un-Stevensian, albeit parabolic, awareness of natural fact.

First, though, the unpoetic ornithology: *Seiurus aurocapillus*, a ground-walking warbler, is common in deciduous woods; it builds a domed nest on the ground and sings from an exposed perch on the understory. That an American poem addressing—or addressing itself to—this thrush-like bird might consider its ground-built, oven-shaped nest, would seem obvious, with interpretations of some sort of pragmatical sublime, being well-grounded instead of lofty, immediately offering themselves. But the poem we are to consider does not.

> The Oven Bird
>
> There is a singer everyone has heard,
> Loud, a mid-summer and a mid-wood bird
> Who makes the solid tree trunks sound again.
> He says that leaves are old, and that for flowers,
> Mid-summer is to spring as one to ten.
> He says the early petal-fall is past
> When pear and cherry bloom went down in showers
> On sunny days a moment overcast;
> And comes that other fall we name the fall.
> He says the highway dust is over all.
> The bird would cease and be as other birds
> But that he knows in singing not to sing.
> The question that he frames in all but words
> Is what to make of a diminished thing.[14]

Robert Frost's sonnet was started in New Hampshire around 1906 but probably finished in England around 1914, far from the shared habitat of bird and poet. Its ending leaves us with a kind of riddle. The opening puzzles us also, slightly, but in a different way: sonnets don't start out with couplets, unless they intend to continue—and as they rarely do—with six more of them. But both octave and sestet of this one are initiated by couplets, and in the latter instance, somewhat strangely for other reasons as well. From the outset, too, we notice at once how casual and how problematic its rhetoric is. "A singer *everyone* has heard?"—come now, people in London who have no more heard that singer than a New Englander could hear a nightingale? No: this is the conventional palaver of nature-writing, of a newspaper *feuilleton* of the sort that you might still find in a rural newspaper in England (or, more likely, being sent up in a Monty Python routine). But the low-literary, prosaic tone is modulated with a jolt, as the second line declares its ulterior agenda, with a "**Loud**, a mid-**summ**er and a **mid**-*wood* **bird**": because of the contrastive stress marking the new coinage "mid-wood," the spatial reciprocal of the ordinary, temporal "mid-summer," the line ends with three stresses (you might call it two overlapping spondees), confirming the opening, intrusive, almost self-descriptive, "Loud."

The bird "makes the solid tree trunks sound again," but at a first reading this always itself sounds strange. It is not just the densely alliterative pattern, first pointed out by Reuben Brower. "Sound again"—have they been unsound? No, not Germanic "sound" (Modern German *gesund*) but French and Latin sonorous "sound"; still, why do we pause momentarily? Do we mistake this bird for a kind of woodpecker, hitting the trunks directly, and thus making them less *gesund* as they make them resound? But it is this purely English and non-Latin way of putting *resound* that then allows the matter of an echo of a prior sounding—that of the earlier—and perhaps for this poem, ordinary and, despite literary cliché, unpoetic—spring birds, since silent.

Then comes the first of the three reiterated assertions of his asserting: "He says . . ."; it will be apparent later why it is not the seventeenth/ eighteenth-century locution, the transitive "he sings," or its version in the nineteenth century and later, "he sings of [whatever it is]" etc. What "He says" first is hardly celebratory, but pragmatically observational quite this side of sounding dirge-like.

The next thing he says is more interpretive, at first reminding us of the dropping of spring blossoms, and of how we tend to read these as nothing more dire than the end of a particularly gorgeous overture or prelude, but then letting the resonance of the term "petal-fall" linger on. As if to make us think, "Yes, they do fall, don't they. . . ." We half notice, too, the phonological patterning here, in which one dactylic foot embracing a hyphenated compound is echoed by another on another (unhyphenated) one: ". . . early [**petal**-fall] is past / When pear and [**cherry** bloom]. . . ." But woven across this is an alliterative pattern, in which **petal/past/pear** enact a different kind of connection, followed by the analogous but more potently expressive assonance of "went **down** in **showers**". Yet this line is not end-stopped here, but flows into the phonologically plain "On sunny days a moment overcast." But there is another mode of resonance at work, one of word rather than of word-sound. There is a subtle aroma of nuance here: the leaves are cast under, in—and for—a moment, even as the sky is momentarily overcast; the point isn't loudly made nor brandished triumphantly, but allowed wonderfully to happen.

But then things become problematic again. *Who* says "And comes that other fall we name the fall"? This line is all the more complex and problematic here because it initiates the sestet, and we want the full stop at the end to be a comma, as if to say "When fall—that other fall—comes, he says [with respect to that] that the highway dust is covering everything." The normal grammar would be that of "come the fall" ("come Sunday," etc.); the present third-person singular verb form here suggests a counter-thrusting inversion ("And [then] comes that other fall . . . etc."). But the first reading would also reaffirm syntactically a linkage that the couplet-rhyme (again, in an anomalous place for a sonnet) is implying. Yet the couplet is broken. And we are reminded by the disjunction that the covering of highway-dust—the stasis in between petal-fall which initiates fullness of leaf, and leaf-fall which initiates bareness of branch—is midsummer stuff, and we can't have the syntax the way we'd like to. As for the coming of the *real* fall (the early "petal fall" is the "other")—we'd needed the oven bird to point out to us that it was a version of the primary one, a shadowy type of the truth of autumn. And, by Miltonic extension, the autumnal "fall" as type of the fall from Paradise, the Original one we name The Fall, which brought about the remodelling of Paradise into Nature, fracturing spring from fall, promise from conditional fulfillment.

Relations between literal and figurative falling are made even more interesting by the fact that in the romance part of English, "cause" and "case" are based ultimately on *cadere*, as in the Germanic part we still have residues of the earlier usage "it fell . . ." for "it happened." There are all those other falls, too. (I'm not sure whether the poem's relative reticence on this question keeps them at a safe distance or not—or is there any safe distance from The Fall?) Poirier remarks of this moment in the poem that "any falling—of leaves, of snow, of man . . . can be redeemed by loving, and the sign of this redemption is, for Frost, the sound of the voice working within the sounds of poetry."[15] Certainly, the cadential full stop at the end of this line makes us momentarily more aware of the working of the poet's voice. But in any case, the peculiar one-line sentence, which makes us keep wanting to open it out into a dependent clause and a full couplet with a comma, gives us meditative pause. Perhaps it works as something of a springboard *pour mieux sauter* into a final quatrain which, in sonnet form, can seem itself to initiate a moment of (at least, structural) renewal.

Some of that quatrain's complexity emerges in a straightforward paradox: what does it mean *not* to sing in singing?[16] Well, if the "singing" birds do herald and celebrate spring and the morning—or, as with swallows, fill the sky with skitterish evening hymns—then the oven bird's repeated disyllabic utterance is not that. "He says," "he says," "he says," "he knows" "he frames" (and here, another kind of figurativeness in the trope of material construction); we call the sounds birds make singing, but this bird demands that we suspend the overtones of the word "sing." His are not songs, but propositions: the very subtle rhythm of the line makes this clear, for in order for the rhyming syllables to be sufficiently stressed, it must go not as "in singing **not** to sing," as the intoning of the paradox seems to demand, but rather "in singing not to **sing**"—not to be claimed by allegorizing human attention as music, but instead as speculative discourse.

By this point in the poem, the casual older fiction of bird song—like that of wind in the trees sighing, and brook babbling—cannot be acknowledged. So it is that he frames a question "in all but words," a formulation which is rhetorically quite reticent (birds don't *really* talk, of course but . . .). The very grammar of the phrase "knows in singing" is unusually resonant: (1) as has been suggested, the bird knows—while singing, not to "**sing**," but rather discursively to raise questions; (2) the bird knows not to sing (literally) in-and-by singing (figuratively); (3) knowing-in-singing: like Sidney's "loving in truth," a kind of knowing in singing? or as if singing were itself a kind of mental process here? In any event, this song is a matter of knowledge, not of charm, of sense making a claim on tra-la-la: I think here—regarding the issue, always crucial for Frost, of the sound of making sense—of how great jazz musicians would often play their purely instrumental solos to the words, singing the text (with a complex systems of rhythm all its own) internally, in order properly to inform the inventions of the melody alone. In the oven bird's case, perhaps, we implicitly reject "frames in all but music"—birds song being only figuratively that—and leap over any literal musical agenda even as a poet's "*cano*" means "I write."[17]

It could also be observed that this sonnet itself, like so many of the other poems in *Mountain Interval*, "knows in singing not to sing." This is not in the way of Yeats's "Words for Music Perhaps" (a phrase which in its way defines all lyric poetry in English from Wyatt and Surrey on); this is more of an implicit revisionary construction of the lyrical of high modernism, and may in some ways anticipate the rejection of the thrush's musical pseudo-invitation in "Come In."

Be that as may be, we come to the oven bird's question itself, which may indeed be two questions. Our colloquial phrase "to make [something] of X" can mean to reshape it, use it as material for some new Y, etc. But to ask "what do you make of X" means "how do you explain, analyze, interpret X?"—"What's with X?" These strangely paired meanings are those of *to construct*, and *to construe*. They both come from the same Latin verb (and are indeed, with unfortunate consequences about fifteen years ago, both designated by the same French word, *construire*). The first of the bird's implied questions, then, is that of what to do with something residual—in this case, summer, but by implication life itself: we are *nel mezzo del cammin* here—something diminished by half. How shall we live the rest of our summer?

The oven bird does not celebrate spring, whether cheerfully, or even problematically, like the cuckoo of *Love's Labors Lost*; it does not pierce the night, in cheerful lieu of illumination, like the winter owl paired with it at the end of that same play. It is neither skylark, singing invisibly at the height of the day, nor the alternatively invisible nightingale. It talks neither of beginnings nor endings, but of a time that is both, in a Janus-like July, looking back and forward at once to an original and a final fall. Mid-points are strange, and they tend not to generate the ceremonies that beginnings and endings do. Midsummer in England tends to mean the solstice, June 21 or thereabouts. But that is not what he celebrates. We tend to think of our Northeastern American "midsummer" as somewhere around July 30 or so, and this is the oven bird's time, a somewhat indiscernible *middle* (rather than a clearly marked *center*).

And thus the bird's other possible question points toward and away from this matter: "what to make of"—how to construe, understand, interpret, the residual. "Is the bottle of summer half full or half empty?"—the invitation to consider the question is not that of the ordinary, crackpot realist cynical put-down of epistemology. I think that the invited discourse on the question, and what it would mean about you and summer to answer it either way, would lie along a line of pragmatic approaches to questioning somewhere between William James and later Wittgenstein. Poirier looks at the question from the point of view of the imaginative energies it generates, referring to "the creative tension between a persistent rising and a natural falling—a poise of creativity in the face of threatened diminishments."[18]

Another way of putting this suggests that one of these diminishments might be thought of as that of the prior tradition itself—Richard Wilbur's "winged words / gone rather stale"; and in that kind of subsequent allegorizing that strong poems tend to exude, one thing to make of *that* diminished thing is, by means of newly animated words, "The Oven Bird" itself. And then, as is the case with very powerful and deep poetic ambiguities, the invitation extends to considering the relation between the two kinds of *making of*, between construing and constructing, in which representation is creation, and understandings are imagined: this relation is poetry's realm (as it may not be philosophy's, despite the woodpecker hammering at such a suggestion of the kind of institutional construing recently called deconstruction). And finally, we observe how the line itself ("what to make of a diminished thing") sings its way into the reader's attention with its assonantal *dimin*ished th*ing* that itself diminishes the accentual and thereby the rhetorical weight thrust upon the word "thing" by being put in terminal rhyming position (not "**dimin**ished thing" but "**dimin**ished **thing**").

The way in which the oven bird, "as other birds," too, got to speak, learned what we might call not his sing-song but his say-song—and his way of framing questions "in all but words"—is also part of Frost's concern. Virgil invents what Ruskin would call the pathetic fallacy in his very first eclogue, in which the shepherd Tityrus, *lentus in umbra*—at ease in the shade—*formosam resonare doces Amaryllida silvas*—teaches the woods to resound with the name of his girlfriend Amaryllis, and thereby teaching nature to talk poetically to us for the first time.[19]

Another one of Frost's great sonnets, "Never Again Would Birds' Song Be the Same," tells its own aetiological story of how birds got to talk, and it is worth considering here for a moment in its relation to the oven bird poem. (A much weaker earlier poem, "The Aim Was Song," propounds another version of such an aetiology.) That story involves the imprinting of a human "tone of meaning, but without the words" onto birds' song, an added "oversound" (perhaps as Frost's revision of the ambiguous post-Spenserian word "under-song").[20] The "He" of the opening line ("He would declare and could himself believe") frames the fiction that Eve's voice, "When call or laughter carried it aloft," added to previously unmeaning birdsong "Her tone of meaning but without the words." That "he" seems to be both Adam, or a poet (writing, and then possibly even "believing," his myth). The oven bird's question obviously comes along fairly late in the development of avian discourse. A linkage perhaps more than trivial with the earlier sonnet can be also found in the much more dramatic use of the broken—here, final—couplet. The poem looks at first to conclude with a "bottom line," as it were, the consequential reiteration of the title: "Never again would birds' song be the same." But then, after the full stop, comes the carefully intoned afterthought: "And to do that to birds was why she came" (leaving the implicit question "To do exactly *what* to birds, by the way? to teach them? infect them? trope them? what?") resonating after this second ending. Ultimately she made them into makers of what Poirier in another context calls signs that are "forever mixed into the wilderness of only possible meaningfulness."[21] In yet another major sonnet, "Design," there is a similarly broken final couplet that leaves a final implicit question hanging. In that poem it is effected by the slightly more melodramatic punctuation of a dash following a question mark pointing the last of three questions that comprise the sestet: "What but design of darkness to appall?— / If design govern in a thing so small."

I should like to return to one comment from the *Field Guide to North American Birds* that I omitted when referring to it earlier in this discussion. The oven bird's song is characterized as "a loud and clear *tea-cher* repeated about 10 times, louder and louder." (It has been argued that, since the oven bird, like many others, also produces a different, high-flying song for a time in spring, that the poem is either suppressing discussion of this with a rhetorical strategy of its own, or repressing it. I do not believe that either of these is the case, and that the lesser-known fact is not, in this instance to be considered as being deployed in the poem—either for the fact of early, youthful spring-song vs. sober, didactic middle-age, or, more complicatedly, for the fact of its being very little-known).[22] Like many good teachers of certain kinds, his lesson goes far beyond what "he says" into parable, and into questions about questioning. As a poetic fiction of a teaching bird, he seems to be a very guarded, transumptive revision of a particular earlier one, Wordsworth's throstle in "The Tables Turned":

> He, too, is no mean preacher;
> Come forth into the light of things,
> Let nature be your teacher.

The last of these lines is rather awkward in its sound: the near-rhyming, echoic relation of nature/teacher is so out of character for the language of poems from *Lyrical Ballads* like "We Are Seven," "Expostulation and Reply," and this one that it feels inadvertent and out of control. This awkwardness casts modern doubt on the authenticity of the quoted expostulation. Thus all birds, even pulpited ones, are not true teachers, and I must note in closing how Frost's bird again recalls a sub-tradition—but a less diminished one—of poems which consider not merely eloquent, but questioning birds. The young Milton's first sonnet was on the nightingale, and what to make of it: for the young, poetically ambitious, virginal poet, was the bird's song a call to attend to a muse or a lover? was it about sex or poetry? The poem ends with this question, the bird in question in this case involving Milton's nightingale knowing in singing not to say.[23]

This can also be a lighter matter, of course. There is something uncannily Frost-y about Christopher Pearse Cranch's "Bird Language" (from an 1875 collection), particularly at the opening:

One day in the bluest of summer weather,
    Sketching under a whispering oak,
I heard five bobolinks laughing together
    Over some ornithological joke.

What the fun was I couldn't discover
    Language of birds is a riddle on earth,
What could they find in whiteweed and clover
    To split their sides with such musical mirth?[24]

The "riddle on earth" seems at first here a social conundrum of the dinner-table sort, whose solution will elicit unaffected laughter but will open up no deeper riddles. But at the poem's conclusion, it becomes clear that the riddle is indeed a funny mystery of a sort:

Vain to conjecture the words they are singing;
    Only by tones can we follow the tune . . .

"By tones" allows of the paraphrase of birdsong by human musical constructs only, and not by discursive glossing. This is not Eve's "tone of meaning but without the words": inscribed in Cranch's bird language is at most natural laughter at the strivings of the pathetic fallacy in human interpreters.

In any event, birds seem to have learned to put questions—at any rhetorical level—fairly late in poetic history. Coleridge's almost hilariously fustian owlet Atheism (from "Fears in Solitude") "Sailing on obscene wings athwart the noon, / Drops its blue-fringèd lids, and holds them close, / And hooting at the glorious sun in heaven / Cries out 'Where is it?'" Conversely, the owl who thought he was God in one of James Thurber's *Fables for Our Time* is misconstrued as interrogating in only one of its three calls, "*Hoo*" [?]. Of more epistemological interest—and closer to those of the oven bird's concerns, are the "wakened birds" in Stevens's "Sunday Morning," who "Before they fly, test the reality / Of misty fields, by their sweet questionings."[25]

Frost's oven bird, then, is not a universal, but a local singer, framing a question of which you can make a number of things. He is not, like Minerva's owl, an emblem of wisdom, but rather an instance of acquiring wisdom—"doing philosophy" in the parlance of Anglo-American analytic philosophers, rather than standing for it. As a poetic bird, he is an American poet-teacher. And the teacher-poet who makes a poem out of him is fully able to acknowledge that. There are all sorts of complex attitudes—let alone, whatever it had come to make of Eve's "call or laughter"—which must be gleaned from modern birdsong. And yet it sometimes sounds as if the song of the threshold—the qualifications, retractions, considerations, economies of the powerfully unsystematic—can only be philosophy.

## Notes

1. In a letter to Robert P. Tristram Coffin, quoted in Richard Poirier, *Poetry and Pragmatism* (Cambridge: Harvard University Press, 1992), 190.
2. Poirier, *Poetry and Pragmatism*, 184.
3. There is an engaging discussion of the mythologized nightingale before Milton in Leonard Lutwack, *Birds in Literature* (Gainesville: University of Florida Press, 1994), 1–17.
4. John Crowe Ransom, "Philomela," in *Selected Poems* (New York: Alfred A. Knopf, 1969), 63.
5. Richard Lewis, "A Journey from Patapsko to Annapolis," in *Gentlemen's Magazine*, 2 (London, 1732), 669. This passage is immediately followed by a visual parallel with the hummingbird. There is a brilliant discussion of "The Mocking-Bird as a Figure of Echo" in Eleanor Cook's "Birds in Paradise: Uses of Allusion in Milton, Keats, Whitman, Stevens and Ammons," *Studies in Romanticism* 26 (1987), 421–443, particularly 421–428.
6. In the "Sounds" chapter of *Walden* (New York: The Library of America, 1985), 420.
7. Joseph Rodman Drake, "The Mocking-Bird," in *American Poetry: The Nineteenth Century* (New York: The Library of America, 1993), 1:204.
8. *American Poetry*, 1:85–86.
9. *American Poetry*, 2:423.
10. *American Poetry*, 2:564.
11. Richard Wilbur, *New and Collected Poems* (New York: Harcourt, Brace Jovanovich, 1988), 269-70. The high-modernist debunking of romantic fictions is at once exemplified and parodied in Aldous Huxley's Mark Rampion (a quasi D. H. Lawrence) in *Point-Counterpoint*, when he complains on behalf of the skylark that its birdhood was compromised by Shelleyan mythmaking, and that any self-respecting skylark would have "dropped something in his eye."
12. Edward Connery Lathem, ed., *The Poetry of Robert Frost* (New York: Holt, Rinehart, Winston, 1969), 334.
13. Wallace Stevens, *Collected Poems* (New York: Alfred A. Knopf, 1955), 160. Also see Harold Bloom, *Wallace Stevens: The Poems of Our Climate* (Ithaca: Cornell University Press, 1977), 91–92.
14. Lathem, ed., *The Poetry of Robert Frost*, 119–120.
15. Richard Poirier, *Robert Frost, The Work of Knowing*, 2nd ed. (Stanford: Stanford University Press, 1990), 74.
16. An overtone of Keats might lurk in what may possibly be an allusive "cease" ("The bird would cease and be as other birds") echoed from Keats's nightingale ode: not only cease = desist from singing, but Keats's cease = stop existing. But I'm not at all sure of this.
17. See my *Figure of Echo* (Berkeley and Los Angeles: University of California Press, 1981), 135.
18. Poirier, *Robert Frost*, 75.
19. And "never again": the reciprocal of this might be the little fiction about the poet Stesichorus in an epigram in the so-called Garden of Meleager, to the effect that "just after his birth, a creature of the air, a nightingale from somewhere, settled secretly on his lips and struck up its clear song." Trans. W. R. Paton, in *The Greek Anthology Book II* (Cambridge: Harvard University Press, 1916), 1:69. This

provides an interesting comment on some of the ancient Greek prejudice against the music of wind, rather than of Apollonian stringed instruments.

20. See my *Melodious Guile* (New Haven: Yale University Press, 1988), 161.

21. Poirier, *Poetry and Pragmatism*, 103.

22. The issue of the alternative song is discussed by Guy Rotella in "Metaphor in Frost's 'Oven Bird'" in Earl J. Wilcox, ed., *Robert Frost: The Man and the Poet* (Conway, Arizona: UCA Press, 1990), 18–27. He discounts the neglect of this question by other critics, but may perhaps wrongly adduce a relevance himself. The point is, I think, that either the earlier high-song figures here or not, in which case Frost either (a) didn't know of it himself, or (b) forgot it. It is wrong here, I think, to argue that the high-song is some bit of natural lore that Frost expects the reader to have been versed in, and can therefore totally suppress mention of, in order that the reader acknowledge and interpret both the lore and the ad hoc suppression of it. This indeed might be the case with a suppressed quasi allusion by Nabokov, for example. But not here. Frost does want his readers to be versed in natural things (such as the fact that wet braided ropes expand along their length, rather than contracting, as they dry—unlike, say, leather thongs—and thus can be said to "relent," as in "The Silken Tent") as, indeed, to be versed in scriptural verses (such as Mark 4:11–12 in "Directive") or classical verses (so as to be able to recognize that "For Once, Then, Something" is in Catullan hendecasyllabics, thereby to frame some agenda of counter-reproach). But in all these cases, the allusion is manifest. Could, indeed, the earlier high-song be legitimately introduced, it should not be in some ad hoc literary historical way, but rather as a matter of poetic thought; the high-song, a skylark-nightingale of romantic tradition, is revised by an inverse sublime or modernist transumption. Yet I still feel that the high-song isn't in or around the poem.

23. Milton's mode of querying birdsong about its discursive content—almost in the impatient manner of an ecphrastic query to a picture to speak up and explain itself—continues up through the middle of this century, at least, e.g., to the great Hoagy Carmichael-Johnny Mercer "Skylark" of 1941, which opens with the singer's asking the bird if it has anything to tell him/her.

24. *American Poetry*, 1:623–624.

25. It may be of some minute significance that in copying these lines an initial typo yielded "questionsings."

# CHAPTER 10

# Frost's "obvious" Titles

ANNE FERRY

*W*hen I told friends I was working on a book about the titles of poems, they almost always responded "Then you must be writing about Stevens." Sometimes they added "and Eliot," "and Williams," once in a while "and Moore," but no one said "Then you must be writing about Frost." This pattern of response can tell a good deal about our habits of reading and some of the assumptions they are predicated on: what we think titles are and how they work—with the poem and for the poet or reader. The fact that no one thought to name Frost also says a good deal about his work, generally in relation to American poets who were his contemporaries, and particularly in his ways of titling, where he is no more "undesigning" than in his other formal decisions.[1]

We rightly assume of most titles what has been nearly always true—at least since the later seventeenth century—that they are chosen to fill the space above the text of the poem by the poet to tell something about it to the reader in abbreviated form, to answer some question the reader might ask, like what the poem is going to be about; what genre it belongs to; who is imagined saying or hearing it. Because historically titles have evolved in conventional forms designed to assert their presentational function, we usually take them for granted, calling them "straightforward," by which we mean they can be trusted to do just what they claim. Habitually we ignore titles when reading poems, as if they were external to the whole design, demanding no more interpretive work than a sign on a door telling what we will find once we open it.

Challenges to these assumptions have come from those recent titles, and their rare predecessors before the late nineteenth century, that make some obvious bid for attention. If the language of the title itself seems to need interpretation, then we read it asking the same sorts of questions we habitually ask when we read poems. Stevens's titling would come to mind as a subject to write about because he is perhaps the first poet to make such attention-getting titles a specialty. Well-known examples are the elaborate wordplay of "Le Monocle de Mon Oncle," the insistent metaphorical possibilities of "The Sense of the Sleight-of-hand Man," the wacky inconsequence of "The Woman Who Blamed Life on a Spaniard." Similarly, the allusive incongruities in Eliot's "Sweeney Agonistes," Williams's play with grammatical and lexical double meanings in "Spring Strains," the suggestive incompleteness of Moore's "Nevertheless" signal that we must ask questions about the title as a prerequisite for reading the text of the poem.

Idiosyncratic, expressive titles like these earlier twentieth-century examples get the attention they ask for because critics know what to do with them. In contrast, most titles are overlooked (almost literally) because they seem to be simply declarative, redundant once we have read the poem like the sign on a door when we have opened and gone through it. Even so, Frost can show us, they are not ignored by poets who must make the decision to use them, a choice more loaded for twentieth-century poets because it is made from the widened range of title forms available in the past hundred years.

This practice of disregarding titles unless they prevent us from doing so is clearly visible in critical discussions of Frost because his insistent preference, especially in his first five volumes, which define him for most readers, was for simple, declarative titles designed to state what the poem is about: an un-qualified noun or gerund, or a noun specified by "The" or "A" and modified by an adjective, the most common of traditional title forms.

Titles in *A Boy's Will* establish from the beginning Frost's preference for these paradigms: "Stars," "October," "Reluctance," "Waiting," "Mowing," "The Vantage Point," "A Late Walk." Such titles seem close to being as unsus-ceptible of interpretation as a sign on a door, as transparent as a window pane. Their expressive neutrality is made stronger by Frost's habitual choice of grammatical modifiers that are not evaluative. Typically they are common nouns doing the work of adjectives: from his first book examples are "Ghost House," "Storm Fear," "Wind and Window Flower," "A Dream Pang," "A Line-Storm Song." Their apparently matter-of-fact naming shows clearly in contrast with the more descriptively charged adjectives "Gala" in Stevens's "Of Bright & Blue Birds & the Gala Sun" or "Black" in Williams's "The Black Winds."

There seems little or nothing to raise questions about Frost's apparently self-evident choices of transparently declarative titles, and in fact there has been no critical discussion of them. Virtually the only exceptions among the titles of poems in the whole of Frost's work to have been given more than passing mention are those few untypically designed to invite attention to themselves, and therefore to their ways of working with the poem, because they do something more than or other than answer some question the reader might be expected to ask about it. These five or six critically noticed titles are worded so that they have multiple or even contradictory implications which make them less informative than ambiguous or enigmatic. Since what Frost called "doubleness, double entendre, and duplicity and double play" is the dimension he always said was the essence of a poem, the fact that such titles are extremely rare in his work, and when his American contemporaries were having fun with them, raises questions to be explored in this essay.[2]

"Design" is the title of Frost's most often included in discussions of the poem, probably because the interpretive questions it invites about itself are of a familiar kind, the same we ask about the language of the poem. Since we have been trained to think that double meanings are the stock-in-trade of twentieth-century poets, readers are likely to recognize the hints in "Design." It signals that the poem will have to do with patterns (including its own, since it is also a commonplace of criticism that twentieth-century poems are likely to be self-referential), and that at the same time it will be about schemes (which might more obliquely include a reference to the poem, since if students of Frost know anything about him as an artist, they know he was, by his own admission, "not undesigning").

The signals of the title are answered in the octave by the poem's interest in the intriguing pattern of small natural creatures all "white" (the key word in the unconventionally repetitive rhyme scheme of the sonnet). The pattern these little white things surprisingly make is likely to be "assorted" with the randomness of happenings along the road, but might be "assorted" like a carefully "mixed" variety of ingredients in a recipe (an alphabet soup of "characters") or in a potion for a magic rite ("right"). Then the sestet, while carrying on the sense of "design" as pattern (just as the "white" rhyme is carried forward), brings still closer to the surface its suggestion of sinister plotting. By the couplet the two meanings come frighteningly close to being synonymous in "design of darkness" (made out of, made by darkness), before the fear is questioned, pushed away, covered up by the partly skeptical, partly parenthetical, partly evasive last line: "If design govern in a thing so small."

"Design" is Frost's only title constituted entirely of a double entendre, and scarcely any double meanings of single words occur in his other titles for poems, except in "The Need of Being Versed in Country Things" and "Nothing Gold Can Stay" (although they appear from the beginning in the titles of volumes: *A Boy's Will*, *Mountain Interval*, *A Further Range*). The singular use of such a title for this poem might be accounted for by its appropriate significance. The insistent formal design the poem makes may be a figure for the designing act the poet performs to counter the darkness. Frost said of the poem both that it is "a set little sonnet . . . a kind of design," and that "It's a kind of poker-face piece." He also said, with more telling implications for its singular title, that the sonnet is "very undramatic in the speech entirely," which may be a hint that its movement is—uncharacteristically—predicted if not predetermined by its title, which was among the many changes Frost made in recasting the earlier poem with the very different title "In White."[3] All the other revisions seem to follow from or be designed to support the double meaning of "Design."

The few other titles given more than a mention in discussions of Frost excite interest because they also offer multiple possibilities of interpretation, but by different means: "The Most of It," "For Once, Then, Something," and especially "Come In." Here there are no words like "Design," "Versed," or "Stay" to signal their inherent doubleness; no unfamiliar words to be puzzled out like "Gerontion"; no words oddly combined, as in "The Emperor of Ice-Cream," to suggest other than their declared meanings. There is, in fact, nothing unordinary about these phrases except their presence in the title space, where they refuse to act like titles because they seem not to predict anything of what the reader will find in the poem. Instead, these unusual title phrases signal the need to begin by asking questions about them before reading the poem, and then about their relation to it after we have read it, which is a curious reversal of conventional roles since the title, coming first, has traditionally claimed to prepare the reader for what follows it.

If we have some idea of the questions to ask about this kind of title, it is because Frost has taught us in his poems and by what he eloquently and often proclaimed were the prerequisites for reading them. We can recognize these titles to be made out of what he called a "sentence-sound," a verbal package familiar as an everyday idiom we have often heard or might hear in certain ordinary situations where it would be spoken in precisely definable but often multiple or even contradictory tones of voice. In lectures, essays, conversations, and letters Frost gave urgent instructions for reading this kind of phrase: to remember that it is "apprehended by the ear"; that it is "definitely and unmistakeably indicated by the context"; and that it "often says more than the words. It may even as in irony convey a meaning opposite to the words." That is to say, the sentence-sound must be read as dramatic speech, by contrast with the simple "declarative sentence used in making a plain statement" which "is one sound."[4]

These lessons apply also to titles. Frost's characteristically declarative titles make only one sound, as everyone knows who tries to say the title as well as the poem out loud. Even "Design," despite its double signification, does not allow a variety of tones because it is formally abstracted from speech like a sign on a door saying "Entrance," while a sentence-sound in the title space offers multiple possibilities to the "ear," which is "the only true reader."[5] "Come In," the title of Frost's least-often ignored (after "Design"), can serve as a paradigm of the way these sentence-sounds work differently in the title space from a sign saying "Entrance." Fittingly, Reuben Brower, who gave to many students and their students what he learned directly from Frost about reading, has given us a demonstration of the questions we might begin to ask about "Come In."

Brower set an example still too rarely followed of reading the title as part of the whole design of the poem. His discussion begins by listening to the way the title "anticipates" in the sounds of its own voice the "doublings of tone in the poem." "'Come In' combines the homely 'come-in' said to someone at the front door with the romantic invitation to 'come into the garden,' into a night retreat of Tennyson or Keats."[6] Brower's demonstration then follows the sounds of this "delicate poise of tones" through the poem. For instance, "'Hark' belongs on one side to poetic and religious wonder, on another to . . . daily speech a generation back. Grandmothers used to say 'Hark' when they surely wanted to be heard." With this kind of attentiveness to spoken tones, the discussion traces a pattern of details that suggest how strongly the voice in the poem expresses longing for and resistance to the seductions of the bird's invitation, "Almost like a call to come in."

Following one of the lessons Frost preached and Brower passed on—that the questions invited by the rich possibilities of a poem's language have no set limits—we can explore in more detail the way the sentence-sound in the title space takes part in a dramatic interchange with the poem. Standing alone, "Come In" has to be an imperative, but its stresses are undetermined, so Brower could hear it as both a neighborly iambic invitation and a trochaic romantic seduction. It could also be an uninflected pyrrhic or an imperious spondee. The stress pattern would be determined by who says "Come In" and to whom, but the title itself has no settled dramatic situation unless the poem provides it.

There the title phrase is said twice by the first-person speaker of the lines, but not as an imperative and not in the cadences possible in the title. In stanza four it belongs to an anapest—"Almost like a call tŏ cŏme ín"—but in the fifth it is ambiguously anapestic and iambic—"Ĭ wóuld nŏt cŏme ín" and "Ĭ woŭld nŏt cŏme ín." These repetitions give no support for an easy identification of the speaker with whoever says the title, while the logic of the story actually disallows it unless the speaker is imitating what the bird's song "Almost" sounded like, a seductive call. Or he might be warding off its temptations by domesticating it, making it sound like a neighbor's invitation.

Another possibility is that the imperative said before the poem is an echo of what the speaker first called out, which would predict the situation in the poem (though not its title) placed shortly after in the same volume, "The Most of It": nature returns to the human being who calls out for a response from it "the mocking echo of his own" words. Or, since the poem "Come In" is itself a kind of echo of "Ode to a Nightingale" (with undertones of "The Darkling Thrush"), the voice heard in the title space may belong to poetic tradition, or to Keats's bird luring the later poet "into the forest dim." In this script, the question of tone is still quizzically and mischievously left unanswered. Does romantic poetry invite a twentieth-century poet seductively; as if to a friendly neighbor; indifferently; impatiently, because whoever is at the door stubbornly refuses to "come in"?

All of these possibilities are allowed by the title "Come In," making it a perfect fit for Frost's description of how sentence-sounds—"Talking contraries"—work in his poems to open readings that "unsay everything I said, nearly."[7] That typically mischievous "nearly" works in precisely the way "Almost" (itself ambiguously iambic or trochaic) in the poem interferes with a settled hearing of the bird's "call to come in."

No instructions for reading them come with Frost's simply declarative titles, and no traditions of criticism have trained us to pay more attention to them than as a way of identifying which poem is to be discussed. "Birches" is an exemplary instance: in its simplicity and directness it expects correspondingly simple acceptance as a self-evident or inevitable choice. There has been no speculation about the reasons for Frost's decision to use that title, or how it works with the poem or for the poet and the reader, although the often mentioned fact that Frost first referred to the title in a letter of 1913 as "Swinging Birches" shows that characteristically he did not arrive at it simply or directly, that it was not self-evident to him.[8]

"Swinging Birches," as well as "Birches," would belong to Frost's much preferred title forms. Both seem modest in claiming to do no more than answer in advance the simplest question the reader might ask, what the poem is going to be about. Grammatically abstracted from the sentence and free of ambiguous meanings or the associations built into spoken idioms, they are in themselves expressively neutral. They seem to give the reader no interpretive work to do with them or with their straightforward relation to the poem. Still, Frost's deliberateness of choice here, as in all his artful simplicity and directness in other features of his poems, should alert us that we need to read at least some of his many titles in unobtrusive forms with as much attention as the few more obviously puzzling ones, though reading them must be a rather different process, requiring that we learn to ask new and different kinds of questions.

"Swinging Birches" would be a congenial choice for Frost, who was the first poet to make present participles a preferred source for titles, a source which has since been so much favored by more recent poets that it no longer seems remarkable. Frost early discovered titling by present participles as a device for getting effects he seems specially to have prized in his first four volumes, where he chose them often and for poems he considered among his best, which are now best known. In *A Boy's Will* there are four, one of them "Mowing" of which he wrote, "I come so near what I long to get that I almost despair of coming nearer."[9] *North of Boston*, with two such titles, gives "Mending Wall" the privileged opening place in the volume. *Mountain Interval*, where "Birches" appears, includes "Meeting and Passing," "Putting in the Seed," and "Range-Finding." Of the three in *New Hampshire*, "Stopping by Woods on a Snowy Evening" is the poem Frost called "my best bid for remembrance."[10]

The opportunities he exploits in these titles are made possible by unique features of the present participle. One is that it has the awareness of time that belongs to verbs, but in the special form of a continual present. This gives it the kind of immediacy we also hear, for instance, in the sound of the speaking voice in the poem "Mowing," while the grammatical suppression of the mower as the performer of the action allows the title "Mowing" to generalize it. This double effect would not have been achieved by a title in one of the other forms prominent in Frost's early volumes, supposing the poem had been called "The Hay-Maker" or "Scythe Sounds."

Besides its power of generalizing without sacrifice of immediacy, the present participle may have attracted Frost as a source for titles by other effects of its unique capacity to act as a verbal noun and a pure nominative. In its gerundive sense it names an action which presupposes a performer who is unnamed, while as a noun it names something done, an event which has grammatical status as a thing. Frost hinted at the figurative richness of this double possibility when he wrote:

> Everything is an event now. Another metaphor. A thing, they say, is
> an event. Do you believe it is? Not quite. I believe it is almost an
> event. But I like the comparison of a thing with an event.[11]

"Mowing" names an event, an ongoing action of someone making something happen, "my long scythe whispering to the ground," and it names some thing whole and free-standing, like the "hay to make." The present participle of the title says that the poem is indivisibly about a process and about some made thing, Frost's characteristic definition of what a poem is:

> Something you can do. Make a basket. Make a dress. Make an order
> of an hour in a class, you know; shape it. It's a momentary stay
> against confusion.[12]

The choice of present participle allows the title itself to make a figure for the poem "Mowing," and for all poems.

There is one more feature of the present participle that may help to account for its attractiveness to Frost, and even for its special fitness to title "Mowing," as well as the poem originally to have been called "Swinging Birches." The gerund has a marked stress built into it which in both these titles initiates a rhythm that can suggest the kind of movement the title names. In "Mowing" this is carried forward most prominently in the rhyming sounds and rhythm of "whispering," "Something," "something," "anything." In those lines of the later poem describing the actions of the "swinger of birches," the rhythmic pattern that would have been set in motion by the original title builds in a crescendo of present participles: "riding," "launching," "climbing," "kicking."

What these observations about Frost's remarkable preference for titling by present participles are meant to show here is that the change from "Swinging Birches" to "Birches" for the title of so characteristic and important a poem was likely not to have been a casual decision, but one involving some sacrifice of expressive possibilities that Frost had already made much of, and continued to develop, in the titles of other poems equally characteristic and important. This claim can be tested only by more observations and questions.

Frost left on record one fact about the poem that may suggest a reason for the change of title: "'Birches' was two fragments soldered together so long ago I have forgotten where the joint is."[13] The revised title may have been designed to disguise the division, because it distributes the reader's attention through the whole poem, whereas the original title would focus it on the act of "Swinging Birches" described in lines 23–42. This emphasis would sharpen any sense of division between that passage and the earlier description, almost identical in length, of what ice-storms do to birches. It would also disturb the balance between the two descriptions: the "matter-of-fact" account of ice-storms and the "dream" preference for the game of swinging birches. By weighing the balance heavily toward the second passage, the unrevised title might have threatened the seriously fooling play in the use of "matter-of-fact" to describe the high poetic language about the reality of ice-storms, while the memory reimagined as a wishful "dream" is detailed in precisely measuring, spoken language. The poem would be ruined if it seemed to value "dream" at the expense of "matter" and "fact."

There is another piece of the poem's history that may say something more about the change of title. Frost also revised the text of the poem by taking out a parenthetical line that came after line 22 between the two long descriptive passages as "Birches" originally appeared in *The Atlantic Monthly* of August, 1915, and again the following year in the first edition of *Mountain Interval*:

> But I was going to say when truth broke in
> With all her matter-of-fact about the ice-storm,
> (Now am I free to be poetical?)
> I should prefer to have some boy bend them.

It seems plausible that this line was a clumsy attempt to solder the joint between the two fragments, but because the changed title did the work less crudely, the disastrously over-explicit parenthesis was expendable. Together these revisions point to larger issues at stake in Frost's decision to retitle the poem.

The title phrase "Swinging Birches" would make the second description the heart of the poem; the presupposition of an agent built into its present participle would bring to the foreground the performer of the continuously present action. Then the "swinger of birches," delicately mythologized by that epithet, becomes the hero of the poem whose "play," one of Frost's favorite metaphors for making poems, is a game "he found himself." He is a "boy" like one Frost in a talk on "Attitudes toward Poetry" described playing the game of hopscotch:

> You know how to play hopscotch. It's laid out for you or you lay it
> out, and you come onto it, you step onto it, and step a figure in it . . .
> a boy began like this long ago. . . he was—fifteen years old, not much
> more than that. . . . And he sketches on the ground for himself that
> way, the court that he makes like hopscotch. Now he's got to step into
> that again and again and make pretty figures out of his sentences.[14]

When Frost, to illustrate this story of "long ago," recited the first stanza of "Ode on Solitude," the boy hero turned out to be Pope.

The figure of "some boy" in "Birches" is less like Alexander Pope than he is like Wordsworth's mythologized Winander boy, but he is made to act as Pope does in Frost's talk, as a figure for all poets, and in particular for Robert Frost: "So was I once myself a swinger of birches." The detailed account of precisely how the boy played his game confirms the poet's own boyhood practice of it long ago, and by analogy describes his later game of making poems. It must be played "carefully," by keeping one's "poise," by taking "the same pains you use to fill a cup / Up to the brim, and even above the brim." It involves dangers to be conquered by learned skills—not "launching out too soon, / And so not carrying the tree away / Clear to the ground"—like the dangers attached to mastering a metaphor as Frost described them in "Education by Poetry": "You don't know how far you may expect to ride it and when it may break down with you":

> All metaphor breaks down somewhere. That is the beauty of it. It is touch and go with metaphor, and until you have lived with it long enough you don't know when it is going. You don't know how much you can get out of it 'and when it will cease to yield. It is a very living thing.[15]

Although Frost said "Birches" perhaps more often at public readings than any other poem, he never dropped characteristic hints—like those he gave about "Design," for example—in talks or elsewhere that would alert readers to the dimension of the poem the unrevised title and unexcised line would have pointed to: that it has to do with making poems, and his poems. Perhaps again wanting to suppress this dimension, he later took out the revealing present participle from the title originally to be "Making the Most of It." That revision prevents the title from giving a clue to whether its truncated sentence-sound is spoken by the maker of the poem or "He" who acts in it. What if anything it signals is the poem's refusal to answer that question or its corollary, whether "He," another figure with ties to the Winander boy, is or is not a lesser or younger self of the poet.

The only recorded instance when Frost, before saying "Birches," offered the audience what he said was the "kind of explication I forbid," shows him slyly supporting rather than undoing the title's artfully straightforward claim to introduce a poem describing birch trees. His confidential explanation to his audience was only that "I never go down the shoreline [from Boston] to New York without watching the birches to see if they live up to what I say about them in the poem."[16] Still, even in this blandly noncommittal remark there may be a playful hint about the poem which might typify all poems: that the "matter" it works with—precisely how "birches bend"—is "fact."

This conviction would support Frost's preference for simple title forms pointing directly to a thing or event in the poem that anyone after reading it might choose as its obvious focus, by contrast with more idiosyncratically expressive titles like those interesting to Stevens, Eliot, Williams, and Moore. These contemporaries could appropriately be included among poets who, in

Richard Poirier's words, "have proved far more accommodating than has Frost to critics who like their poems to be about poetry":

> The reason, I think, is that while it is possible . . . to infer from Frost's poems an interest in the drama of poetic "making," he is some of the time even tiresomely determined not to surrender the human actuality of his poems to a rhetoric by which action is transformed immediately into ritual. . . .[17]

"Directive" is treated with the same uncritical acceptance as Frost's titles in simple, declarative forms like "Mowing" or "Birches," as if he had chosen instead to call the poem "Giving Directions" or "The Road Back." These hypothetical titles match the ordinary language of the poem itself, whereas the voice convincingly dramatized in the lines by idiom and cadence could not conceivably say "The road there, if you'll let a guide give you a directive," or "The road there is a directive way back." Listening to the hypothetical alternatives, we can hear that "Directive" is not that kind of title, does not do the same work of pointing directly to some event or thing the poem is obviously about.

The reason for its difference is that, uncharacteristically, Frost chose for the title of this poem a specialized term, scarcely if ever used in daily speech, associated exclusively with certain rare and limited but precisely definable situations. These are spelled out in dictionary definitions for "directive" as both noun (which is how we tend to read it in the title space) and as adjective (which is how the *OED* says it began, accounting for its suffix, from medieval Latin *directivus*):

> That which directs; specif., a general instruction as to conduct or procedure; as, subject to the *directives* of his political party.
> A form of general orders, usually emanating from a supreme [military] headquarters. . . .

And:

> Serving or qualified to direct, guide, or govern; regulative; as, the *directive* power of the Ten Commandments.
> Serving to point out direction; showing how to act or where to move; as, the *directive* function of a compass; the *directive* influence of ideals. . . .[18]

To take "Directive" as a pointer, like Frost's earlier preferred titles, to some event or thing in the poem, we would have to put a common word such as "Directions" in its place by simply translating it, which Frost always argued was the way not to read his poems:

> I'm always hinting, intimating, and always on the verge of something I don't quite like to say out of sheer delicacy. And the only thing I

have against my friends, the teachers, is some of them are indelicate. They won't leave it where I left it. . . . I don't complain. I have complained of translating what I write. . . . And I've complained of people who've sat side of me when I've cracked a joke and said, "He means. . . ."[19]

Instead of translating the title "Directive," we should raise questions about it, beginning with those we would ask by treating it as a kind of sentence-sound. This is possible, though paradoxical—since it is a toneless term to be met more often in written documents than in speech—because it has built-in associations with certain definable situations. It pertains to the delivery and reception of general regulations from a distant authority that dictate correct behavior under its jurisdiction. It is a jarringly inappropriate word to refer to the situation of a traveller in an unfamiliar countryside being given directions by a native of the place to follow a road that leads to an abandoned town.

Once we take the precise choice of the word "Directive" seriously, the fact that it belongs to an area of vocabulary unlike and even alien to the ordinary language Frost habitually uses, in both poems and titles, shows it to be carefully designed, but not to give us guidance for reading the poem. It does not focus attention on an event or thing in it, as would "Giving Directions" or "The Road Back," but instead raises the expectation of difficulties to come in our experience of it. Frost hinted at those pitfalls on relatively rare occasions when he included the poem in a public reading. For instance, "I'll do it slow and you take it straight. But it's full of dangers, sideways, off, and all that," and again, "One of my diffidences is about poems like this to read aloud. Some of them, you know, are more open work, and this is a little more closed." After saying the poem he added, "See, I don't read it with the same certainty that I should. I feel a little afraid of it."[20]

Uncertainties and fears begin to stir early in our experience of reading the poem as we submit, with some degree of resistance, to being directed by a self-styled "guide" like Spenser's Archimago, who "only has at heart" our getting lost. This common idiom, which makes the line sound convincingly like the guide's own speech, is one that should make us uneasy. "I only have at heart" is among those packaged insincerities like "let me say frankly" or "for your own good" that familiarity has taught us to be wary of. Another is "You must not mind." It is a repeated reassurance here that actually assures us we do mind, and have reason to as we hear the guide describe the ugly and threatening signs of nature reasserting itself over the abandoned town, its houses, orchards, and fields.

What the guide wills us to see along the road "back" has none of the grandeur and freedom of the natural scene readers are led back to by the voice saying the opening lines of "Tintern Abbey." In place of "lofty cliffs" there are giant boulders heaving up like the "great monolithic knees" of some primordial monster. All that remains are cellar holes the guide compares to "eye pairs" spying on us and a "few old pecker-fretted apple trees," while Wordsworth's revisitor found "plots of cottage ground" and "orchard-tufts." Where he saw grass growing up to "pastoral farms / Green to the very door," this guide describes a field shrunken to a raw and ugly "harness gall," and nothing is left of the farmer's house but an overgrown cellar hole "now slowly closing like a dent in dough" in silent parody of domestic living.

The guide's reassuring commands go on disturbing us. He tells us to soothe our fears with self-deceiving sentimentalities, for instance with a comfortable picture of country life and work easily mocked by its differences from Frost's farm poems: "Make yourself up a cheering song of how / Someone's road home from work this once was." To "Make . . . up" is not Frost's verb for making poetry, nor is the verb in "Then make yourself at home," a still more fatuous self-deception in a place where all traces of home-making have been "lost," presumably in failed struggling against the galling rural hardship and poverty Frost's poems often describe. Most mockingly sentimental is the guide's imperative to shed complacent tears over the meager "dishes" left "shattered" where the children once played "house": "Weep for what little things could make them glad."

If we have been made uneasy enough by now, having listened with appropriate suspicion to the guide's directions, we are "lost enough" to be prepared for his final imperative:

> Your destination and your destiny's
> A brook that was the water of the house,
> Cold as a spring as yet so near its source,
> Too lofty and original to rage.

This is high poetry: certainly "lofty"—for instance in using the noncolloquial sense of "original" as primal, the origin—and loaded with traditionally portentous words like "destination," "destiny," "source" (though the placing of the contraction "destiny's" at the end of the line lightly emphasizes a slight dip in elevation). These lines are not the colloquial speech we are used to hearing from the voice in the poem, nor do they sound like descriptions of nature in Frost's other poems, which we are reminded of by the next two casually parenthetical lines:

> (We know the valley streams that when aroused
> Will leave their tatters hung on barb and thorn.)

The personal pronoun "We" here is the first plural (since the seemingly sympathetic and communal "us" of line one) to join the speaker and the reader. In "We know" we are linked by familiarity with the same countryside, following some dozen uses of "you" that had, often it seemed with hostility, separated stranger from initiate.

Having made this appeal to our shared experience, the guide lets us in on the secrets of what he has been up to:

I have kept hidden in the instep arch
Of an old cedar at the waterside
A broken drinking goblet like the Grail
Under a spell so the wrong ones can't find it,
So can't get saved, as Saint Mark says they mustn't.
(I stole the goblet from the children's playhouse.)

This is not the way the guide has talked to us before. The voice here is confiding, and confident that "We" will catch the playfulness in the casual "like the Grail," and in the rustic epithet "the wrong ones" for the nonelect. Now fully included among the initiated, we are ready to receive the final imperative:

Here are your waters and your watering place.
Drink and be whole again beyond confusion.

These lines return to the "lofty" solemnity and weighted symbolic language that introduced this closing passage, but its unfolding allows us to "get" them as the last move in the game the guide has told us he was playing. The fooling in the lines just before can only prepare us for this final, ringing directive if it is taken as a teasing shock, which Frost seems to have hinted in a talk "On Being Let in on Symbols" given in 1953, six years after "Directive" appeared in *Steeple Bush*:

A parable is a story that means what it says and something besides. And according to the New Testament the something besides is the more important of the two. It's *that* the nonelect are supposed to miss and so not go to heaven. Saint Mark says so. . . . And these things are said so as to leave the wrong people out. I love that because it sounds so undemocratic. That's not because I'm smart either, but I just love to be shocked, don't you? I like to come right up against something like that.[21]

Since we have arrived where we were going—as travellers along the road to the abandoned town, as readers to the end of the poem—we have found, have been taught, what is "Back out of all this now too much for us." There is no escape "beyond confusion," but to go "back" to the "source," living through our fear and uneasiness, is to know "confusion," and in that knowing to be initiated into the game a poem plays to make a stay against it. Frost liked to tell audiences about an exchange he had with a man who complained to him of being confused:

"All right, let's play the game of Confusion. Are you ready?
First I'll ask you. Are you really confused?"
"Yes, I am."
"Now you ask me."
"Are you confused, Mr. Frost?"
"No—I win!"[22]

The discussion of "Directive" to this point has proposed that the title plays its part in the unfolding of the poem by its jarring inappropriateness. Its unfitness involves it in the game of getting the reader lost, whether it encourages translation into a more helpful and undisturbing word like "Directions," or if instead it promotes acceptance of a dictionary definition of "Directive" in good faith as a straightforward statement of what the poem is about. It would then require the reader to transform the actuality of the poem into a kind of allegory pointing beyond the traveller, the guide, the road leading back to the abandoned town, the brook, to a stratum of significance where the title would not jar. In this way "Directive," because of its association with abstract or general commandments from a higher power, might be designed to tease the unwary into turning events and things in the poem into "symbol" and "meaning," habits Frost often made fun of: "I've grown to hate the word *symbol*. . . . I wish we could change the subject a little and say *typifies*"; "I want something that hasn't any meaning; I'm sick of meaning."[23]

In such an allegorizing of the poem, the title would be an appropriate sign pointing directively to the high poetry, the allusively symbolic language of the closing passage. It would from the beginning prepare readers for the final imperative. The "wrong ones," the type Frost also called "these ultimate people" for their tendency to "deal in" ultimate symbols and meanings rather than to "play with them," would hear it as a solemn "Directive."[24] The guide, no longer a cranky countryman or even a Spenserian wizard, would be transformed utterly into a higher power commanding us to drink from the communion chalice (the broken goblet the guide had stolen and hidden for his own secret game) and be saved.

Commenting on the critical reception of "Directive," Frost hinted that those who elevated it above his other work might be "ultimate people" guilty of overlooking—looking "beyond"—the dramatic situation, the things and events of the poem, so that they have hold of the meaning but miss the experience:

> This is the poem that converted the other group. The one these fellows
> have taken to build my reputation on. The boys [followers of T. S.
> Eliot] call it great. They have re-estimated me. This is great and most
> of the rest, trivia.[25]

This identification of wrong readers of "Directive" with the "converted" recalls one of Frost's most famous wordplays, which could serve as a gloss on the reading proposed here of the last line. Comparing himself to Eliot, he wrote: "We are both poets and we both like to play. That's the similarity. The difference is this: I like to play euchre; he likes to play Eucharist." In "Directive," the moves in "euchre" follow the steps in "the game of Confusion."[26]

Paradoxically, "Directive" has more in common with titles by Eliot and other modernist contemporaries than is usual among Frost's titles. Its resemblance is in being oddly angled to the poem by using a vocabulary alien to it, though far less insistently so than, for example, the liturgical title "The Burial of the Dead" for part one of *The Waste Land*, or than Stevens's "No Possum, No Sop, No Taters" for a somber description of a frozen landscape. Again paradoxically, but not uncharacteristically, the far less obvious mismatch of Frost's title makes it seem more straightforward while it is actually trickier, harder to pin down. It may be mainly for this reason that critical discussions of the poem have ignored the title. They assume it to be as transparently simple and direct as might be expected of Frost, even while recognizing that the poem itself quite obviously takes special risks in allowing traditional symbolic language and overt allusion into descriptions of the events and things out of which, typically for Frost, it is made.

From the beginning Frost preferred to title his poems in declarative noun forms that seem clear to the point of transparency, almost invisible like a window pane we look right through at what is beyond it. Such titles give up not only "the pleasure of ulteriority" in the doubleness of words and tones of voice so prized by Frost in poems, but also what he called their essential effects of "wildness" and "surprise."[27] Even so, because titles in these simple noun forms are clustered so thickly in Frost's volumes, especially in the first five, which he came to be best known by, they accumulate a certain unassertive expressiveness. They convey a respectful sense of the familiar solidity and integrity, the inviolable thingness of things, and "thing" is a key word in the poems.

In a letter to Untermeyer letting him in on the fun to be had from ulteriority, Frost gives a clue to why the very simplicity and familiarity of his titles made them serve his designs better than the more exciting effects of expressively charged modernist titles:

> I should like to be so subtle at this game as to seem to the casual person altogether obvious. The casual person would assume that I meant nothing or else I came near enough meaning something he was familiar with to mean it for all practical purposes. Well well well.[28]

Certainly Frost's characteristic titles, the many that are habitually ignored, seem "altogether obvious" and "familiar." They invite the reader to "Come In" (and it is to the point here that Frost repeated the enigmatic title of that evasive poem as the title for a volume of poems aimed, with the help of its illustrations and Untermeyer's commentary, to appeal to young readers). They offer an easy way into the poem, predicting that it will not raise difficulties, or keep secrets, or intimidate the uninitiated. The seeming straightforwardness of his titles, then, is a form of ulteriority that contributes powerfully to the appearance his poems have of being accessible, perhaps what he hinted in a journal note: "A poem would be no good that hadn't doors. I wouldn't leave them open though."[29] It is this appearance of accessibility that most immediately divides them from a quintessentially modernist poem, which assaults the reader with a title that predicts the poem's obscurity by its own. Frost's supposedly obvious and self-evident titles are a finely crafted feature of his art, giving their unobvious support to Poirier's claim that "Frost is a poet of genius because he could so often make his subtleties inextricable from an apparent availability" to a large and inclusive audience of readers.[30] When in the early 1930s William Rose Benét asked Frost to choose for inclusion in *Fifty Poets: An American Auto-Anthology* the one poem he would most like posterity to know him by, and to explain his preference, Frost named what was then his most popular poem, "Birches." With characteristic dislike of explanations he wrote, "If I must defend my choice, I will say I took it for its vocality and its ulteriority."[31]

### Notes

1. Robert Frost, *Selected Letters of Robert Frost*, ed. Lawrance Thompson (New York: Holt, Rinehart and Winston, 1964), 84.
2. Reginald Cook, *Robert Frost: A Living Voice* (Amherst: University of Massachusetts Press, 1974), 42.
3. Cook, *Robert Frost*, 265, 126.
4. Frost, *Selected Letters*, 111, 80, 113, 80.
5. Frost, *Selected Letters*, 113.
6. Reuben Brower, *The Poetry of Robert Frost* (New York: Oxford University Press, 1963), 32.
7. Richard Poirier, "Robert Frost," *Paris Review* 6 (1960), 113.
8. Frost, *Selected Letters*, 89.
9. Frost, *Selected Letters*, 83.
10. Robert Frost, *The Letters of Robert Frost to Louis Untermeyer* (New York: Holt, Rinehart and Winston, 1963), 163.
11. Robert Frost, "Education by Poetry," in *Selected Prose of Robert Frost*, ed. Hyde Cox and Edward Connery Lathem (New York: Holt, Rinehart and Winston, 1963), 38.
12. Cook, *Robert Frost*, 171.
13. Stanley Burnshaw, *Robert Frost Himself* (New York: George Braziller, 1986), 129.
14. Cook, *Robert Frost*, 146–147.
15. Frost, "Education by Poetry," 39, 41.
16. Cook, *Robert Frost*, 232.
17. Richard Poirier, *Robert Frost: The Work of Knowing* (New York: Oxford University Press, 1977), 137.
18. *Webster's New International Dictionary of the English Language*, 2nd ed., s.v. "directive."
19. Cook, *Robert Frost*, 140.
20. Cook, *Robert Frost*, 84, 114.
21. Cook, *Robert Frost*, 37.
22. Lawrance Thompson, *Robert Frost: The Early Years 1874–1915* (New York: Holt, Rinehart and Winston, 1966), 482 n. 12.
23. Cook, *Robert Frost*, 140–141, 59.
24. Cook, *Robert Frost*, 141.
25. Elizabeth Shepley Sergeant, *Robert Frost: The Trial by Existence* (New York: Holt, Rinehart and Winston, 1960), 394. The bracketed phrase is Sergeant's.
26. Louis Untermeyer, *Bygones: The Recollections of Louis Untermeyer* (New York: Harcourt, Brace and World, 1965), 46.

27. Frost, "The Constant Symbol," "The Figure a Poem Makes," in *Selected Prose*, 24, 18–19.
28. Frost, *Letters to Untermeyer*, 47.
29. Thomson, *The Early Years*, 397.
30. Poirier, *Robert Frost*, x.
31. William Rose Benét, ed., *Fifty Poets: An American Auto-Anthology* (New York: Duffield and Green, 1933), 30.

# CHAPTER 11

# *"What is the matter, trow?":*
# *A Rhetoric of Obscurity*

FRANK KERMODE

All places yield to him ere he sits down,
And the nobility of Rome are his.
The senators and patricians love him too;
The tribunes are no soldiers, and their people
Will be as rash in the repeal as hasty
To expel him thence. I think he'll be to Rome
As is the osprey to the fish, who takes it
By sovereignty of nature. First, he was
A noble servant to them, but he could not
Carry his honours even. Whether 'twas pride,
Which out of daily fortune ever taints
The happpy man; whether defect of judgement,
To fail in the disposing of those chances
Which he was lord of; or whether nature,
Not to be other than one thing, not moving
From th'casque to th'cushion, but commanding peace
Even with the same austerity and garb
As he controll'd the war: but one of these—
As he hath spices of them all, not all,
For I dare so far free him—made him fear'd,
So hated, and so banish'd: but he has a merit
To choke it in the utt'rance. So our virtues
Lie in th'interpretation of the time,
And power, unto itself most commendable,
Hath not a tomb so evident as a chair
T'extol what it hath done.
               —*Coriolanus*, 4.7.28–53[1]

*A*ufidius, marching on Rome with his
new ally, the exiled and irresistible Roman Coriolanus, is answering a question
put by his lieutenant. Aufidius has just remarked that although Coriolanus seems

to be strong and honest in the Volscian cause he, Aufidius, is keeping a record of whatever will count against the Roman in a final reckoning of the rivalry between them. The lieutenant, no doubt feeling that there won't be much of a case against Coriolanus if his campaign continues to succeed, invites his general to give an opinion on this possibility: "Sir, I beseech you, think you he'll carry Rome?" The result is the speech in part set out above. It is not strictly speaking a soliloquy, since the lieutenant is standing there, but he says nothing more.

Coleridge thought the speech beautiful "in itself" but called it "the least explicable from the mood and full intention of the speaker of any in the whole works of Shakespeare. I cherish the hope that I am mistaken, and that, becoming wiser, I shall discover some profound excellence in that in which I now appear to detect an imperfection."[2] This is an odd judgment, not because a speech can't be at once beautiful and obscure, but because Coleridge seems to be measuring it against some private and prior knowledge of Aufidius's "mood and full intention"; by definition it doesn't derive from the speech itself. The speech is deliberative, the mood speculative, and the intention of the speaker in one sense obvious: he is trying to make clear to himself or the lieutenant just how mixed were his feelings on the subject, how difficult he finds it to take a position on the standing of his ally, who has in the past been a bitter rival and may be a rival in the future. He thinks Coriolanus will easily take Rome, and puzzles over the circumstances which led to the exiling of such a superman, taking account of the reasons why he "could not / Carry his honours even," and introducing some general considerations concerning the nature and risks of power. If the speech is roughly explicable in some such terms, what was it that Coleridge found so baffling? It was no doubt the speed and complexity of the speech, its rapid movement from particular to general, from one idea to the next, the metaphors flashing by, never pausing to be exfoliated, leaving the auditor, even the reader, no time to judge their aptness in themselves, as distinct from their part in the representation of excited thought. Yet it must have been just those qualities that persuaded Coleridge that the speech was "beautiful."

This is far from the only passage in this play the sense of which has puzzled and continues to puzzle editors and readers. Its obscurity is hectic, its deliberative violence such that the word for it is not really "beautiful" and not really "sublime" either; we need to explain why we reach feebly for a modern word like "awesome." But as in other instances, Coleridge's judgment is interesting simply because he is willing to confess bewilderment and allow that the speech, though impressive, is somehow, in its essence, eluding him. He takes the blame for his incomprehension on himself. Johnson, less concessive, finds lines 51–53 at the end of the quoted passage "a common thought, but miserably expressed."[3] Philip Brockbank, in his excellent Arden edition, intelligently keeps the peace: "The obscurity of the speech is part of its dramatic force, as if Aufidius's thoughts are imperfectly clarified even to himself." I myself, thirty-odd years ago, spoke of the verse of *Coriolanus* (with this passage among others in mind) as having "its own absolutely decorous power,"[4] doubtless content that it was safe, in a brief introduction, to say so without being called on to justify the remark; but now I reflect that for remarks of this kind the honored recipient of these essays has habitually demanded justification. I will try to provide it by using the instrument of comparison, and my first example is from the early tragedy *Titus Andronicus*:

> Who is this—my niece that flies away so fast?
> Cousin, a word. Where is your husband?
> If I do dream, would all my wealth would wake me;
> If I do wake, some planet strike me down
> That I may slumber an eternal sleep.
> Speak, gentle niece, what stern ungentle hands
> Hath lopped and hewed and made thy body bare
> Of her two branches, those sweet ornaments
> Whose circling shadow kings have sought to sleep in
> And might not gain so great a happiness
> As half thy love? Why dost not speak to me?
> Alas, a crimson river of warm blood,
> Like to a bubbling fountain stirred with wind,
> Doth rise and fall between thy rosed lips
> Coming and going with thy honied breath.
> But sure some Tereus hath deflowered thee
> And, lest thou shouldst detect him, cut thy tongue.
> Ah, now thou turn'st away thy face for shame,
> And notwithstanding all this loss of blood,
> As from a conduit with three issuing spouts,
> Yet do thy cheeks look red as Titan's face,
> Blushing to be encountered with a cloud.
> Shall I speak for thee? Shall I say 'tis so?
> O that I knew thy heart, and knew the beast,
> That I might rail at him to ease my mind!
> Sorrow concealed, like an oven stopped,
> Doth burn the heart to cinders where it is.
> Fair Philomela, why she but lost her tongue,
> And in a tedious sampler sewed her mind;
> But, lovely niece, that mean is cut from thee.
> A craftier Tereus, cousin, hast thou met,
> And he hath cut those pretty fingers off,
> That could have better sewed than Philomel.
> O, had the monster seen those lily hands
> Tremble like aspen leaves upon a lute
> And make the silken strings delight to kiss them,
> He would not then have touched them for his life.
> Or had he heard the heavenly harmony

Which that sweet tongue hath made,
He would have dropped his knife and fell asleep,
As Cerberus at the Thracian poet's feet.
Come, let us go and make thy father blind,
For such a sight will blind a father's eye.
One hour's storm will drown the fragrant meads:
What will whole months of tears thy father's eyes?
Do not draw back, for we will mourn with thee;
O, could our mourning ease thy misery!

*Titus Andronicus*, 2.3.1–57[5]

This speech has been an embarrassment to theatrical directors. It is one of the longest and in some respects one of the most elaborate in the canon, yet it occurs at a point where such responses as silent horror or bustling action might seem more appropriate. In the memorable Peter Brook production of 1955, Vivien Leigh as Lavinia entered with red ribbons trailing from her wrists and mouth, and the whole speech was cut—Marcus wasn't even onstage. In 1972 Trevor Nunn cut twenty-nine lines from the speech. In her version of 1988 Deborah Warner, always adventurous and here adventurously conservative, included every word.

Jonathan Bate, the new Arden editor, having offered this information, adds that Marcus needs a long speech because he has to learn to confront suffering:

> The working through of bad dream into clear sight is formalized in
> Marcus' elaborate verbal patterns; only after writing out the process
> in this way could Shakespeare repeat and vary it in the simple, direct,
> unbearable language of the end of *Lear*: "Look there, look there!" . . .
> And a lyrical speech is needed because it is only when an appropriately
> inappropriate language has been found that the sheer contrast between
> its beauty and Lavinia's degradation begins to express what she has
> undergone and lost.[6]

This is a pretty but surely misguided attempt to recruit the speech of Marcus to the category of subtle psychological representations that are routinely called for, and plausibly discovered, in later plays like, for instance, *Macbeth* and *King Lear*.

Maynard Solomon, in his biography of Mozart, makes the interesting suggestion that certain youthful and ephemeral music—mostly serenades and divertimentos written between 1772 and 1776 for Salzburg entertainments (and perhaps given only a single performance) can be seen as essential preparation for the greater achievements of the composer's maturity.[7] The remark is not vaguely general, but has specific applications. Thus Susanna's aria "Deh vieni, non tardar" in the fourth act of *Le Nozze di Figaro*—dramatically unusual for two reasons: the serenader is a woman, and involved in a vengeful intrigue—is high, pure operatic Mozart, exquisite in itself yet actively involved in the ironic complexities of the opera's dénouement; yet it probably could not have existed without the precedent of that more or less routine Salzburg "social" music, written when the serenade, with its imitation guitar accompaniment, was so much in demand that "serenade" became the word for the entire suite of which it formed a part. The point is the transformation of this type of pizzicato-accompanied melody, already not without its simple irony, into the complexity of the later operatic use. Susanna's song, considered simply as a serenade, may be the most perfect ever written, but it takes its unexpected place in a context of inexhaustibly varied music and at the climax of an entangled plot ("Eccoci della crise al grande istante") with all manner of ironies, ethical, psychological, and political. The young Mozart had gone through, and developed, a set of exercises, and the mature Mozart drew on them in this remote unequalled moment; for it will probably be agreed that the serenade in *Don Giovanni*—in fact accompanied by a mandoline—for all its charm lacks the originality of Susanna's (for which Mozart made what seems to have been an unusual number of sketches) and has a far less complicated relation to plot and character.

Just as it would be supererogatory to seek in the Salzburg serenades, however polished they may be, true as they are to a satisfying musical rhetoric, evidence of dramatic or psychological complexity, so it is entirely misleading to look for more than a highly elaborate rhetorical performance from Marcus. In the first shock of the encounter he compares Lavinia to a tree with lopped branches, plays with the antithesis "gentle/ungentle," and then, since she ignores his request that she should speak, turns his attention to her missing tongue. From a tree he moves on to a garden ornament; the blood pouring from her mouth is as a fountain stirred with wind. He is inevitably reminded of the rape of Philomela (as well he might be, since it is the archetype of the present tale, and is known from its conceited treatment by Ovid, as the play more than once reminds us). Marcus makes other allusions to the mythological repertoire: Lavinia's cheeks, despite her loss of blood, are as red as the setting sun, as Titan's face encountering a cloud.

Marcus then proceeds with what is really a formal oration. He will have to do the speaking, since she can't. By way of establishing that he is so upset by what he has seen that he needs to talk about it, preferably (and, by later standards, with a certain effect of absurdity) by giving the culprit a good scolding, he cites the familiar saw that sorrow must have expression or kill the victim (see under "Grief pent up will break the heart" in *The Oxford Dictionary of Proverbs*).[8] He now reverts to the tale of Tereus and Philomela, making a more elaborate comparison between Lavinia and Philomela: Lavinia, he notes, couldn't, like her model, reveal the truth in a piece of needlework, since, having had her hands cut off, she cannot be expected to sew; and then on to Cerberus and Orpheus, and, continuing the theme of mutilation, the speculation that the sight of her will blind her father.

This speech is not meant to communicate horror or psychological adaptation; it is a rhetorical discourse on the topic of enforced silence, rather as there are rhetorical discourses on the topic of inexpressibility, with mythological parallels both central and marginal. With its continual reminders of the way in which the Tereus myth is being cleverly amplified, and with its leisurely exploitation of the literary ironies implicit in Lavinia's plight, it is altogether a remarkably sophisticated piece of writing, but of another kind than the dramatic texts that will follow it—more akin to *Venus and Adonis* than to *Hamlet* or *Macbeth* or *Coriolanus* or *Antony and Cleopatra*—this last possibly a fairer comparison, since it also is a play that seeks to relate an ostensibly historical narrative to a more or less occult mythological plot.

Shakespeare later found other ways of dealing with silence, as in the characters of Virgilia in *Coriolanus* and Hermione in *The Winter's Tale*.[9] The contrasts they offer to this earlier scene are instructive. What Marcus says would be very little different if this were a narrative poem, a prose tragedy; the moment calls for a set piece in which the enforced silence of one character draws forth a particularly elaborate form of speech from the other. The silence of Virgilia is entirely different: it is counterpointed against the din of Coriolanus, and also the insistent talk about the "voices" required to elect him; the sheer *noise* of *Coriolanus* called for a "gracious silence" to emphasize it. Hermione is a silent statue; the sight of her silences Leontes. Perdita speaks only to explain why she is kneeling; it is altogether a scene of silence, staged by the talkative Paulina, who has earlier been told off for chattering but now speaks as the presenter of a sort of numinous climactic dumbshow. All these silences belong essentially to the theater; they could not be done on the page. Purely theatrical, for instance, is the silence of Gloucester in *King Lear* 5.2. The old man is left alone on the stage while Edgar goes off to join the fight. While the battle is fought he simply sits there, for as long as actor and audience can bear it—a most memorable moment in Peter Brook's 1962 production. Edgar returns with the news that the battle is lost and Cordelia and Lear captured; the whole scene has eleven lines and might play for five minutes, the silence of Gloucester offset by the distant noise of battle. The rhetoric of *Titus* clearly belongs to the past, or has been developed into something almost unrecognizably new.

The next example, from *Hamlet*, is intended to clarify the contrast:

> Pray can I not,
> Though inclination be as sharp as will,
> My stronger guilt defeats my strong intent,
> And like a man to double business bound,
> I stand in pause where I shall first begin,
> And both neglect. What if this cursed hand
> Were thicker than itself with brother's blood,
> Is there not rain enough in the sweet heavens
> To wash it white as snow? Whereto serves mercy
> But to confront the visage of offence?

And what's in prayer but this twofold force,
To be forestalled ere we come to fall
Or pardon'd, being down? Then I'll look up.
My fault is past—but O, what form of prayer
Can serve my turn? "Forgive me my foul murder"?
That cannot be, since I am still possess'd
Of those effects for which I did the murder—
My crown, mine own ambition, and my queen.
May one be pardon'd and retain th'offence?
In the corrupted currents of this world
Offence's gilded hand may shove by justice,
And oft 'tis seen the wicked prize itself
Buys out the law. But 'tis not so above:
There is no shuffling, there the action lies
In his true nature, and we ourselves compell'd
Even to the teeth and forehead of our faults
To give in evidence. What then? What rests?
                    *Hamlet*, 3.3.38–64[10]

Here is a man in a dilemma, feeling the urgent if hopeless need to decide, to do something; in that respect at any rate differing from Marcus, who is more like a Tudor musician adorning his melancholy theme with "divisions." This dilemma of Claudius, as editors note, echoes Hamlet's; a decision in favor of confession and the renunciation of goods he has obtained from the murder is all but unthinkable, and so he cannot pray; his meditation only explains how he has lost the name of action, just as Hamlet does a few moments later. This is in fact the only soliloquy in the play that isn't spoken by Hamlet, and in its mode and language it is not very different from all the others. It proposes two alternatives, as in "To be or not to be," but far from systematically expounding them it subjects them to the press and slippage of the metaphors that rise up from intelligence in crisis. The point is no longer the skill with which the topic is augmented and expounded. A fine distinction is fleetingly suggested between "inclination" and "will" (more complex just because in Shakespeare "will" so often means "desire," including, rather eminently, sexual desire—after all one of the murderer's motives). The figure of the man to double business bound is terse and neat; it illustrates the point without flourish and is not expanded into an anecdote. The hands washed white allude, decorously, to the Bible, not to Ovid. The figuration is evanescent, not sustained: Mercy confronting "the visage of offence" is an idea where a sort of melted down personification, Mercy, is brought into proximity with an even more amorphous figure, Offence—a figure, however, with a face—and "confront" suggests a challenge; this Mercy is not invariably tender, is less about to wipe Offence's face than to purge its deformities. When he asks, already knowing the answer, whether pardon can be had by one who retains the benefits of a crime, Claudius reflects that on earth, in his world, the law may be bought; Offence, now coming into allegorical focus, becomes a powerful figure with a guilty golden hand with which, having no need to wheedle, it simply shoves Justice aside. And these considerations of earthly law and justice ensure that when he comes to draw the contrast with how things are "above" he is forced to envisage an implacable justice confronting "the teeth and forehead of our faults," a wonderful compression: Offence is no longer a powerful agent, shoving and shuffling, but a mere face, the face of the faults of the man on trial, and so his face.

All these qualities—the play of figures, echoing one another as it were contrapuntally, the pace at which the King's deliberations are rendered, the failure or refusal to follow the old course of slowly milking similitudes, the changing depth of focus on Mercy, Offence, Justice, the colloquial roughness of "shove" and "shuffle," the legal references ("the action lies" and "evidence") testify not only to a different range of metaphorical usage but to a different, dramatic manner of representing a man thinking. The end of Claudius's speech lapses into an older style ("O wretched state! O bosom black as death"), but so, in the lines deplored by Johnson, does the speech of Aufidius with which we began. They serve to remind us of a continuing but increasingly tenuous relationship.

Such reversions to the old stock ("Virtue cannot so inoculate our old stock but we shall relish of it") may seem to us let-downs, like the closing couplets of some of the Sonnets; but they are, as it were, Salzburg survivals, vestigiary evidence of where the groundwork was laid down, and should not affect our judgment of the originality of the passages they terminate. Great changes came over theatrical language about the time of *Hamlet*, as the play itself as well as its hero seem to be fully aware. To confirm this none too startling observation one needn't go all the way back to *Titus Andronicus*; compare, for instance, the great speech of Richard II, "I have been studying how I may compare / This prison where I live unto the world" (5.5.1ff.), where topic elegantly, movingly, follows topic, and intelligence illuminates the whole, but without giving the lines the fierce, disjointed animation we find in Claudius's meditation. Or, to take a moment rather closer in time to *Hamlet*, consider Brutus making up his mind about the need to kill Caesar ("It must be by his death," *Julius Caesar*, 2.1.10ff.), which uses the simple figures of the adder, the ladder, and the serpent's egg, but hews closely and decorously (even allowing for a proper measure of obscurity in the account of motive) and without metaphorical extravagance, to its deadly political subject.

The difference of manner is plain; it is necessary only to set these speeches against the soliloquies of Hamlet or Angelo (*Measure for Measure*, 2.4.1ff.) or Leontes (*The Winter's Tale*, 1.2.108ff., 138ff.). Soliloquies were first made to explain to the audience "some necessary question of the play" (a service they continued to perform, even in *Othello* and later plays), but Shakespeare came to see them as admirably apt for the expression of thought under emotional pressure. In the soliloquy language and silence coexist, and create a situation in which the registration of the emergencies of private thought, as expressed by Claudius and Hamlet, Angelo and Macbeth, calls for those new figurations, metaphors appearing and disappearing like ghosts, indecisions expressed undecisively but with an awful vigor, crazed convictions expressed with manic force.

Leontes's outpourings of pathological jealousy may stand as a paranoid extension of this dialect, but we hear it in its most extensive form in *Coriolanus*. This is not the place to discuss the language of the play throughout its length: its extraordinary forced expressions, its obscurity of syntax and vocabulary, its contrasts of prose and harsh verse, its interweavings of the domestic and the brutal military. The speech of Aufidius must serve as my sole example. The osprey and the fish, a bestiary illustration, is tersely adequate in its assertion of natural superiority; the oxymoron "noble servant" illustrates with precision the dilemma of Coriolanus. There follows a series of tentative explanations: "whether . . . whether . . . or whether": pride attendant on continuous success; inability to act in peace with the same assurance as in war (but note the strange illustration of casque and cushion, and the hendiadys of "austerity and garb," hendiadys being a way of making strange, of splitting an expression in two, so that it calls for explanation as a minute metaphor, a trick of which Shakespeare was for a time exceptionally fond). Most remarkable of all the device here used for simulating the movement of thought, the working out of a knotty problem, is the conclusion of this exploration of possibilities:

> but one of these—
> As he hath spices of them all, not all,
> For I dare so far free him—made him fear'd,
> So hated, and so banish'd; but he has a merit
> To choke it in the utt'rance.

One theory is right, he has a touch of all these defects—no, not all, only one is needed to explain his fate; and even so one finds it hard to say so, his virtues being so great. That is roughly what the lines mean if one takes the antecedent of "it" to be the chief of the faults mentioned; if it is "merit," then Johnson's explanation that the merit is choked by boasting about it ("utterance") is the right one. Brockbank is hesitantly willing to admit Johnson's reading as constituent of a valuable ambiguity. That seems unlikely, but the present point is merely that given this new way of representing turbulent thinking as against plainly formulated thought, obscurities are bound to engage the commentators. It is an example of a new rhetoric, developing from the time of *Hamlet* and to be noted also in the Romances, where we even reach the stage when one character may be defeated by the disturbances in the speech of another. "What is the *matter*, trow?" asks Imogen, puzzled by a difficult speech of Iachimo (*Cymbeline*, 1.6.47; my emphasis). It is a question many editors, more comfortable with the earlier plays, must ask when confronted with the later Shakespearean rhetoric.

## Notes

1. *Coriolanus*, Arden edition, ed. Philip Brockbank (London: Routledge and Kegan Paul, 1976).
2. Coleridge's comment on the passage is cited in the Brockbank edition.
3. Johnson's comment is also cited for the passage in the Brockbank edition.
4. In G. Blakemore Evans et al., *The Riverside Shakespeare* (Boston: Houghton Mifflin Co., 1974), 1394. In the absence of other indications, Shakespearean references are to this edition.
5. *Titus Andronicus*, Arden edition, ed. Jonathan Bate (London: Routledge and Kegan Paul, 1995); editorial stage directions have been omitted.
6. Bate, ed., *Titus Andronicus*.
7. Maynard Solomon, *Mozart: A Life* (New York: Harper Collins, 1995), 122–123.
8. F. P. Wilson, ed., *The Oxford Dictionary of Proverbs*, 3rd. ed. (Oxford: Clarendon Press, 1970).
9. See Frank Kermode, "Shakespeare's Silences," in Y. Takada, ed., *Surprised by Scenes: Essays in Honour of Professor Yasunari Takahishi* (Tokyo: Kenkyusha, 1994), 16–26.
10. *Hamlet*, Arden edition, ed. Harold Jenkins (London: Routledge and Kegan Paul, 1982).

# CHAPTER 12

# *Making It Expressive: Ibsen's Language*

## ROBERT GARIS

$O$ne of the rewards of studying Ibsen is getting to know the strange imagination that produced the great prose plays—an imagination more graceless in its earnest working than one had thought an imagination could be. And it is moving and rather splendid to watch this remarkable faculty doing what it does best, solving hard problems, particularly when the problem is so central and difficult as the one that concerns me here: how to make language in the prose plays expressive.

Language isn't generally considered one of Ibsen's strong points; his plays are always discussed in terms of large-scale structure and ideas. He wrote eleven plays in verse in the first half of his career, including the masterpieces *Brand* and *Peer Gynt*, but there has been no serious discussion of the way this verse works. Some Ibsen critics may have been silent out of prudence, because they don't know Norwegian (perhaps I should follow their example), but for whatever reason Ibsen's dramatic verse has been accepted, without analysis, as merely the fitting garment for the dramatic structure, not an intrinsic part of it—and this may be the right way to handle it, since Ibsen himself probably identified the function of his dramatic verse in this way. As for the prose drama of ordinary life that Ibsen began to write in the 1870s, the language in these great plays has also been taken for granted and that too may be the right way to handle it, for we tend to think the language in realistic prose drama should be a transparent medium, not an object of attention in itself.

Yet the prose of Ibsen's realistic plays remains stubbornly noticeable, if only for the wrong reasons. Not knowing Norwegian, yet wanting to feel some confidence in my dealings with Ibsen's language, I made the experiment many years ago of comparing in detail four different English translations of *A Doll's House*; I confirmed my hunch that Ibsen's dialogue is almost bare of rhetorical inflections, of expressive devices—far more so than the language we use in our own everyday lives. Ibsen's prose really is exceptionally inexpressive. It's all a matter of sending messages, of communicating information. The English translators never ventured into any special tones or inflections in English, which persuaded me that Ibsen hadn't done so in Norwegian either. Nor is one ever struck by Ibsen's "ear," a gift for catching the nuance of vivid speech. This must be what James meant when he called Ibsen's later style "the very prose of prose."[1]

James came to admire the stageworthiness of Ibsen's plays, his gift for creating characters who come to vivid life in the theater, an aspect of Ibsen he hadn't really noticed until he saw *Hedda Gabler* staged in 1891; what he couldn't in the end handle was Ibsen's charmlessness. He names his deficiencies in a devastating list: lack of style, free imagination, charm, humor and glamour. He identified Ibsen pretty much as I have been doing here, then, with one great difference: for James, the attributes he listed were essential to important art, whereas the fact that Ibsen had been exerting power over me in the absence of style, charm, and the rest was one of the reasons I had been finding him so interesting.

Yeats's frequent attacks on Ibsen in his polemical writing about the theater are less global than James's and he does focus on the language of the prose plays:

> Ibsen has sincerity and logic beyond any writer of our time, and we are all seeking to learn them at his hand; but is he not a good deal less than the greatest of all times, because he lacks beautiful and vivid language? "Well, well, give me time and you shall hear all about it. If only I had Peter here now," is very like life, is entirely in its place where it comes, and when it is united to other sentences exactly like itself, one is moved, one knows not how, to pity and terror, and yet not moved as if the words themselves could sing and shine.[2]

This sounds mildly regretful, as if Yeats were anxious not to offend the Ibsenites, but he actually felt very strongly on this matter. All of his dramatic criticism at the turn of the century takes the form of a campaign to replace realistic prose drama with poetic drama, a campaign in which one might expect Ibsen, with his immense prestige, to figure as the arch-enemy, for he wrote exactly the kind of play Yeats hated the most. But for no very clear reason Yeats puts him in a slightly different category and attacks him in different terms:

> Of all artistic forms that have had a large share of the world's attention, the worst is the play about modern educated people. Except where it is superficial or deliberately argumentative it fills one's soul with dust. It has one mortal ailment. It cannot become impassioned, that is to say, vital, without making somebody gushing and sentimental. Educated and well-bred people do not wear their hearts upon their sleeves, and they have no artistic and charming language except

light persiflage and no powerful language at all, and when they are
deeply moved they look silently into the fireplace. Again and again I
have watched some play of this sort with growing curiosity through the
opening scene. The minor people argue, chaff one another, hint
sometimes at some deeper stream of life just as we do in our houses,
and I am content. But all the time I have been wondering why the
chief character, the man who is to bear the burden of fate, is gushing,
sentimental and quite without ideas. Then the great scene comes and
I understand that he cannot be well-bred or self-possessed or
intellectual, for if he were he would draw a chair to the fire and there
would be no duologue at the end of the third act. Ibsen understood the
difficulty and made all his characters a little provincial that they might
not put each other out of countenance, and made a leading-article sort
of poetry—phrases about vine leaves and harps in the air—it was
possible to believe them using in their moments of excitement, and if
the play needed more than that, they could always do something
stupid. They could go out and hoist a flag as they do at the end of
*Little Eyolf*. One only understands that this manner, deliberately
adopted one doubts not, had gone into his soul and filled it with dust,
when one has noticed that he could no longer create a man of genius.[3]

The broad, simple terms of this passage years ago became the foundation of my
thinking about realistic drama; however self-evident Yeats's distinctions may be,
they came to me with the sense of revelation. His generalization about the
language of educated people became axiomatic, and I completely agreed that
such language couldn't yield expressive results in the theater—witness in our
century the hollow rhetoric of Arthur Miller. So far so good. But Ibsen's plays
about such people hadn't filled my soul with dust and their language hadn't
seemed inexpressive, and I couldn't quite make out the terms of Yeats's
apparent disapproval of Ibsen's methods. For reasons hard to make out, he
doesn't seem quite sure why he has exempted Ibsen from his general censure
(if that's in fact what he is doing). How a provincial atmosphere might help
Ibsen's characters not to put each other out of countenance escapes me—I just
don't get the picture. I too dislike Ibsen's leading-article images—Hedda's vine
leaves and Hilda's harps in the air—but they seem to me just corny mistakes,
not part of the general linguistic procedure of the plays. The snort of contempt
for *Little Eyolf* and its harmless flag is suspiciously excessive, and the last
point, about Ibsen the creator of men of genius, which hopes to clinch the
matter triumphantly, blurs it instead, since it isn't clear whether or not Yeats
has forgotten Ibsen's most famous play about a man of genius, *The Master
Builder*. Nor is it clear whether he's discarding *John Gabriel Borkman* and
*When We Dead Awaken*, both unarguably centered about a great man of genius.

It's as if Yeats had reminded himself, in the middle of his tirade against
the play of modern educated people, that Ibsen had composed some famously

interesting plays in this mode; he feels obliged to acknowledge this fact but isn't in the mood for analysis. In the earlier passage I quoted, he had caught a glimpse of a good way to handle such matters: "When [this sentence from *An Enemy of the People*] is united to other sentences exactly like itself, one is moved, one knows not how, to pity and terror." This is the obvious answer to the question how Ibsen's plays work, but again Yeats doesn't want to conduct the inquiry himself. It is of course exactly in the way Ibsen's sentences are united with each other that they acquire power and expressivity and I propose to look at how that works. I want also to ask how he manages to remain within his basic uninflected, non-figurative, non-rhetorical question-and-answer prose, yet make this mode expressive without making it less ordinary.

By far the chief source of expressivity in all of Ibsen's plays comes from his drastic reshaping of the structure of the well-made play he inherited from nineteenth-century French drama. To take an example, dialogue at the opening of an Ibsen play almost always takes the question-and-answer form familiar from the exposition of well-made plays. We must be informed of what's going on and has gone on, and the normal way of accomplishing this is through the mutual interrogation of the characters, since the laws of realism won't allow such facts to be narrated directly to the audience, as is often the case, for instance, in Shakespeare. But Ibsen's powerful and earnest imagination seizes on the mechanical question-and-answer of the conventional well-made play and makes it expressive in itself, by thematizing it. He presses the questioning mode far beyond its function of eliciting the facts we need to know, until it acquires the force of a full-fledged interrogation, important in its own right: question-and-answer becomes a form of action. Compared with the paltry biographies of characters in routine well-made plays, the leading characters in Ibsen have led lives crammed with choices and actions before the rise of the curtain; consequently it may take virtually the whole first act to investigate what has already happened, so the process of inquiry is emphatically prolonged and sustained. And as we follow and participate in this long and drawn-out investigation, we come to experience another kind of action, a pull backwards into the past we are learning so much about: the sheer amount of detail we learn about the past, and the steadiness with which the detail gradually accumulates, give it mass, which compels our interest as if in an action of gravitation. As all this happens, the character whose life is being questioned also gathers presence, power, and mass in our imagination by virtue of the sheer amount of willing, deciding, choosing and changing she has initiated and carried through.

An Ibsen inquiry is usually conducted by another conventional figure, the confidant, and Ibsen also amplifies and intensifies the service rendered by this figure far beyond the norm in the well-made play. Ibsen confidants are extraordinarily naive and easily shocked; as they respond with never-failing astonishment to the emotionally charged actions and events uncovered by the inquiry, their surprises and astonishments also make up a kind of movement, almost a parody of action, which also forms part of the action of the play. The reactions of the Ibsen confidants are full of the gushing sentimentality Yeats disliked, but in Ibsen's structure these responses bring into relief the superior strength and control, the reticence, the calm, and the capacity for dealing with experience, of the leading character, "the woman who is to bear the burden of fate," in Yeats's words.

As the interrogation grows to fill the first act, it gathers substance and force in proportion to the number of events narrated and the force of will those events reveal. The stage space too, and the space of our imagination, seems to fill up with the image and record of individual will and action. We know who these characters are and what they have done, they have won a place in our minds and imagination, and we are now well situated to move in sympathy with them as they begin to act, and to understand exactly what they are doing and feeling when they do act. Because we understand their past, they need not describe in detail what they are experiencing during the action of the play—need not, that is, become gushing and sentimental.

The ending of the first act of *Ghosts* is the locus classicus of the technique. From the beginning of the play, Mrs. Alving has been shocking her adviser and one-time beloved, Pastor Manders, by revealing momentous changes in her intellectual, religious, and political opinions, and by revelations about her private life, most notably the fact that her late husband, Chamberlain Alving, a pillar of society and solid citizen in the eyes of Manders and the entire community, had actually been a thoroughly dissolute and degenerate man. He had capped his life of drunken disorder, and exhausted Mrs. Alving's patience, by seducing a serving-maid from his own household; at great cost to her own feelings, Mrs. Alving sent their small son away to boarding school to protect him from his father's influence, and she took charge of the financial affairs and the entire public image of her husband. She also took charge of the child born of this seduction, and as the play opens, this child, Regine, has grown up to take her mother's place as the maid of the household. Osvald, the son and heir, who has been living as an artist in Paris, has just returned to live with his mother, to her delight. She had earlier been deprived of the joy of motherhood, and now she is looking forward the more keenly to sharing her life and in particular her new views with her liberated son. It is at this point that the past repeats itself and the ghosts appear, on the last page of the act, when Osvald begins to flirt with Regine (the maid who he doesn't know is his half-sister) in the next room. Here is Mrs. Alving's response:

Mrs. Alving (*Stiffens with horror*): Ah—! (*She gazes distractedly at the half-open door. Osvald is heard coughing and humming a tune—then the sound of a bottle being uncorked.*)

Manders (*In agitation*): But what *is* all this? What's the *matter*, Mrs. Alving?

Mrs. Alving (*Hoarsely*): Ghosts—those two in the conservatory— Ghosts—They've come to life again!

*Manders*: What do you mean? Regine—? Is she—?
*Mrs. Alving*: Yes—Come—Not a word!
  *(She takes Manders' arm and goes falteringly toward the dining room.)*
                                                              CURTAIN[4]

Despite its verbal poverty, the passage (not least Mrs. Alving's "Ah—!") is rich
in exact dramatic substance. The pressure of all we have heard and understood
before this moment fills these all but inarticulate cries with meaning and feeling;
and the exactness of the preceding inquiry leads to a sense of corresponding
exactness in Mrs. Alving's response, so that even "Ah—!" creates the illusion
of specificity. The task her language is performing is not expression but
information—passing along to Manders the message that Regine is the daughter
of the former maid and therefore Osvald's half-sister—and therefore we don't
find the gushing sentimentality Yeats might have predicted. It is simply not
relevant that Mrs. Alving is provincial. The language is certainly James's "the
very prose of prose": it doesn't go beyond the pointing and signaling functions
of language. But it is the sufficient vehicle for a powerful charge of emotion
and meaning.

The exposition of *Ghosts* is the normal mode in Ibsen; it is voiced in the
ordinary everyday prose he thought required by the realistic convention, but by
creating the other kinds of "action" I have described—the persistent inquiry, the
perpetual astonishment of the confidant and so on—he brought expressivity to
the very mechanicism of exposition. In *A Doll's House* and *Ghosts*, Ibsen
invented still another device with which to make his structure expressive, to
drive it ahead and to contribute yet another kind of action to the exposition. He
laced a couple of banal pieces of language in through the action—"the
wonderful thing" in *A Doll's House* and "the joy of life" in *Ghosts*—to serve
as tracers guiding us through the action, to increase suspense, and to help carry
the burden of the play's major meaning. The action of the whole play, in fact,
turns on these phrases. They are entirely representative of the way Ibsen's
imagination works: they combine emphasis with vagueness to a degree rarely
encountered in drama, and Yeats himself could hardly have hoped for a more
egregious instance of gushing sentimentality than "the wonderful thing." The
vagueness of the tracer phrases might in fact place them beneath discussion, if
Ibsen didn't aggressively call it to our attention. When one of them is first
introduced by a leading character, it puzzles other characters, who immediately
ask what it means; but the character who introduced the phrase can't explain it,
and it remains tantalizingly undefined. The process of defining it may in fact
stretch through the whole play and if it does so, the gradual definition gets
linked to a major development in understanding on the part of the leading
characters and of the audience.

The action of *A Doll's House* turns on Nora's shock at her husband
Helmer's disappointing response to learning about her forgery, a shock
registered in the fact that "the wonderful thing" doesn't happen. Years before,

when he had taken sick, she had secretly forged her father's signature as security for a loan she got from a disreputable man named Krogstad, in order to pay for the trip abroad considered essential for Helmer's recovery. The fact that Helmer was ill and that it was Nora who was making decisions about his cure had to be concealed from him, for his manhood would suffer if he knew that a woman was in control of his life. As the play opens, the plan has worked out well: Helmer has recovered and prospered, having been promoted to president of his bank just before the play opens; Nora has reverted to her role as Helmer's "little lark" and the playmate of her own children, while at the same time secretly conducting her own life of business, working at lowly piece-work jobs like copying to pay off the loan. Then everything begins to unravel.

Krogstad, wanting to regain respectability, tells Nora he knows she has forged her father's signature, and threatens to reveal the secret unless she persuades her husband to give him a job in the bank. When Helmer refuses, Krogstad proceeds with his plan and two-thirds of the way through the second act, he drops a letter incriminating Nora into the Helmer mail box. Now "the wonderful thing" makes its first appearance, the phrase but not the fact. Nora waits for Helmer to find the letter with mixed feelings: she is afraid of his anger, but she is also in an exaltation of happiness because, as she tells her confidante Kristin, "the wonderful thing" is about to happen. When Kristin asks what she means, Nora says she can't explain and sends Kristin away. Our first clue about the meaning of "the wonderful thing" comes in the soliloquy that follows:

> Five o'clock. Seven hours till midnight. Twenty-four hours till the next midnight and then the tarantella will be over. Twenty-four and seven? I've thirty-one hours left to live.[5]

We must wait until the final discussion between Nora and Helmer for the full exposition of "the wonderful thing," but in the meantime we are building an understanding of the phrase out of the bits and pieces of information that come our way. As we listen to this soliloquy, for instance, we know we're hearing something about "the wonderful thing" because there's nothing else to attach it to; and therefore we see that the wonderful thing will involve Nora's death, though we know nothing more detailed. In the big dramatic dialogue between Nora and Helmer after his discovery of the forgery (67–69), there are many such pieces of information out of which we continue to build our knowledge of the wonderful thing. When Helmer asks "So it's true! It's true what he writes?" and Nora answers, "It *is* true! I've loved you more than all the world," we gather from the clue of her lofty rhetoric that she and he are living in different worlds, with her language coming from the high heroic world of "the wonderful thing." Thus we assemble our understanding of the phrase, which is never defined explicitly but eventually stands before us as a work of our own imagination, deriving much of its power and all its expressivity from this fact.

Nora's wonderful thing is a thrilling way of living and dying. She has constructed a scenario in which Helmer will try to take the blame for her crime on himself, whereupon she will kill herself in order to prevent his loss of honor. To Nora this scenario is marvelously heroic; to Helmer it is foolish. To us it isn't quite foolish, for our investment in Nora's life guides us to understand how this scenario underpins and guarantees her having consented all these years to play the role of "little lark" in the doll's house. She has always been vaguely aware of loss of freedom and individuality when she plays that role in Helmer's drama of power, discipline, and self-regarding protectiveness, and her occasional acts of rebellion—the forbidden macaroons, the whispered "damns," the sexual innuendo in her conversation about food with Dr. Rank, and so on—are among the most inspired things in the play in their witty registration of the exact degree of her self-awareness. She has been willing to play this humiliating role because she believes that underneath the power-politics of her relation with Helmer lies the promise and guarantee of heroic love and sacrifice on his part. She hardly notices his petty abuse of power in his everyday relation with her because she thinks him capable of heroic and selfless power; it is this great strength, she believes, on which the conventional gender roles in marriage are based, the roles and the corresponding privileges that Helmer has asked for or simply taken so often in the play.

The sublime sacrifices of Nora's drama differ entirely in scale and tone from the ordinary actions of the world Nora and we have been living in since the play opened: the world of promotions at the bank, of forbidden and smuggled macaroons, of forged signatures, of anxiety about the letter box. They also differ from the panicked efficiency with which Helmer now handles her crime. Her act has put her in the category of criminals, from whom certain actions are to be expected and toward whom certain administrative measures must immediately be taken: separating her from her children, keeping up the false front of the household, and so on, ideas and procedures in which Helmer proves disgustingly fluent. We measure the pitiful insufficiency of his strength against the vague and inflated heroic feelings, actions and expressivity conveyed in the phrase, "the wonderful thing."

Helmer is a brutally accurate critic of Nora's heroic drama and specifically of her language. When he calls her promises of self-sacrifice and her threats of suicide "silly nonsense" and "play-acting," her rethinking of her life begins immediately—it is the measure of her stature as an Ibsenite heroine. Three lines after Helmer has scorned her for "play-acting," she looks at him "fixedly," speaks with "a stiffening expression," and says, "I think I'm beginning to understand for the first time"—these are the familiar and effective if not notably subtle signs of dawning understanding in Ibsen's dramaturgy. A moment earlier the cliché lyrical cadence of "I've loved you more than all the world" had been her song; now, when Helmer says, "You think and talk like a silly child," she answers in quite another linguistic mode: "Perhaps." Against the melodrama of Nora's belief that Helmer will take the blame for the forgery on himself, which suits the gush of "the wonderful thing," the play poses the flat conventionality of Helmer's response: "One doesn't sacrifice one's honor for love's sake." But Helmer's lecture is instantly demolished by a calm generalization from Nora that is one of the great strokes of the play, "Millions of women have done so" (75). Ordinary language is made expressive through its contrast with "the wonderful thing," which has helped point out the insufficiency of Nora's life and her whole culture.

Ibsen has given his little device a job to do beyond what it "means" or "expresses"; it is an organizing agent, without subtlety or finesse, to be sure, but appropriate for the moment of the action at which it is introduced. "The wonderful thing" is brilliantly placed for maximum excitement: after the theatrics of the tarantella rehearsal, when Nora has tried to distract Helmer from the letter box by seducing him into the manly role of coaching her in dancing the tarantella (with, it need hardly be said, the refined and restrained femininity he had taught her on Capri during their trip). Nora's ruse is useless; Helmer retreats into his study and we hear Krogstad's letter dropping in the letter box. Now the phrase enters the action at this height of nervous tension, and sustains the tension of anticipation over the act break. The phrase has created a force field in which we listen with highly focused attention to Nora's eventual explication, the vapidity of the phrase preparing us for her discovery that her ideal image of the relation of the sexes in marriage is exactly what Helmer calls it, the stuff of play-acting and histrionics. As this cheap theater is exposed, the falsities of the whole relationship between Nora and Helmer fall away, and the stage is cleared for the final conversation, the first of those "discussions" for which Shaw made Ibsen famous.

Remarkable as we have seen the ending of the first act of *Ghosts* to be in its economy and its dramatization of Mrs. Alving's strength, Ibsen had even bigger plans for her, for his play, and for his experiment with language. She has exercised her will powerfully and effectively in the past, and she grasps what is happening in the present with resourcefulness and resilience: despite her initial horror at the sight of Osvald and Regine flirting, she soon entertains the thought that they should marry, to Manders's consternation. But Ibsen planned to have Mrs. Alving face some even less thinkable truths about herself and her fate. And he chose an extension of the technique we have been examining in *A Doll's House* to make this happen.

In *Ghosts*, "the joy of life" functions as a guiding tracer through the play, as "the wonderful things" had functioned in *A Doll's House*, but Ibsen has also passed it through major redefinitions. *A Doll's House* holds "the wonderful thing" before us undefined for a long time, to give the moment of definition maximum impact, but once the definition is made it remains constant. "The joy of life" goes through several meanings, each signaling a new step in Mrs. Alving's understanding of her husband and her past, her son and her future. But she does more than merely understand: she creates herself and an entirely new conception of her husband, Chamberlain Alving, with each new use of the phrase. And because the phrase is concretely present in our imagination, we have the illusion of actually seeing the process by which new language creates new life.

Osvald's Parisian life has something to do with "the joy of life," but though a large, simple opposition is set up between Parisian sun and freedom and Norwegian rain and self-denial, the phrase itself doesn't appear in this connection. When the phrase actually appears, Osvald uses it more pointedly to praise Regine:

> *Osvald*: I'd never noticed her much before, Mother—but suddenly I saw
> her there—so beautiful—so vital—she stood there as though waiting to
> come into my arms—
> *Mrs. Alving*: Osvald—!
> *Osvald*: I suddenly realized that she could save me; she was so full of the
> joy of life!
> *Mrs. Alving*: *(Startled)* Joy of life—? Is there salvation in that?
> *(Regine comes in with the champagne.)* (128)

Mrs. Alving, the daughter of her culture, has associated salvation with self-denial but Osvald now suggests that salvation might come through pleasure. We see Ibsen's heavy-duty workmanship in Mrs. Alving's startled response and the explicit pointedness of the whole discussion that follows; but the play is making a huge leap forward and can use all the steadying and focusing Ibsen can give.

> *Mrs. Alving*: Osvald—What were you saying about the joy of life?
> *Osvald*: Yes—the joy of life, Mother—you don't know much about that
> here at home. I could never find it here.
> *Mrs. Alving*: Not here with me?
> *Osvald*: No. Never at home. But you don't understand that.
> *Mrs. Alving*: Yes—I believe I'm beginning to understand it—now.
> *Osvald*: That—and the joy of work. They're really the same thing, you
> know. But of course, you don't know anything about that here either.
> . . . You must have noticed, Mother, everything I paint is filled with
> this joy of life; always and forever the joy of life! My paintings are
> full of light, of sunshine, of glowing, happy faces. That's why I'm
> afraid to stay here, Mother.
> *Mrs. Alving*: Afraid? What are you afraid of—here with me?
> *Osvald*: I'm afraid that all the strongest traits of my nature would become
> warped here—would degenerate into ugliness.
> *Mrs. Alving*: *(Looks at him intently)* You really believe that is what would
> happen?
> *Osvald*: Yes—I'm convinced of it! Even if I lived the same life here as I
> live abroad—it still wouldn't *be* the same life.
> *Mrs. Alving*: *(Who has listened intently, rises; a thoughtful look in her
> eyes)* Now I see it! It's all becoming clear to me—
> *Osvald*: What do you see?

> *Mrs. Alving*: The whole pattern—for the first time, I see it—and now I
> can speak. (128–129)

Ibsen means it to be thrilling when Mrs. Alving suddenly makes the connection
between what Osvald is describing and her despised husband, and it is in fact
a moment worth the heavy emphasis of the deafening stage directions. It's
excitingly appropriate that what Mrs. Alving so liberatingly sees should be "a
pattern" that she can't yet describe nor we understand. The moment has great
energy because of the intellectual and imaginative exertion it asks of us.
Nothing is given, everything is promised. But if we don't yet see the pattern,
we incontestably see the way it was arrived at. For it is when Mrs. Alving
hears Osvald unknowingly describe what happened to his own father, as he uses
the terrible word "degenerate" to describe what would happen to him if he
stayed at home, that her mind makes the heroic leap between father and son.

The process of Mrs. Alving's understanding is now interrupted by world
drama's most heavily symbolic fire, as the Chamberlain Alving Memorial
Orphanage is completely destroyed. This building represents the alarming wit
Mrs. Alving has grown capable of: she built it with the exact sum of money
which Chamberlain Alving had brought to the marriage, and its function
expresses an even more blatant irony. But this bitter planning came long before
the changes we have just watched. When Mrs. Alving reverts to "the joy of
life" in Act 3, her new conception of her husband and his relation to the great
creating phrase "the joy of life" has deepened and softened. She has not only
seen the pattern; she has re-seen her husband himself with a fresh imagination
that amounts to re-creation:

> *Mrs. Alving*: You should have known your father when he was a young
> lieutenant. He was filled with that joy of life, I can tell you!
> *Osvald*: Yes—so I've heard.
> *Mrs. Alving*: He seemed to radiate light and warmth—he was filled with
> a turbulent, joyous vitality.
> *Osvald*: Well—?
> *Mrs. Alving*: And this boy, so full of the joy of life—he was like a boy
> then—was cooped up in this drab little provincial town—which could
> offer him no real joy—only dissipation. (137)

Joy of life has in fact produced salvation, and right in front of us; it has "saved"
Mrs. Alving's husband by helping her recreate him. "Joy of life" has burned
away her angry resentment of her husband and of his life but not only that: it
has given birth to a new young man of radiant beauty and health. It is the
moment of growth and hope in the play, the emblem of a great revolution and
the promise of more. James and Yeats might worry about the indifferent language in which Mrs. Alving's vision is embodied, but if one is inside the play,
living according to its laws, all is well.

But the revolution promised by Mrs. Alving's discovery is aborted, for the redefinition of the "joy of life" is still in process, and its final meaning will have the force of Nemesis. The phrase has up to now been unambiguously positive. When Osvald speaks of being saved by Regine, it is an unambiguous celebration of her youthful animal vitality—he gets a sense of life from merely looking at her. And that meaning has carried over into Mrs. Alving's new picture of her husband: a sense of glowing well being comes from merely being in the presence of these exemplars of the joy of life. But Mrs. Alving's creation of her husband's joy of life, and her joy in seeing him again in her imagination, is followed almost immediately by the discovery of the syphilis which his son has inherited. This terrible discovery brings the key phrase into play again, carrying a radically new meaning and value.

The question at the end of the play is how Osvald is to be taken care of when his illness appears; we are dimly aware of the options because of Osvald's frequent insistence that "Regine would have done it," but we don't fully understand what he means. When Regine is directly asked to perform the service of taking care of Osvald in the years of his failing powers, we think we have the answer:

> *Regine*: I can't waste my time out here in the country looking after invalids.
> *Osvald*: Not when it's your own brother, Regine?
> *Regine*: I should say not! I'm poor—all I have is my youth—I can't afford to waste it. I don't want to be left stranded. I have some of that joy of life in me too, Mrs. Alving! (138)

Regine appropriates the phrase for her own purpose and meaning: looking out for number one. She means to cheapen the phrase and might succeed, but the play won't exactly let her, for it has in mind a terrible variation on her meaning. When Osvald foresees that Regine's "magnificently light and buoyant nature . . . wouldn't put up long with an invalid," the play finds its central deadly irony, for though the descriptive language seems positive, the implications are not: what Osvald welcomes with sardonic pleasure as magnificent is Regine's absence of scruple, of inhibition, of conventional piety, and he finds it magnificent because it will help him kill himself. In a hint of popular Darwinism, we see Regine working in the service of the survival of the fittest. The "joy of life" in the avatar of Regine brings salvation because it brings death, for the drive toward survival must sometimes destroy what has grown corrupt, the debilitated ideals and habits of its own fashioning—loyalty, duty, reverence for life, love. Life itself must kill the diseased Osvald to protect the race.

These ideals are for us richly embodied in Mrs. Alving's generous love and marvelous adaptability, but her strengths seem to him useless in his present need:

> *Mrs. Alving*: Can't you trust your mother to do that?
> *Osvald*: You! *(Smiles)* You'd never do it. *(With a melancholy laugh)* You!

*(Looks at her gravely)* And yet you're the only one who has the right to do it. (136)

In the end, with Regine gone, it is Mrs. Alving's terrible task, and her right, to give her son the morphine in an act of love. The language with which she faces this demand reminds us of the situation she handled at the end of the first act.

> Osvald *(Tonelessly as before)*: The sun—The sun.
> Mrs. Alving *(Springs up in despair, tears at her hair with both hands and screams)*: I can't bear it! *(Whispers, paralyzed with fear)* I can't bear it! Never! *(Suddenly)* Where did he put them? *(Passes her hand rapidly over his breast)* Here! *(Draws back a couple of steps and cries)* No; no; no!—Yes! No; no! *(She stands a few steps away from him, her hands clutching her hair, and stares at him in speechless terror.)*
> Osvald *(Immovable as before)*: The sun—The sun.
>
> CURTAIN (145)

These minimal articulations bring back in a kind of rhyme the ending of the first act in the compression of their signalling and the density of their substance. It's a rhyme stretched out over a huge stanza, but it really works.

### Notes

1. Henry James, "On the Occasion of *Hedda Gabler* (1891)," in *The Scenic Art*, ed. Allan Wade (New Brunswick: Rutgers University Press, 1948), 246.
2. W. B. Yeats, *Plays and Controversies* (New York: Macmillan, 1924), 118–119.
3. W. B. Yeats, *Essays* (New York: Macmillan, 1924), 339–340.
4. Henrik Ibsen, *Ghosts*, in *Eight Plays by Henrik Ibsen*, trans. Eva le Gallienne (New York: Random House, 1982), 107.
5. Henrik Ibsen, *A Doll's House*, in *Eight Plays by Henrik Ibsen*, 55. Page references to *A Doll's House* and *Ghosts* will hereafter be incorporated parenthetically in the text.

# Horace, Ode iv.8: To Censorinus

DAVID FERRY


*I*f I had plenty of money, Censorinus,
    I could give other kinds
        Of presents to my friends,

Bowls, and bronzes, and tripods, antique Greek treasures,
    Things painted by Parrhasius,
        Or things that Scopas sculpted,

Skillfully representing gods or heroes.
    And you would by no means have
        The least of these. But I

Don't have the power to give such gifts as these,
    Nor do you need such trifles.
        It is poetry you love.

It is poetry I can give, and I know its worth.
    Marble can tell the story
        Of what the dead hero did,

Bringing him back to life engraved in stone,
    Or how Hannibal fled,
        His threats on his own head,

And how Scipio by his conquest came
    Home with a new name;
        But stone cannot tell as well

As poetry can the tale; nor would you have
    The praise you merit if
        Your story went unwritten.

Who would Romulus be, the son of Ilia
    And the son of Mars, had silence
        Envious of his deeds

Held back the telling? And who was it who rescued
    Aeacus from the Stygian
        Waters of oblivion

And brought him safe ashore on the Blessèd Isle?
    It was poetry rescued him.
        Poetry forbids

That he who deserves our praise will be forgotten.
    The blessing of the Muse
        Is on the hero's head.

Thus Hercules, an honored guest, is welcome
    At Jupiter's banquet table;
        And the shining stars, the brothers

Castor and Pollux, quiet the waters, and
    The storm-stricken vessel
        Makes it home to port;

And over the woodland festival Bacchus presides,
    Wearing his crown of ivy,
        All promises having been kept.

# CONTRIBUTORS

MILLICENT BELL is Professor of English Emerita at Boston University, and the author of *Hawthorne's View of the Artist* (1962), *Edith Wharton and Henry James* (1962), *Marquand: An American Life* (1979), *Meaning in Henry James* (1991), editor of *The Complete Novels of Nathaniel Hawthorne* (1983), *New Essays on Hawthorne's Tales* (1993), and *The Cambridge Companion to Edith Wharton* (1995).

LEO BERSANI is Class of 1950 Professor of French at the University of California at Berkeley. His most recent books are *Acts of Impoverishment: Beckett, Rothko, Resnais* (with Ulysse Dutoit, 1994), and *Homos* (1995).

DAVID BROMWICH is the author of *Hazlitt: The Mind of a Critic*, *A Choice of Inheritance*, and *Politics by Other Means*. He is the Housum Professor of English at Yale University.

THOMAS R. EDWARDS, a friend and colleague of Richard Poirier for many years, is Professor Emeritus at Rutgers University. He is the author of *This Dark Estate: A Reading of Pope*, *Imagination and Power*, and *Over Here: Criticizing America 1968–89*.

ANNE FERRY has taught at Hunter, Wellesley, Harvard, Boston College, and MIT. Her books include *The "Inward" Language*, *The Art of Naming*, and, most recently, *The Title to the Poem* (1996).

DAVID FERRY teaches at Wellesley College. His two most recent books are *Gilgamesh: A New Rendering of Verse* (1993) and *Dwelling Places: Poems and Translations* (1993).

ROBERT GARIS is Katherine Lee Bates Professor of English Emeritus at Wellesley College. His *Following Balanchine* was published in 1995.

JOHN HOLLANDER, Sterling Professor of English at Yale University, is a poet and critic. His study of ecphrastic poetry, *The Gazer's Spirit*, was published in 1994.

FRANK KERMODE, formerly King Edward VII Professor at Cambridge University, is the author and editor of numerous books, including the recently published memoir *Not Entitled* (1995).

BRIDGET GELLERT LYONS is Professor of English and Associate Dean for Humanities at Rutgers University.

ROSS POSNOCK is Andrew Hilen Professor of American Literature at the University of Washington. He is the author, most recently, of *The Trial of Curiosity: Henry James, William James, and the Challenge of Modernity*. Currently, he is working on a study of black intellectuals and the politics of pragmatism.

BARRY V. QUALLS, Chair of the English Department at Rutgers University, is the author of *The Secular Pilgrims of Victorian Fiction*. He has written extensively on the Bible as literature, as well as on Victorian fiction.

MARGERY SABIN is Lorraine Chiu Wang Professor of English at Wellesley College. She is the author of *English Romanticism and the French Tradition* and *The Dialect of the Tribe*. Her recent essays about British imperialism and literature, and about the activity of reading, have appeared in such journals as *Raritan*, *Essays in Criticism*, and *Victorian Studies*.

EDWARD W. SAID is University Professor of English and Comparative Literature at Columbia University. Among his most recent books are *Representations of the Intellectual* (1994), and *Peace and Its Discontents* (1996).